THE ULTIMATE GUIDE TO
WATERFOWL HUNTING

Tips, Tactics, and Techniques for Ducks and Geese

TOM AIRHART • EDDIE KENT • KENT RAYMER

Skyhorse Publishing

Skyhorse Publishing books may be purchased in bulk at special discounts for sales promotion, corporate gifts, fund-raising, or educational purposes. Special editions can also be created to specifications. For details, contact the Special Sales Department, Skyhorse Publishing, 307 West 36th Street, 11th Floor, New York, NY 10018 or info@skyhorsepublishing.com.

Skyhorse® and Skyhorse Publishing® are registered trademarks of Skyhorse Publishing, Inc.®, a Delaware corporation.

Visit our website at www.skyhorsepublishing.com.

10 9 8 7 6 5 4 3 2 1

Library of Congress Cataloging-in-Publication Data is available on file.

Cover design by Tom Lau
Cover photo credit: Jay Cassell
Interior Photos by the authors, unless noted otherwise.

Print ISBN: 978-1-5107-1674-2
Ebook ISBN: 978-1-5107-1675-9

Printed in China

Contents

Preface

What in this world were we thinking when we decided to write a new waterfowl hunting how-to book? Answer: there are a lot of new hunters afield and they could use some solid, up-to-date, twenty-first-century hunting information salted with well over a hundred years we accumulated during the century gone by. Welcome folks! Some of the factors that have improved waterfowl hunting for everyone include the expansion of electronic communications, information access, and entertainment; improved Internet search engines that have made all this information readily available; improvements in the availability of ducks and geese; real-time, accurate information on bird migrations and on weather patterns; plus, travel is now reasonably affordable, so that a dream trip to a faraway or not-so-faraway hunting mecca is within the reach of those of us of modest means. These are the new good old days. Credit goes to a lot of people who care. The ending of the drought down the center of North America sure hasn't hurt either.

We believe that the fascinating world of waterfowl hunting (or wildfowling or waterfowling, if you prefer) has been, up to now, too wide and too deep to be covered in detail by a single volume. It would take a better library than most of us could assemble, much less read and assimilate, and still fit some hunting and practice shooting into our schedule. The solutions up to now have either been a very general coverage of the big picture, or a more detailed effort that covers a specific aspect of waterfowl hunting, such as identification; calling and decoying; wingshooting; retriever training; boats; and decoy arrangements. This book is intended to be different, to cover it all in as much detail as the reader can stand. We've made pointers throughout for the reader to combine all of that information with our years of inexperience. The interesting terms can be searched on the Internet. Using search engines, you can turn these words into your own gargantuan library. Limitless information, experience, and, sometimes, informative opinions reside, online, just waiting for you. Most of the terms can be found in topic headings.

Internet or not, we'll cover the total spectrum of waterfowl hunting. We'll cover it in enough detail for you to know what's going on, to be able to go hunting on your own, then dive into any specialty as far as you can stand. We've intended to hit all of the topics. There are detailed instructions to help you adequately master the fundamentals of all aspects of hunting ducks and geese. There are practice techniques designed to make you consistently successful. The emphasis is on ducks and geese because that's what most hunters are after.

We follow a progression: simple and inexpensive to begin, then progressively more complicated and not so inexpensive. This approach will help you gain experience and decide if you want to take the next steps as you become ready on your own. As an alternative, you can assimilate that progression through these pages and begin greater adventures with the assistance of professional outfitters and guides. Most waterfowl hunters seem to progress eventually into specializing in a specific type of waterfowl hunting: ducks or geese; small or big water; lots of hunting of familiar local areas or a few long-anticipated adventures in remote locations; or, the eternal amateur, always sampling something different. Newcomers to the waterfowl hunting world, and maybe some of the old-timers who've fallen into a rut, could use an up-to-date source of information and instructions for all aspects of the sport.

We recommend that the beginner first go after ducks on small waters. Why? Why not make it about hunting ducks everywhere? Here's the deal. If you can't get 'em on small water, you can't get 'em anywhere. Solve that, and you're ready to handle the corollary, which is where the real wisdom resides. If you can get 'em on small water, you can get 'em anywhere, from small water close to home to far marshes or big waters. Far, really far, extends to every continent around the globe. But we'll try to contain ourselves to our own backyard: North America.

Our intent is to make this project the waterfowl hunting guide for everybody: for the casual reader with a beginning interest in the topic, it can be reviewed by scanning the illustrations and reading the captions to get the general idea the easy, entertaining way; for the reader seriously thinking about or committed to that first hunt, or who has made a few trips without having any luck, it's our take on how to be successful; finally, for the dedicated, experienced, hell-bent hunter, there will be at least some stuff you haven't seen before.

Introduction

First get the feel; then the facts.

The Essence of the Hunt

We'll approach duck and goose hunting the way a marsh comes out of the dark and haze of early morning. Let's say it's your first time duck hunting, probably with a duck hunting friend. You set up and get all ready and it's so dark you can't see a duck unless it lands in your lap; then you can see the old dog, actually almost in your lap, turning his head and looking with his ears; you see that the black above is turning dark gray; then there's water to your front; the bank and the shapes of your hunting buddies off to the side come into view, then the decoys. Suddenly it's shooting light. "Shootin' time?" "Time's good." The Lab turns to look downwind to our front. He whines. Shapes whistle in. "Take 'em!" Slightly felt recoil and orange spouts of flame into the dark. "Baaackkk!" The dog explodes into the water. And you're seeing dark turn to simple shapes that turn to marsh below and limitless sky above. Starting from blackness, you can now see and feel it all.

We'll start with the progression mentioned in the preface, the least complicated, least expensive duck and goose hunting, and cover it in detail; then we'll progress into duck hunting as a shared experience with good companions close to home, or as high adventure, with tips on how to survive it.

Ducks and Geese

Ducks and geese have optimally adapted to their aquatic habitat over a very long time. Theirs is predominately a terrestrial world on a transcontinental scale, yet their habitat consists of the aquatic nooks and niches scattered across or narrowly stretching through the expanses of dry land. For many, habitat will include feeding areas in cultivated fields.

According to the fossil record, the history of waterfowl goes all the way back to a time when birds were evolving from specialized dinosaurs. Fast-forward about 100 million years, give or take, up to the present. The current dominant species have recently evolved during the extended period of recurring ice ages punctuated by periods of abrupt warming cycles. A short while back, on the timescale we're using, humans came upon the scene. Prior to written history, subsistence hunting with primitive gear and equipment came to include waterfowl hunting. The few decoys preserved and uncovered would indicate that primitive hunters used some of the same methods, if not the same equipment, as the bunch going out early tomorrow morning. Within the micro-time of present human history, there has been overexploitation of waterfowl resources followed by a conservation movement actively supported by waterfowl hunters.

Duck and Goose Habitat on the Continental Scale

Ducks, geese, and other waterfowl make continental-scale migrations in order to utilize natural resources throughout the annual cycle of bounty during spring and summer in the North, then head south to escape the cold and ice and exploit the resources of their southern range in fall and winter. It should be noted that ducks and geese are not overly susceptible to the cold; some sea duck species even spend the winter in the arctic ice, diving deep to feed on mollusks. But the majority of species feed on aquatic vegetation, grain, nuts, and small aquatic animals that either become absent and/or inaccessible by thick snow and ice.

Duck and Goose Habitat on the Predator Attack and Shotgun Range Scale

Along and at either end of the continental-scale migrations, ducks and geese need habitat that furnishes daily subsistence and minimizes predation. Natural predators, from arctic foxes to brown bears, are the greatest threat to all waterfowl in their summer nesting and molting habitat. Predation is most severe on nesting females and newly hatched young. In the case of ducks, avoiding threats to eggs and setting hens primarily involves hiding on the nest. The drakes, which are not effective fighters and just draw attention, leave the hens to fend for themselves after breeding. Species survival depends on large clutches of eggs and favorable rainfall to furnish subsistence and water-borne escape from terrestrial and aquatic predators.

Geese are generally more successful in summertime survival than ducks. Their natural nesting areas are in the high Arctic, where human cultivation and high concentrations of predators are still minimal. In contrast to ducks, geese (both male and female) not only hide, but are also fighters and will put up a spirited, and often successful, defense of the nest and hatchlings. Biting with bills and striking with wings are often effective on foxes. Bears usually win, however. Geese mate for life, and the family unit of the breeding pair and young from the recent past hatchings stay together to provide more eyes looking out for threats.

The greatest threat to both ducks and geese during the fall migration is from human hunters. Successful game management of waterfowl was determined early on to primarily consist of management of the human hunters. Open and closed seasons, plus bag limits, are primary reasons why we have such good waterfowl hunting available today. The situation has also improved with the activities of organized outdoor enthusiasts to promote conservation of habitat, control excessive predation, and other efforts too numerous to review. Our old beat-up felt hats and new camo beanie caps are off to them.

Duck and Goose Hunters

Duck and goose hunters seem to fall into at least two groups: the passionate waterfowlers who'll hunt on the dark morning of the worst blizzard of the century alone except for their devoted retriever; and the outdoor sports types who may go on a once-a-year big-game hunt and need an excuse to get out with kindred spirits during the rest of the fall and early winter. Both groups are represented by your authors, and you can easily tell who is who over the course of the instructions to follow.

Our goal is to make this a waterfowling guide for everybody—from the naturally gifted hunter who instinctively knows where to be half an hour before sunrise, to the rest of us. Waterfowl hunting has a lot to offer, no matter what your level of expertise may be. Happily, duck and goose populations, and waterfowl hunting, are on the rise after some hard times going back over the past couple of decades. One of us has been afield for five decades before that. In review, we'll cover some introductory topics with a general approach: identification of all species of waterfowl and habitat on the continental scale. Then the reader can see how hunting ducks on small water fits into the broader scheme of things. In the final analysis, it's a thirty-yard-range proposition. Which brings us to . . .

Waterfowl hunting is characterized by a series of mindsets: eager anticipation during the trip to the hunt location, preparation of the setup, and the wait for the first flight to appear; a rush as birds drop toward the decoys and into range, sometimes after a cautious pass or two or more; absolute focus as the world stands still and it's just you and the target as you make the appropriate lead of the barrel and the gun fires as something detached; exhilaration if the shot is made, the immediate sinking feeling if a miss.

Using This Book

This book is intended to be the definitive guidebook for waterfowl hunting in all of its many forms. We've addressed it to everybody across a broad range of resources: physical capability, financial resources, and time. Do it yourself or get help, professional or otherwise. Hunt on public land outside of town or travel to a famous lodge. Set up your own boat with cover for a few hundred dollars or go all out and buy a fully tricked-out boat for $50,000.

Part I is a practical introduction to the nature of ducks and geese. The initial focus is on waterfowl characteristics and behavior, as all hunters need to be able to identify ducks and geese for compliance with game laws and bag limits. After some insight into the nature of the game, we'll then take you hunting, covering the basics of waterfowling, before continuing into advanced insights for readers already familiar with the basics, but who're interested in moving up a notch in their techniques and tactics. Part I is the prerequisite to the skills development and selection of equipment in Part II.

Part II takes you past that point of reading as an observer. You're in preparation for participation. We don't take for granted that you grew up in a family full of hunters. A lot of folks haven't gone through the phases that Tom and Eddie, a generation later, survived: BB guns at whatever age we could get our hands on one; a .22-caliber single shot at age nine to eleven on, depending on maturity; and a single-shot .410 shotgun, or the old 12-gauge around every farm because that was what was available; and, finally, a "big gun," otherwise called a "deer gun," which translated to a high-powered rifle of some kind, often a lever-action 30-30. And we just followed our interest from there on. And, with this progression of equipment, we disposed of varmints and pests, and took game for the table.

Kent came along almost contemporary with Eddie, but a world away in the suburbs, with a perspective probably close to that of many of our readers. Toward the end of his high school years, a friend invited him to come along on a duck hunt. Somewhere between "shoot 'em" and "reload," Kent came down with a severe case of waterfowling fever, something he carries to this day.

Part II is a crash course on the things that many of you missed during your youth: shotgun actions, gauges, powder, shot, shells, leads, ammo, decoys, calls, blinds, hides—everything it takes to make the shot. Then all of the rest of the assorted gear you need to get out there: camo clothes, waders, raingear, gloves, boats, GPS systems, and so on. We also touch on shooting practice, which is as important as anything else you need before going hunting.

Part III goes into the nature of hunting across North America. This is essential in making arrangements for your hunt, be it in your local area or far away. We'll show you how to follow the migrations as they roll over your local area, as well as how to go intercept the migration in other regions. Arrangements for the hunt are less complicated, faster, and relatively less expensive than they were in the good old days. Airline or interstate travel can now make that dream trip a reality, another aspect of the good new days.

Waterfowl hunting is in a state of expansion and diversification after decades of contraction. Ducks, with their requirement of northern prairie potholes (water-filled depressions formed by the weight of melted glaciers) and other water-based habitat for nesting and sustainment, were reduced in numbers. Bag limits followed suit. Complicated bag limits of points based on species and whether ducks taken were drakes or hens moved some of us to vacate the ponds and marshes for a time. Nowadays, thanks to the efforts of a great many individuals and organizations, the ducks are back, as are the specialized duck hunters. The geese came through better due to their diet and the fact that their arctic nesting areas remain safe from agricultural development. Grazing on agricultural cropland along migratory routes and wintering areas, in fact, has sustained population growth of all but the most specialized of geese species. Overpopulations of snow geese have put so much pressure on some arctic habitat that extended seasons and liberal bag limits became a necessity.

We intend that this book can be opened at any page and make sense. We refer to other chapters throughout, with links throughout. And finally, for those who didn't read the preface, here's what you missed: The book has been designed so that the reader has the option to make maximum use of Internet searches. That's where all of the details reside, just waiting for you to look. The terms in the index are designed to be searched. A lot of them can be found in topic headings. We've dropped them into the main text where needed. That's the magic that covers all the details.

PART I

Ducks and Geese and How to Hunt Them

Chapter 1

Identification and Behavior Patterns

The objective here is not to make you a wildlife biologist, but to provide you with background for identification of ducks and geese, so you're in compliance with regulations. Identification has to be sure, according to species and in some cases male or female. This chapter will address physical description, flight characteristics, predation avoidance, and nutrition. Ducks and geese are intertwined with their habitat. Habitat and migration patterns will be introduced here, and covered more thoroughly in Part III. Familiarization with waterfowl and habitat will prepare you for instruction in techniques, tactics, and strategies of hunting.

General Survival Adaptations Common to All Prey Animals

There's a beauty in nature that attracts and fascinates us. The balance and symmetry are mostly beyond our comprehension. But here are some fundamentals of nature as they pertain to animals.

All animals are in a constant state of threat. They exist on the edge of starving or being eaten, and sometimes both. They exist in a habitat for which they're uniquely adapted. Suitable habitat for prey animals provides means of subsistence and avoidance of predation.

To avoid extinction, prey species have to successfully avoid predation and reproduce sufficiently to balance mortality. Each species, each individual of each species, acts according to an overall strategy that is designed to ensure the species' continued existence.

OVERVIEW OF WATERFOWL

Ducks and geese lead a hazardous, terrestrial existence that's inexorably tied to flight and water habitat. But even the species most adapted to an existence on, under, and over water still return to dry land for the annual extended and hazardous summer task of the female ducks and pairs of geese: to lay and brood the eggs and bring forth the next generation. And shortly thereafter, while the newly hatched young are incapable of flight, both male and female adults shed their feathers and are incapable of flight for weeks. Then some species head back to their preferred diet of fish from the big, deep waters of northern lakes and migrate toward the coast to spend the winter on the briny. Other species are adapted to overnight on water for safety, and then venture onto dry land for grazing on tender shoots and foraging for high-quality food sources like grain, fruits, and acorns.

The highly successful survival strategies of waterfowl mimic those of small animals of all orders, including small game: keen vision and wariness; speed, agility, and endurance; and, most critically, the capability of reproducing in numbers sufficient to replenish annual losses. Survival of individuals, and ultimately the species, is threatened by losses suffered in northern breeding grounds. Females in particular are vulnerable while sitting on nests. Sudden weather changes may freeze the eggs or emerging young, while drought can devastate breeding habitat.

INTRODUCTION TO DUCKS AND GEESE

The first order of business is for you to become acquainted, in a general way, with ducks and geese. Waterfowling 101, if you please. We'll give a general overview of the major divisions of ducks and geese, then get into identification.

Dabblers, the Puddle Ducks

One large branch of duck families, commonly termed the *dabblers*, is adapted to feed primarily on aquatic vegetation and to seek refuge on small, shallow bodies of water: prairie potholes of northern nesting areas on the plains of Canada; streams, flooded timberland, sloughs, farm ponds, and freshwater swamps along the migratory routes to the South; marshlands and shallow bays in wintering areas of the Gulf Coast; and back north again in an annual cycle.

Dabblers feed by foraging from the surface of shallow water near shorelines or in small ponds by tipping tail up, head down to feed on the bottom. Their preferred nutrition sources and feeding habits are ideally suited for small-water habitats. Mallards, teal, wigeons, and American black ducks are frequently cited as typical

Puddle ducks take to air. Credit: JoAnne Airhart.

dabblers. (The official definition of the verb *dabble* is "to splash around or paddle in water.") The dabblers are very agile aerodynamically, capable of fast flights to avoid danger and long-duration migration flights at an efficient, lower, energy-saving speed. They have the ability to come into a landing at low speed but then, if alarmed, can explode into the air from a resting position on the water surface and fly straight up to escape danger or clear trees before flying off at top speed.

The above photo by a startled but smooth operator illustrates an unexpected encounter with a combined flight of mallards (foreground), gadwalls (various stages of springing up from the water surface), and a few pintails (drake with wings flat against the water surface for push-up left of center) as they all jump up from the water surface.

The legs of dabblers are set in the middle of their body mass so that they walk with reasonable efficiency on open fields to feed on wasted grain after fall harvest and early grain sprouts during winter and early spring. Dabbler flotation is balanced to allow them to easily tip forward to feed on shallow bottoms with very low energy output. They're also capable of diving to moderate depths to feed on deeper bottoms, if necessary. A visual identifier of dabblers noted in references is an iridescent speculum, or wing patch.

Diving Ducks

Almost all of the rest of the ducks are deep divers, feeding primarily on small aquatic invertebrates, fish, and shellfish in large, deep bodies of water along migratory routes from Canada and the northern United States to wintering areas along the northeast and mid-Atlantic coastlines, and over the mountains to the west and along the Pacific coast. Divers may also be found in smaller numbers across the central migration routes with the dabblers, as well as along both eastern and western routes.

Freshwater divers share waters and habitat with dabblers. Divers effortlessly roll over forward into a dive to feed in terrestrial waters at considerable depth, if required, but small inland waters usually require just a few feet to find the wide variety of plants, fish, insects, mollusks, and crustaceans preferred by each species. Cited in references as typical freshwater divers are the small ring-necked duck, even smaller merganser, and the relatively large canvasback.

Another branch of the diver family of ducks is adapted to dive deep into large waters to feed primarily on a wide range of aquatic animals found in large freshwater lakes, along saltwater shores, and far offshore. They're referred to collectively as the sea ducks. Some sea duck species make long migrations deep into the interior of Canada to nest; others nest along rocky shorelines of the sea, where they'll spend the winter far offshore. Sea ducks range in size from the very small bufflehead, at around one pound, to the very large eiders, at well over six pounds.

Diving ducks, in both fresh and salt water, have small, strong wings that propel them at high velocity through the air. In aerodynamic terms, they have a high wing loading that results in less aerodynamic agility than the dabblers. They have to fly hard and fast to fly at all; if they slow down, they can't stay airborne! They'll often fly low over the water surface to take advantage of ground effect (the additional lift provided by compression of the air under a flying body against a very close rigid surface, ground or water). They land on the water hard with poor control compared to the dabblers, and have to take off using long, hard runs across the water surface with wings beating fast in order to build up speed sufficient to get airborne. Once airborne, they generally have a top speed greater than that of the dabblers.

Their legs are set far back on their bodies to allow their large feet to efficiently propel them through the water while diving. They stand with an awkward-looking upright stance and are poorly adapted to feeding on land.

The first instinctive impulse of the dabblers is to explode off the water and fly away from danger. And they're fully capable of just that. The divers have a tough time taking off under the best of circumstances, however. They're inclined to dive under the water surface and swim away from immediate danger. Compared to dabblers, divers are at a distinct disadvantage in flying away from danger.

Aerodynamic curse of the divers. Hooded merganser hen demonstrates small wings on a chunky diver body. Credit: JoAnne Airhart.

Speed vs. Gravity. With a trail of splashes, a hooded merganser goes airborne after a short run across the water. Credit: JoAnne Airhart.

Advantages of being a dabbler. Diver and dabbler in the middle of an escape. With an even start, a diver and dabbler compared illustrate why the diver is better served with a dive rather than flight. Credit: JoAnne Airhart.

A diver and a dabbler together on the water and startled simultaneously illustrate the difference.

Perching Ducks

Perching ducks, which comprise a small fraction of all ducks, have evolved to go back to the trees with the rest of the birds to seek safe refuge, rest, and nest in the arboreal habitat, but still feed in the aquatic realm.

Geese

Then there are the geese, very distant cousins of the ducks. Geese on the wing in their ever-changing "V" formations mark the passage of the seasons: fall heading south, spring headed back north. They're an inspiration to poets, songwriters, photographers, and artists. But let us not forget the goose hunters.

The most sweeping summary to convey the character of geese is big: big in size, in distance of migration, and in numbers. Geese as a family of species are the largest waterfowl game, several times the weights and dimensions of ducks. Migration of some species is between the coasts of the Arctic Ocean and the Gulf of Mexico. And they gather together to travel as a single gaggle (goose term for flock) made up of a couple thousand of their closest friends and family. The reference to family is literal. A mated pair of geese, with offspring, often multiple generations, will hold together amid the thousands of their kind. And these thousands are composed of many, many individual close families. The family bond begins with the pair that mates for life, with both parents protecting and caring for hatchlings.

In the sometimes brutal, hard workings of nature, geese have fared much better than duck populations as humans have intruded into the domain of waterfowl. Human impacts, added to the cyclic, natural rhythms of flood and drought, have led to cyclic calamities on duck populations. Expanding agricultural interests have encroached upon duck breeding grounds on the northern prairies. Geese of many species, in contrast, migrate in their massive numbers to breeding grounds in the high Arctic, largely untouched by human enterprise. Large numbers of some goose species have adapted their diets to utilize what humans cultivate. Several subspecies of Canada geese, in particular, have partially moved in with humans. They range north a short distance, if they go at all, and do just fine among humans, their golf courses, and their well-irrigated croplands. Grain crops contribute to the subsistence of migrating geese just when they need it: wasted grain missed by combines in the fall for the southbound migration; tender emerging sprouts of the new crop for the springtime trip back north.

Why Identification of Waterfowl Is Such a Big Deal

It's imperative that the waterfowl hunter understand the importance of identification. A copy of (state) hunting regulations for the location you're going to hunt is the first priority of gear you should acquire; understanding the content is the first insight you'll need. State regulations incorporate yearly guidelines of the United States Fish and Wildlife Service (USF&WS) for seasons and bag limits for migratory game birds. USF&WS recommendations go by "flyways," which are administrative designations of north to south zones across the continent east to west: Atlantic, Mississippi, Central, and Pacific. They're not to be confused with the migration corridors that waterfowl actually use, as will be covered in detail in the later chapters.

The following table gives typical daily limits for several states distributed across the United States. Our numbers are current as of this writing (and that's as good as we can figure them), but certainly won't be good for your state when you read them. As we mentioned first thing, your first order of business when you think about waterfowl hunting is to get a current copy of the hunting regulations for your state. You'll find there are a lot more rules than the daily bag limits, and the consequences of breaking them are going to be more severe than any parking ticket. So, as soon as you've been made aware that the daily bag limit isn't the same for all species, the next order of business is to develop the skills to identify the different waterfowl game species you'll encounter. That translates to being able to identify either gender of all the duck species (limits may be different for males and females, and, in most cases, they wouldn't resemble each other at all during hunting season). Among the geese, goose and gander are identical except in size. But, maybe more important, we'll illustrate the protected nongame waterfowl species.

Many of the nongame (no shoot) species are threatened with or even in danger of extinction, and the consequences of killing a member of one of these species can be severe.

EXAMPLES OF BAG LIMITS OF TYPICAL STATES FOR DUCKS AND GEESE

(They change every year for every state.)

SPECIES	TX EAST	TX WEST	AR	ND	LA	ME	CA	UT	WI	SC	OK	MD	IN
Duck Total Daily Limit	6	6	6	5	6	6	7	7	6	6	6	6	6
Mallard Total/Hen	5/2	5/2	5/2	/1	4/2	/2	7/2	/2	4/1	4/2	5/2	4/2	4/2
Redhead	2	2	2	2	2	2	2	2	2	2	2		2
Scaup	3	3	3	2	3	2	3	3	3	2	3	2	3
Pintail	2	2	2	1	2	2	2	2	2	2	2	2	2
Canvasback	1	1	1	1	1	1	1	1	1	1	1	1	1
Mottled Duck	1	1	1	1	1	1			1	1		1	1
Black Duck			1	1	1	1			1	1		1	1
Wood Duck	3	3	3	2	3	3		2	3	3		3	3
Duck Notes	No species limit (except as noted for particular states); Daily limit applies: Teal, Gadwall, Wigeon, Shovelers, Ring-Necked, Scoters (4 in MD, Sea Duck SC), Goldeneyes, Ruddy, Buffleheads, Long-Tailed (5 in MD, Sea Duck SC), Fulvous Whistling Duck (1 in ME), Eider (SC).												
Merganser Total Ex Other Ducks/ Hooded	5/2	5/2	5/2	5/2	5/2	5/2			5/2	5/2	5/2		3/2
Sea Ducks						7 + Regular Ducks				Duck Notes			
Canada (Dark) Geese Total/White-Fronted	3/2	5/1	2/2	3/2	3/2	3	10 (of 25T)		12/1	5	3/2	2 Atl/ 5 Res	3/2
Snow, Blue, Ross's (Light) Geese	20	20	50	50	20	25	15 (of 25T)		20	25	20	25	20
Coot	15	15	15	15	15	15			15	15			15

Note: The generalization into light and dark is used by state wildlife/game management: dark geese are all of the Canada subspecies, Atlantic and black brant, and white-fronted goose; light geese are snow geese (both phases) and Ross's goose.

Summary Data and Portraits of Widely Hunted Ducks and Geese

The professional grade photos, with drakes in full breeding plumage, are easily distinguished from what the average duck and goose hunter encounters afield. Most of our photos include some up close or in hand (*at hand* is the common term); some in the field at distance on the water or land sans benefit of large telescopic lens (unhandy while hunting); some in flight. Don't expect most of our photos to meet the standards of professionals. They do represent what ducks and geese actually look like to the hunter, however. Bad lighting; drakes not always in full breeding plumage; and often appearing out of the fog and darkness and over your blind, going like bats out of hell before you can even get the safety off. And if your blind and/or camo doesn't measure up, the flight of ducks will explode in all directions, or the formation of geese, wings locked, will veer off to the side in a majestic sweep and you won't see them again, for that day at least.

Our discussion of characteristics and identification of waterfowl places the most emphasis on species hunted the most often. That would be the species with the greatest bag limits and the most easily reached with the lowest cost in terms of time and money. Our firsthand experience, and that of the majority of our readers, is primarily close to home on small private waters or public land.

Identification of Ducks and Geese Under Hunting Conditions

The complexities of waterfowl identification go beyond the already mentioned drastic differences in appearance, primarily in duck species, between males and females. The males, drakes, change in appearance from summer when they're on the northern breeding grounds, through fall and winter on into early spring, when breeding takes place. All general publications, and many publications directed at waterfowlers, are only illustrated with the males in full breeding plumage. This makes for nice pictures, but are of limited use to the newly minted hunter heading toward the potholes of the northernmost tier of states for the opening of the season. The drakes are just beginning to start to look like a drake rather than an ugly hen. This annual transformation doesn't progress at the same rate for all species, either. When the mallards show up in Texas, they're in their glory of breeding plumage, or fast approaching it, while the northern shovelers, with arguably the most spectacular breeding plumage of all the ducks of North America, will look motley for another two months or more.

Classic terms of identification are *on the wing* and *at hand*. We've taken the liberty to sometimes expand terms to include: *on the wing, close,* and *distant, good* and *poor light; on the water near* and *distant;* and *at hand* (sometimes termed *in hand*).

Poor lighting and fast-moving targets are the overriding obstructions to visual identification in the real world of waterfowl hunting. Following are the techniques used to overcome what would, at first glance, appear to be the impossible. With these beginning instructions and a lot of practice, it becomes intuitive.

There's one set of techniques when the flight is close enough to see and hear with some accuracy: patterns of flight (dynamics of individuals and group), and characteristics of flight (speed and wingbeat); calls during flight; number of birds in the flight; size of individual birds; body and wing configuration; takeoff and landing characteristics; flight altitude; recognizing ducks and geese by their silhouette against the dimly lit sky; unique habits and behavior; sound of wings beating through the air (each species is unbelievably distinct) at speed. New hunters can dig up apps off the Internet that have wingbeats and vocalizations. We have them internalized—best if Eddie is in the boat. A general rule is that the diver's wingbeat is much faster than that of the dabbler.

Clues to identification on the wing at distance include: flight characteristics such as rapidity of wingbeat and stroke arc distance; internal dynamics of individuals within the flock; patterns of the shape of the collective flight; plus a general wariness and reluctance to land if suspicious of danger in a particular location on the water or ground. Discussion of characteristics of each species will include notable attributes of flight. Some flight characteristics between species and collections of species can also be made.

All ducks and geese fly high in migration as a general rule. Geese will fly from three hundred feet up depending on the best level for tail wind. They drop lower as they become tired during long flights, down below two hundred feet to about one hundred feet if they're completely worn out and need to rest on water. Dabblers are the most wary ducks as a group and the highest fliers. Mallards and their close relatives take the high road, well over one hundred feet if suspicious of something down there. The pintail is a high, agile flier and can drop like a rocket if it wants to. The gadwall and wigeon fly high when they're on the way somewhere. The rest of the dabblers, the northern shoveler, and all teal are upper-mid-level fliers. The wood duck is all over the place, mid-level high or down through the trees. All of the divers fly lower. The freshwater divers, scaups, ring-necks, redheads, goldeneyes, and canvasbacks fly higher than the sea ducks: long-tailed, scoters, eiders, mergansers, and buffleheads. Coots fly low. The experienced hunters thinking in terms of plate covers know that the good-eating ducks are the high fliers.

Good afternoon scouting is one way to identify ducks in the dim light of tomorrow morning. The ducks coming through this afternoon will be the same ones diving out of the darkness in the morning.

The discussions of each species coming up will include insight into behavior, such as characteristics of feeding activities and schedule; location of feeding according to preferences of feed; and routes between overnight sanctuary and feeding locations. There will also be information about plumage markers visible at a distance, accounting for progression of male breeding plumage for each species with particular emphasis on white markers under conditions of poor visibility.

At hand identification is discussed for individual species.

Effect of Low-Light Conditions

The effect of dim light conditions: shades of dark gray, wigeons in gloom.

A little more light creates wigeons in color.

Drake mallards in dim light. Drake mallards at a distance in poor lighting are distinctive with white sides and dark stripes along sides of back. White can be seen in dim light. Green heads are black without direct sunlight, a point to remember when repainting your decoys.

Identification on the Wing in Poor Light

Wigeons against the early morning sky.

Shifting flight pattern. Note that wigeon wings have a unique crescent shape. With only an outline against the sky, identification clues are limited: flight characteristics, sounds of calls and wing beats, unique shapes of different species, and, best of all, scouting and migration reports indicating waterfowl in the area.

Identification and Regulation Compliance; Scouting Methodology and Information; and Hunting Methods, Tactics, and Arrangements

There are a few generalizations that will pertain to identification of the two general types of ducks regardless of lighting effects and distance. Note in the photographs that follow that puddle, or dabbler, ducks float high in the water, while divers hardly clear the water surface except for the head. Old hands note this characteristic, since the dabblers are almost always good on the plate, while the divers can range from strong to awful. You don't fill your bag limit with the "little black divers" when dabblers might show up at any time. We've mentioned before some of the ways that old-timers sort out the best tasting. You'll probably read some more.

Identification Techniques Useful for All Ducks

With a little practice, you can get a rough idea of a particular duck species in flight, at least within a general range, based on appearance. We define size according to four ranges, which is about as accurate an estimate as you can make for identification. Weight and length/wingspan measurements of ducks typical of each of our four ranges are: small (blue-winged teal, one pound and fifteen to twenty inches); medium (gadwall, two pounds and twenty to thirty inches); large (mallard, three pounds and twenty-five to thirty-eight inches; canvasback, three pounds and twenty-two to thirty-two inches); and very large (king eider, four pounds and twenty-five inches). Within each species, drakes will be a little over these averages, hens less. Flight speed and characteristics, individual and as a group within the flight, are very useful for identification at distance.

During migration, all species tend to fly at a range of elevations, often very high. As previously noted, flight during the daily routine is more distinctive. First order of identification is between the two families of ducks: dabblers pop up off the water and fly, depending upon species, twenty to eighty or more feet up, much lower in fog; divers run across the water surface to get airborne and then fly close to the water, very close in the case of the sea ducks, going out of their way to avoid flying over land. Distinguishing markings at distance and at hand will be noted for each species.

Comments that pertain to scouting and hunting particular species, and in some cases, families of species, are included in this section for reference. In order to be successful, both scouting and hunting use a range of information: behavior, feeding patterns, the progression of migration, and, in the case of the consistently successful, a certain element of intuition. Presentation of this section will follow a general format to keep the reader from getting completely lost, but, hopefully, with enough variation to avoid that annoying eye-glaze effect.

Total populations and distribution of species, at different places and times, will be addressed in Chapters 9 and 10 as part of the information a hunter needs to know when planning a hunt.

Puddle Ducks

In this section we'll discuss the extended family referred to as puddle ducks, dabblers, and unprintable on lots of days toward the end of the season. Common identifiers are physical characteristics and capabilities, behavior, and foraging habits. The common denominator is that they're adapted to feed on dry land as well as very shallow waters, both open to predation by highly efficient land-bound carnivores. Over eons of time, the survivors of these hazards have developed center-balanced legs from front to back. They're remarkably efficient at moving about foraging for high-quality nutrition on those aquatic webbed feet. In high gear after elusive prey, the duck waddle is barely perceptible. Dabblers minimize time spent exposed to hazards. If they're surprised on land or in shallow water, their strong, nimble wings will lift them straight up out of harm's way. A back flap of the same wing action can allow them to drop straight down through a small hole between closely spaced oak trees to feed on acorns.

Puddle Ducks: Habits and Habitat

Puddle ducks of North America typically nest across Canada, and winter across the southern United States and parts of Central America. Many puddle ducks nest in the Prairie Pothole country of central Canada. This exposes their populations to the hazards of cyclic drought. Drastic population fluctuations can occur when the potholes dry up. Nature helps them deal with this by having them disperse over wide regions. Dispersion and scattered nesting sites also deny predators the concentrated windfall of plundering eggs, nestlings, fledglings, and nesting female adults.

A few generalizations can be made concerning distribution of specific species. Black ducks are restricted to the East. Pintails can be found across the continent, but are more numerous in the West. Mallards are everywhere, year-round in some places, mixing in with domestics. Gadwalls and wigeons are widespread. Few of the stay-overs in the South are able to reproduce in any kinds of numbers, as the young usually fall victim to predators. Wood ducks, once rare and even threatened as a species, are now numerous in their favorite habitat of large trees with hollows. They also take advantage of man-made nesting boxes.

Every puddle deep enough for dabbling from the surface is habitat for these ducks, which includes about everywhere in North America except the wind-blown peaks. And that extends to the coastal marshes out to where the sea ducks take over. Pursuit of these elusive ducks is consequently available for most hunters in the country.

You'll see in our reviews of the different species that we've put more emphasis on the ducks and geese most available and most hunted. The italics will direct your search for more information concerning insight into the nature, availability, and unique characteristics of any particular species.

Mallard Drake (Greenhead), Hen (Susie)

<u>Identification at distance and in flight</u>: Mallards in flight at a distance can be recognized by their steady, straight-ahead movement and easy, deliberate, and rather shallow wing strokes. Their cruising speed is around thirty miles per hour.

A large flock of forty to fifty individuals at altitude will form up in a "U" or a "V" pattern, transitioning to multiple patterns if the flight becomes larger. If startled in flight, the flock immediately explodes in all directions, using deep, rapid wing strokes to hit escape speeds of sixty miles per hour.

Mallard pair. Credit: JoAnne Airhart.

An individual mallard at distance will appear as a large duck with a chunky body. As wings flap down, iridescent purple-blue speculum feathers between white edges at the top of the wings are evident on both the male and the female. Drakes appear to be dark in front and over the back, with a light, almost white underbelly. They weigh around three and a half pounds and measure about twenty-five inches in length. The wingspan is thirty-eight inches, with the wings being noticeably wide in relation to other dabblers. Hens are golden brown and smaller at two and a half pounds, with a length of twenty-two inches and a wingspan of thirty-four inches. Distinction between mallard hens and drakes is important in that specific species bag limits of one or two per day apply to hens. Drakes outnumber hens two to one due to predation during nesting, which has to be taken into account by game management.

Identification by landings and takeoffs: Identification can be made by landing and takeoff characteristics. Wings are normally locked in a glide to the vicinity of the selected landing spot. Speed drops rapidly as the wings make a couple of backstrokes and the feet extend to touch the water. There's a short slide over the water surface before the belly settles into the water. A mallard can alternately drop straight down through trees using vertical wing strokes and lightly splash down to a spot landing. The mallard can spring straight up from the water surface using deep, powerful wing strokes. After clearing the water surface, a mallard can immediately move off in any direction, but usually forward, or continue to climb vertically straight up through dense timber.

Identification up close and at hand: Markings noted at hand are the drake breeding plumage noted throughout hunting seasons: iridescent green head, crimson front with light underbelly, white along upper sides of body, yellow-green bill. Hens are golden brown with darker brown trim on tips of feathers, an orange bill darkened on top by a black pattern. Both have orange legs and feet.

Range, distribution, and migration patterns: There are more mallards than any other ducks. Distribution is over North America, Europe, and Asia.

Their greatest concentration is central North America. They have the most widely distributed nesting area of any duck. Data from published information indicates ten to twelve million wild mallards available for hunting in North America. Migration patterns are broadly across the continents at a leisurely pace. Most mallards are late to move south in the fall, just ahead of freeze-over.

Habitat and diet: Favored habitat is shallow, freshwater ponds: nesting in the North, primarily around glacier-formed potholes, natural lakes, and marshes; wintering in the Midwest, West, and South, primarily in flooded fields and timber, creeks, sloughs, shallow-water swamps and upper ends of man-made lakes, stock ponds, brackish marshes along shorelines, and irrigation water storage. Diet is omnivorous: predominantly aquatic vegetation, seeds, nuts, and small invertebrates.

Hunting techniques and arrangements: Hunting techniques are shooting over decoys using one to two dozen decoys on small ponds and up to one hundred on shoreline irregularities. Hunters use cover, blinds, and camouflaged boats for concealment.

Mallards are a favorite for do-it-yourself arrangements over small waters and shorelines of larger waters. Hunting from boats is usually by self-arrangement also, but guides and outfitters are available. A hunting tradition has developed around hunting clubs and lodges dedicated primarily to hunting mallards. The lower Mississippi Region is considered the center of mallard hunting, although mallards are so widely distributed that you can start some good debates by saying that in some gatherings.

Additional facts and information: The mallard is synonymous with "wild duck" for most folks with casual knowledge of waterfowl. The spectacular breeding plumage of the male and the aerobatics of mallards could put them in the category of very athletic birds of paradise if they were rare and occurred only on an exotic tropical isle. But they're the most plentiful of all game ducks, have a worldwide distribution, and the makings of fine dining with a little effort in preparation. So it's no wonder that they're highly sought after by duck hunters. A recently evolved species, the genetic dynamics of the mallard have resulted in an array of closely related species and subspecies, both wild and domesticated, which will interbreed and produce fertile offspring. The protospecies mallard was a very large version of the current model. It originated during an interglacial of the recent ice age in what is now eastern Siberia, but part of the continuous landmass of Beringia that connected Asia and North America at the time.

The population of resident and domesticated mallards is significant. Domestics may be recognized by their large size. Many are effectively free roaming and can cause problems for wildlife management by interbreeding with wild populations, primarily by groups of predatory drakes on wild females of closely related species, often resulting in injury or death of the female. Mallard hybridization can result in weirdly spectacular drakes.

Hybrid mallard drakes (both are hybrids). Credit: JoAnne Airhart.

As noted in the identification sections, the mallard population determines the bag limits of the major flyways of North America. Drakes dominate the population due to mortality among nesting hens. The disproportionate number of males versus females results in typical daily bag limits of five total, with a limit of two hens. Expert mallard hunting specialists—such beings actually exist—hunt with the objective of taking drakes only. Really tough with pairs. The rest of us can pull it off when flights of bachelor drakes only occur in late season.

Mallards strongly pair bond, and pairs will separate from large flocks, often in the company of another pair. When alarmed pairs take off, the hen will be in the lead. Good to know for limited bag limits for hens. If the shot is on a pair dropping straight down or flying away in tandem, it's very likely that the shot will take both. If the male is lost, the hen can pick up another suitor almost immediately. The size of flights can range from a pair to hundreds.

"Howyadoin'?" Pair and a spare of mallards in the feed-bed at early morning light. Hens often have multiple suitors since drakes outnumber hens by more than two to one. Hens face greater hazards and higher mortality than drakes, due to predators during nesting.

Mallard pairs up from a stock pond. Pairs are usually aligned and close together.

Black Duck

Identification at distance and in flight: The American black duck is a large duck: males average three and one half pounds, with a length of twenty inches and a wingspan of thirty-eight inches; females average two and one half pounds, with a length of twenty-two inches and a wingspan of thirty-four inches. They have an escape speed of sixty miles per hour, and a cruising speed of thirty miles per hour. In flight at

American Black Duck Drake. Credit: Alan Schmierer.

distance, American black ducks can be identified by their ever-changing flock patterns and strong, full, deliberate wing strokes, all in close resemblance to the mallard. An individual will appear as a large, black duck that shows white underwings, unique to the black duck. The black duck in outline is identical with the mallard. Under conditions of good lighting, their dark color is unmistakable. They may be seen in mixed flights with mallards. They have a deep, strong, and steady wingbeat. The white undersides of the flapping wings flash with each wingbeat. At distance on the water, they appear large and ride high on the water surface, in common with most dabblers.

Identification by landings and takeoffs: Flight characteristics and markings can be used to distinguish black ducks at distance. They are high fliers with a deliberate, straight flight. They have a locked wing glide landing, and a pop-up takeoff. Iridescent purple-blue speculum feathers between the black edges on top of the wings of both male and female black ducks are distinctive.

Identification up close and at hand: Black ducks resemble a darker (dusky), brownish-black version of the female mallard. Drakes are a dusky, blackish brown; the hen is slightly less dark, with a more pronounced brown cast, compared to the drake, which is almost black except for its head. Heads of drakes may vary in darkness. In good lighting, up close and at hand, the feather tips produce a beautiful pattern on the body and folded wings. The mottled appearance formed by the dark tips of the mallard hen can be readily defined on the black duck hen, but is almost completely lost in the blackness of the drake's full breeding plumage. Speculum is blue with black edges (contrasts sharply with the white around the mallard speculum). The drake's bill is yellow (as is the mallard's) with dark shade in the center; the hen's bill is olive. The yellow bill of the drake and the dull green bill of the hen are definitive. Both drakes and hens have orange legs and feet.

Range, distribution, and migration patterns: The range of black ducks covers eastern North America. Breeding grounds are primarily in southeastern Canada. Wintering range is the eastern United States. Makes for a relatively short migration at a leisurely pace.

There is a wide overlap between breeding and wintering areas. Black ducks tend to gather during the fall and winter along the Atlantic and Gulf coasts of the eastern United States. Extensive overlap occurs where the ubiquitous mallard mixes with the black duck. The two flock together during migration and during feeding for the duration of the stay in the wintering area. Pairs seek seclusion during breeding and selection of the nesting spot.

Habitat and diet: Habitat is fresh and saltwater marshes, small ponds, and sloughs. Black ducks are omnivorous. Their diet is predominantly aquatic vegetation, such as pondweed, as well as seeds, acorns, and grain when available from harvest wastage. Invertebrates and crustaceans are a secondary source of food. They feed on animals more than mallards do; mussels and shad are examples.

Hunting techniques and arrangements: Hunting techniques are the same as for the mallard and include decoying using one to two dozen decoys on small ponds and at shoreline irregularities. As with mallard hunting, black duck hunters use cover, blinds, and camouflaged boats.

Black ducks are considered characteristically wary by those who hunt them extensively—even more so than the mallard—and hard to decoy, compared to the mallard.

Additional information: The black duck is closely related to the mallard. In fact, some consider the black duck to be a variant of the mallard. Size, behavior, diet, preferred habitat, and flight characteristics are very similar. They're also close to mottled ducks, Florida ducks, and Mexican ducks. Significant hybridization occurs where ranges overlap. Studies indicate that mixed breeding may result from forced copulation by marauding mallard bachelor flocks on unattended black duck hens. In areas where the species intermingle, aggressive breeding by mallard drakes results in hybrid offspring that often fail to reproduce. Many specialists in wildlife research consider interbreeding to be a main driver in the reduction of black duck populations, but competition with mallards for identical resources can't be ruled out.

Mottled Duck

<u>Identification at distance and in flight:</u> Mottled ducks match mallards in size and weight. They have mallard-like flight characteristics and identical markings distinguished at distance. Appearance gives the impression of a very dark mallard hen.

<u>Range, distribution, and migration patterns:</u> Mottled ducks are permanent residents of the Gulf Coast of Louisiana, Texas, and Mexico.

Mottled Duck Pair. Credit: Alan Schnierer.

<u>Habitat and diet:</u> Mottled duck habitat is coastal marshes and cropland, primarily in close proximity to water. Diet of the mottled duck generally follows that of the mallard. They consume more animal food during summer than the mallard.

Mexican Duck

Mexican duck pair. Credit: Alan Schmierer.

The Mexican duck is very mallard-like in all characteristics. It's a permanent resident of the interior of Mexico.

Blue-winged Teal

The season is on. The blue-winged teal is a favorite with waterfowlers who enjoy a wingshooting challenge.

Identification at distance and in flight: Hunters need to be able to distinguish between teal and other species by size and behavior since the characteristic blue feathers over the tops of their wings are not in place early in the season and, when in place, hard to identify in the early morning light. The blue-wing is a small duck, about a pound or less. They can be recognized in flight

Blue-winged teal drake. Credit: Alan Schmierer.

at distance often in a "V" formation behind a tight group of leads. Within this semiorganized flight formation, individuals will dart along in a somewhat erratic pattern. Like all teal, they're actually not as flat-out fast as the small size would lead the wingshooter to assume. Cruise speed is around thirty miles per hour; escape around forty-five miles per hour.

Identification up close and at hand: Identification at hand is easy in the case of drakes with a large blue area over the wing in breeding plumage. It's often not present during early season.

Range, distribution, and migration patterns: Duck hunters rejoice at the arrival of the blue-wings zipping down the flyways from their northern US, southern Canada Prairie Pothole Region breeding areas each September. Blue-winged hunting is usually a short-term delight. Might even get in a couple of hunts during the special early teal season before they buzz on south for warmer climes. They're first to head south, last to come back north. Teal make the longest migration of the ducks, as far south as central South America in a few cases. That takes an early start. Special early teal seasons are set before the regular duck hunting season starts. About nine million are available for hunting.

Habitat and diet: Habitat and feeding preferences are important to know for scouting purposes. Habitat for the teal consists of sheltered freshwater ponds, potholes, natural lakes, flooded fields and timber, creeks, sloughs, shallow-water swamps, and upper ends of man-made lakes. Diet includes aquatic plants, seeds, grass, smartweed, duckweed, small mollusks, crustaceans, and insects.

Hunting techniques and arrangements: Hunting technique is usually pass shooting over decoys. Many dedicated teal hunters use only teal decoys. Everybody else normally uses whatever they have—usually mallard decoys. The teal's habit is to swoop over decoys and maybe, maybe not, come back around again. They're considered easy to decoy, at least for experienced hunters who've pitched out a few spreads, but minus a reassuring spread of decoys, teal may be very reluctant to set down. They're wary of landing on water without resting ducks already in place, making wide sweeps several times before settling down, or moving on to another place that looks more secure. If ducks (or decoys) are already in place, they usually make a sweep or two and come in to land.

Additional information: All of the teal—blue-winged, green-winged, and cinnamon—have a common attraction for hunters: they offer the most difficult wingshooting available. Their speed, which is not great on an absolute basis, is deceptive due to their small size and darting, twisting flight in tight flocks.

Green-wing Teal

Identification at distance and in flight: Green-winged teal are slightly larger than other teal, a pound to one and a half pounds, but they have many characteristics in common. In early fall, blue- and green-winged drakes, sans breeding plumage, and hens appear to be identical except in size. A major

Green-winged teal. Credit: Alan Schmierer.

difference is migration habits. Green-winged teal move south later in the fall, and they tend to move through on a more leisurely schedule. Many don't go much farther than Texas, so later in the fall, drakes can be recognized by breeding plumage with distinct markings that can be seen at distance: a dark red head with iridescent green patch from eye to back of head; a distinctive white vertical stripe in front of the shoulder.

Flight characteristics are very similar to those of blue-wings: a "V" formation, loaded on the front point, swooping low over the water past decoys; individuals moving fast in their own erratic path. Small size and lots of movement tend to make them look faster than they actually are. It's actually about the same as blue-winged.

Hunting techniques and arrangements: Easily decoyed but wary to land if no other ducks on water. When scouting, look for about the same habitat and feed as the blue-wing. They seem to hang with Northern Shovelers. Around four million are available for hunting.

Additional information: Green-wings may be seen flocking with other species. A spectacular show of green can happen when green-wing and northern shoveler drakes take flight together.

Birds of a green feather. Green-winged teal and shovelers create green on the wing.

Cinnamon Teal

<u>Identification at distance and in flight</u>: The cinnamon teal is a duck of the Pacific Flyway. They are very small: fourteen to seventeen inches long; weight one half to one pound. Drakes in full breeding plumage are spectacular. The cinnamon dark russet color is unmistakable in good light. Iridescent green speculum. Early in the hunting season, the color of the drakes is in transition from the plumage of the hen to breeding plumage. Cinnamon hens, like the hens of all the teal species, are a mottled brown that allows the hen to hide from predators during nesting. Drakes have a dark mottled brown eclipse plumage slightly more red hue than the hen and trace of blue when wings are folded They show a sometimes hard to see powder-like shoulder patch in flight. Hens are indistinguishable from blue-wing teal.

Cinnamon teal, as they appear in the coffee table books. Credit: Alan Schmierer.

Flight characteristics are very similar to blue-wings: small numbers in ragged "V" formation, loaded on the front point, swooping low over the water past decoys; darting flight of individuals moving fast in their own erratic path. Small size and lots of movement tend to make them look faster than they actually are.

Cinnamon teal, as they appear during hunting season.

Range, distribution, and migration patterns: Breeding area is western United States centered on the Great Salt Lake with wintering throughout Mexico. There is considerable overlap between breeding and wintering in Southwest US and New Mexico.

Habitat and diet: For scouting purposes, habitats are marshes and lakes. Preferred foods are seeds of bulrushes, salt grass, and pondweed; secondary foods are mollusks and aquatic invertebrates.

Hunting techniques and arrangements: Easily decoyed but wary to land if no other ducks on water.

Gadwall (Gray Duck, Gray Mallard)

Identification at distance and in flight: The gadwall is a favorite with waterfowlers who enjoy a challenge. A flock of gadwalls in flight looks more like a jailbreak than a coherent formation. Erratic in flight and fast: escape speed is fifty-plus miles per hour and cruise speed is thirty miles per hour. They're wary of putting down before they've made a few (out of shotgun range) passes over a given location. In poor lighting when first flights drop in, identification depends on pattern of the flight and behavior. However, the showy white spectrum over the tops of the wings are easily recognized at distance.

Identification up close and at hand: The gadwall is a medium-sized duck with around four million available for hunting. Drake in breeding plumage is best

Gadwall drake. Credit: Alan Schmierer.

described as stunningly beautiful in an understated way. Notable details are a jet-black rear and tail and a white speculum edged in black, both helpful in dim light, with a rich brown slightly forward. Breeding plumage develops through the early fall. Late in the season, drakes reach breeding plumage. Beautiful but subtle variations of color are hard to see except up close or at hand.

Range, distribution, and migration patterns: Nesting area is the Prairie Pothole Region extending southward east of the Rocky Mountains. A large part of the population migrates along the Central Flyway. A smaller breeding area is around the Great Lakes. Wintering areas are around the coasts and south of the United States, the lower Mississippi Flyway, and Mexico.

Habitat and diet: Helpful in scouting: wintering habitat is shallow freshwater ponds, potholes, natural lakes, flooded fields and timber, creeks, sloughs, shallow-water swamps, and upper ends of man-made lakes; diet is primarily aquatic plants and seeds, with small mollusks, crustaceans, and insects being a secondary food source.

Hunting techniques and arrangements: Gadwall tend to stay out of sight during the daytime, loafing by hiding in small streams with overhanging banks. That makes them susceptible to jump shooting by hunters coursing along the stream or stalking up to known hideouts.

Northern Pintail (Sprig)

Identification at distance and in flight: Pintails are the masters of the air. Pintails have a distinctly sleek body configuration with long neck and tail, elongated tail feathers, and athletic aerodynamic performance. This configuration gives the appearance of a larger duck than it actually is: three pounds

Northern Pintail. Credit: Alan Schmierer.

max for drakes, and two and a half pounds for hens. They're fast fliers—sixty miles per hour in the escape, thirty miles per hour in cruise—and fly with an extended arc, wide wingspan, and rapid beat of narrow wings. They are often referred to as the "greyhound of the air" in numerous publications. Pintails are graceful and aerobatic in flight. The male breeding plumage color pattern emphasizes its graceful movement on the water and in the air. The distinctive spike tail feather is part of the breeding plumage and may not be evident in early fall.

Identification by landings and takeoffs: A flight may be flying a steady course more than one hundred feet up and suddenly decide as a group to extend their wings up and drop like so many rocks toward the water below. They'll make a couple of backstrokes a few feet off the water and lightly settle in.

Identification up close and at hand: Close or at hand, males have a chocolate-brown colored head with a white stripe on either side of the neck. The back of the body is dark, front and belly are white, and there is a white spot on either side of the rear. The tail has two long, black central feathers with gray on either side. The upper wings have an iridescent speculum with a green-black hue. The female has a dark brown, toned upper body and a buff of gray lower body and head. Speculum on their upper wings create a bronze appearance.

Range, distribution, and migration patterns: Pintails are the most widely dispersed species, with a single race across the circumpolar continents of the Northern Hemisphere. They are among the first to migrate to the South in fall; they're also among the first to head back in the spring. A long-ranging, fast flier, they may wander widely across flyways within a single season. The pintail has a vast breeding area centered across western Canada, around Hudson Bay, along the St. Lawrence River and the northern plains of the United States, extending to Alaska and on into Siberia. They winter predominately along the Pacific Coast Flyway into Mexico, but many cross the western United States to the Gulf Coast and Atlantic coast to winter.

Despite their wide dispersal, the pintail population has declined. The population available for hunting is currently around three and a half million.

Habitat and diet: Wintering habitat consists of shallow freshwater ponds, potholes, and natural lakes, flooded fields and timber, creeks, sloughs, shallow-water swamps, and upper ends of man-made lakes. Primary foods consist of aquatic plants and seeds; secondary foods are small mollusks, crustaceans, and insects.

Additional information: They have a distinct short whistle note.

American Wigeon (Bald-plate)

Identification at distance and in flight: In flight, they use deep wing strokes in close formation with erratic individual movement resembling teal. Flight speed is fifty-plus miles per hour in the escape, thirty miles per hour at cruise. A white crown on the head of drakes is prominent at distance on the water or field. Wigeon drakes under some lighting conditions illustrate the old nickname of "baldpate."

Wigeon drake. Credit: JoAnne Airhart.

<u>Identification up close and at hand</u>: At hand or close range, a prominent green iridescent crescent band behind the eye can be seen. American wigeons are medium sized at around two pounds.

<u>Range, distribution, and migration patterns</u>: The wigeon has a large breeding area across the western United States and Canada to Alaska. Wigeons winter around all coastlines of the United States and across Mexico. They leave the breeding area early. Population available for hunting is around three million.

<u>Habitat and diet</u>: When scouting wintering habitat, look for shallow freshwater ponds, potholes, natural lakes, flooded fields and timber, creeks, sloughs, shallow-water swamps, and upper ends of man-made lakes. Feed depends primarily on availability: leafy shallow water aquatic plants, tender sprouts of grain and pasture grass, waste grain when available, and, in coastal areas, widgeon grass, pondweed, and eelgrass.

<u>Hunting techniques and arrangements</u>: Hunting techniques include stalking, pass shooting, and calling over decoys. Wigeons can often be found on dry ground grazing on new growth. They prefer to have some puddles in the vicinity. They keep to open areas so that predators can't stalk to within lethal range.

Northern Shoveler

<u>Identification at distance and in flight</u>: At distance, shovelers appear as a medium-sized ducks; each bird weighs about one and a half pounds. They usually travel in small flights moving along at a steady pace in no particular order. Flight speed is just under that of the teal: escape speed is over fifty miles per hour; cruise speed is thirty miles per hour. They often rest on the water and travel in mixed flocks with other species.

In the fall, breeding plumage is not evident. Drakes transition from the golden brown of the hen after the molt to a very spectacular breeding plumage easily seen from a distance, with iridescent green head, white front, crimson belly, white-trimmed black back, and green speculum. The remarkable spooned bill of both hen and drake can be seen at some distance.

Northern shoveler drake, ready for breeding season. Credit: Alan Schmierer.

Identification by landings and takeoffs: Shovelers are agile and graceful in the air, light to lift off the water surface and light to touch down again after a short glide.

Range, distribution, and migration patterns: Breeding area is the vicinity of northern prairie country; wintering areas are in Mexico along the Pacific Flyway, and to the Gulf Coast along the Central and Mississippi Flyways. Population available for hunting is about four and a half million.

Habitat and diet: Wintering habitat is open marshes, natural lakes, shallow-water swamps and upper ends of man-made lakes, and brackish marshes in coastal areas. They often feed moving along single-file over the water, heads lowered, with bills swinging side to side over the water surface, straining microsized plants and animals through that oversized bill. A secondary feeding method is dabbling for seeds and aquatic plants.

Hunting techniques and arrangements: Shovelers are often taken incidental to hunting other dabblers over decoys.

Whistling Duck

Range, distribution, and migration patterns: Whistling ducks occur around the globe close to the equator. Two species reside in North America.

Habitat and diet: Habitat is shallow waters and wetlands. Flooded rice fields are prime habitat. Nesting is in tree cavities. Whistling ducks have adapted to agricultural feed.

Additional information: Whistling ducks are an ancient group not considered to be true ducks. They are, in fact, closer to geese and swans than ducks. The call of all species is a whistle. Whistling ducks mate for life.

Black-Bellied Whistling Duck

Black-bellied pair. Credit: Alan Schmierer.

Identification at distance and in flight: A medium-sized duck at around two pounds, with a wingspan of around thirty inches. Neck, body, wings, and legs are long. The head is gray with a long, red bill, and the belly is a distinctive black. Front and back are tan. The flight of the black-bellied whistling duck is slow and without order. Wings show white in flight. Male and female black-bellied whistling ducks are identical. Usually in flocks when not breeding.

Range, distribution, and migration patterns: Southern US states are on the northern fringe of the black-bellied whistling duck's range, which extends south through Central and South America.

Fulvous Whistling Duck

Identification at distance and in flight: Resembles the black-bellied whistling duck in configuration. Bill is gray; body is generally tan with dark back. Flight is slow, with loose formation and without coherence. Long legs and feet stick out behind the tail. Call is a whistle.

Fulvous whistling duck pair. Credit: Alan Schmierer.

Wood Duck (Woody) (Summer Duck)

Some waterfowl hunters, Kent among them, prefer to hunt wood ducks above all others. Challenges are thick habitat, fast flight, little targets. With experience, shots can be made. Speed is required, but shooting distance is short through the typical habitat.

Identification at distance and in flight: Sometimes seen in flights of a dozen birds above timber, wood ducks often travel in singles and pairs, darting through thick stands of trees and brush, and often over water or along creeks. In flight, they seem to dodge and dive along at an unbelievable speed to the observer. They're actually not that fast: about forty miles-plus per hour in the escape, thirty miles per hour in cruise. Part of the effect is due to the fact that wood ducks are small, about one and a half pounds.

Identification by landings and takeoffs: They can be heard coming in with wings striking branches just before they splash into the water.

Wood duck drake. Credit: Alan Schmierer.

Identification up close and at hand: Breeding plumage of drakes is spectacular. Predominant color is black with a reddish front. The head is patterned with an iridescent green cap over black with narrow white trims. The bill is generally reddish with a white patch overlay and a black tip. Eyes are bright red. Drakes and hens both have spectacular blue feathers. Plumage is in place in late summer, but the color is less defined than later in the year.

Range, distribution, and migration patterns: Northwest coastal and north into the prairies of Canada. Wood duck breeding areas are the eastern half of the United States, the northwest contiguous US states and northwest into the prairies of Canada. Wintering area is across Gulf Coast states of the US and northwestern coastal areas. Breeding areas are in marshes and ponds in close wooded areas. The population of wood ducks has increased to the point of allowing hunting across their area of distribution.

Habitat and diet: Nesting is in hollow trees. They may use a woodpecker nesting hole or any other hole in a tree that can be found. Nesting boxes have been placed in many areas to increase survival rates. Wintering habitat is wooded wetlands of several types: shallow-water swamps, creeks, sloughs, and upper ends of man-made lakes. Feed is primarily acorns and other nuts.

Hunting techniques and arrangements: For the uninitiated, wood ducks often pass in a blur before you finish your startled jump. First-hand experience of your authors can definitely verify this. You just hope that you don't startle the ducks as they pass over. White splash on your cap often appears.

Hunting techniques are stalking, pass shooting through thick timber and brush, and calling with wood duck calls over wood duck decoys. Finding a place to shoot over decoys, preferably wood duck decoys, is more productive than stalking, although stalking with pauses can work.

DIVING DUCKS

Diving ducks are primarily adapted to deep-water habitat, habitat that is too deep for duck wading and tipping up. In nutritional preferences and feeding habits, they're not as well adapted to typical small, shallow-water habitat as the dabblers.

Freshwater diver species that may be encountered on waters great and small across the continent are: canvasbacks, redheads, scaup, and ring-necked ducks. They'll be discussed first, since they'll be the types most commonly encountered by hunters. Then, sea ducks will be handled apart from the more commonly distributed freshwater divers along the Mississippi and Pacific Flyways. Sea ducks nest in the interior of northern Canada, and winter on the big waters of the Great Lakes, along saltwater shorelines and in deep water offshore. These ducks are hunted by the hardy few.

Diving Ducks: Habits and Habitat

The annual cycle of many diving ducks is to nest in the interior of Canada, some in big lake country, others in the Prairie Pothole country, followed by migration to the east or west coast for the winter. A significant number will be encountered scattered across the southland. The diving ducks in general are easier to call and decoy than puddle, or dabbler, ducks. The challenge is often the time and places where they're hunted. Diving duck habitat, particularly that of the sea duck branch of the family, is not for the faint of heart. Hunting from low freeboard sneak boats on deep water in late-season cold lakes or small fishing boats in the offshore storm swells of the Atlantic shouldn't be taken on by unassisted beginners. The specialized skill-sets and equipment crucial to particular big-water locations under certain water and weather conditions during late season are beyond the scope of this book.

Canvasback (Cans)

Identification at distance and in flight: Canvasbacks weigh about three pounds, the size of mallards, and with their regal bearing, they stand out among other ducks. In flight, a flock often forms a "V." Wingbeat is slower than that of the smaller divers. Escape speed is around sixty miles per hour; cruising speed is thirty miles per hour. Wing arcs are moderately deep. They appear to look all white from the underside.

Canvasback drake. Credit: Alan Schmierer.

Identification up close and at hand: The novice duck hunter needs to recognize the unique plumage patterns of this large duck and not get trigger-happy if a flight sails over low and slow. Canvasbacks have very distinctive color and plumage patterns. The head and front of drakes are a deep russet. The back has the color and texture of weathered sail canvas that gives them their common name. Eyes are red. Hens have a dark reddish head and front and a mottled back. These photos taken in the early morning of a heavily overcast December day don't do their uniquely beautiful plumage justice, but this is probably what they're going to look like if encountered in the wild.

Range, distribution, and migration patterns: Breeding area is the Prairie Pothole Region and extends across western Canada and the interior of Alaska. Wintering areas are the Gulf Coast, across Texas and eastern Mexico; and along the west coast, from Puget Sound to Baha. The canvasback population has been trending lower for some time. Limit is usually one per day. Population available for hunting is about seven hundred thousand.

Habitat and diet: Wintering habitat includes shallow freshwater ponds, potholes, natural lakes, flooded fields and timber, creeks, sloughs, shallow-water swamps, and upper ends of man-made lakes. The canvasback primarily dives and dabbles for aquatic plants: wild celery, tubers, leaves, and sago pondweed; secondary diet consists of insects and mollusks.

Hunting techniques and arrangements: The main hunting technique is over diver decoys using diver calls.

Additional information: Canvasbacks are the largest of the diving ducks and have long been the preferred quarry among the divers. Their diet of plants places them at the top of the divers as table fare.

Ring-Necked Duck (Ring-Billed Duck)

Ring-necked duck drake. Credit: Alan Schmierer.

Identification at distance and in flight: Ring-necked ducks in flight give the impression of small ducks flying fast and low over the water in small flocks. Their fast flight is accompanied by rapid wingbeats. Formation is a compact wedge. On the water at distance, they are recognized by a black head, chest, and tail, with bright white sides and a dark back. On the water, the black back of the ring neck contrasts with the light gray back of the scaup.

Identification up close and at hand: Close up and at hand, the drake very faintly shows a purplish sheen to the head, with a pronounced crown. Chest, back, and rear are black. Sides and belly are white, with a sharp, curved transition. Bill has distinct white ring at base and another just behind the black tip. Close or at hand, the bill appears to have a light blue hue. Quizzically, the ring around the neck of the ring-necked duck is hard to make out, near, far, or at hand. It amounts to a purplish tint for most of the season. The hen has a dark brown head and back, with lighter brown sides.

Range, distribution, and migration patterns: Breeding occurs across the Pacific and Gulf Coasts of the southern United States and eastern Canada, and ranging down into US mountain states. Wintering area is across southern US states and around both coasts of Mexico.

Habitat and diet: Wintering habitat preference is water slightly deeper than the shallows preferred by dabblers. Winter feed is aquatic plants, pondweed, and duckweed.

Hunting techniques and arrangements: Hunting technique is over lines of decoys and diver calls. Freshwater divers are often seen on small waters with dabblers. The divers will be working the deeper water while dabblers work the edges. Good idea for decoy spread.

SCAUPS (BLUEBILL)

Identification at distance and in flight: Lesser scaup can usually be recognized trading back and forth between feeding and resting locations as a small, black-and-white duck flying low over the water in small flights, usually in small

Lesser scaup. Credit: JoAnne Airhart.

flocks. Flight is fast with the rapid wingbeat characteristic of divers. Wings may show the long, white speculum with down beat of the wings. For long migration flights, they'll be gathered into large flocks flying high. On the water at distance, markers are black head and chest, tail more gray than the black tail of ring-necks. Body has white sides and white, slightly gray back.

Identification up close and at hand: Close up and at hand, the black head of the drake has a purple sheen; neck, chest, and rear are black with sides and belly a dark gray, becoming mottled over the back. Hen is brown cast overall, with dark head and mottled brown and gray over the back and lighter shade over the belly. A white ring can be made out at the base of the bill. The blue bill is a defining characteristic. Bill is deep blue on drake and hen, darker on drake. Both have blue-gray legs and feet.

Range, distribution, and migration patterns: Breeding area covers the Prairie Pothole Region and on to the West along the US-Canada border and on to the Northwest through interior Alaska, and across Canada, and on to Alaska. Wintering areas isare the Pacific and Atlantic coasts and the Gulf Coast on into the interior of the southern US states and throughout Mexico. Along the southern coast of the United States, they can be seen gathered in rafts on large lakes and coastal bays.

Greater Scaup

Greater scaup drake. Credit: Alan Schmierer.

Identification at distance and in flight: Greater scaup may be identified in flight as identical to the lesser scaup, even to details of white speculum.

Identification up close and at hand: Close up and at hand, drake has a dark-green sheen over the head, black chest and rear, white sides and belly, and mottled black-and-white over back, withdefining demarcation along sides between back and belly. Hen is dark brown; heads are darker and belly lighter. Both hen and drake have blue-gray legs and feet, and light-blue-tinted gray bill.

Range, distribution, and migration patterns: Breeding area is across far north of Canada and extends across Alaska to the west coast. Wintering is along the Pacific, Atlantic, Nova Scotia to Florida, and the Gulf Coasts and lower Great Lakes.

Habitat and diet: Wintering habitat is coastal bays and estuaries. Winter feed consists primarily of clams; aquatic plants, such as pondweed, celery, and sea lettuce are a secondary food source.

Hunting techniques and arrangements: Most productive hunting technique for both lesser and greater scaup is usually over large decoy spreads near the blind, using long lines of "J" or "Hook" lines of decoys leading to the blind.

Redhead

Identification at distance and in flight: Redheads are often seen in large flocks that appear to have the organization of a stampede. They are usually recognized by their tendency to feed and move about in massive flocks without any discernable order. Normally seen in large flocks in wintering area, sometimes mingling with other divers.

Identification up close and at hand: At hand, drakes have a dark-red head, black chest and rear; back is dark gray and belly is white. Turned-up bill is a dark blue with black tip. Hen is light brown with a slightly

Redhead drake. Credit: Alan Schmierer.

reddish head, a darker brown back, and light belly. Legs and feet on both are gray.

Range, distribution, and migration patterns: Redheads collect on saltwater bays and estuaries along the Gulf Coast. They migrate south in a hurry and are seldom encountered. They normally migrate without stopovers, and thus are rarely encountered by hunters along the migration routes between breeding and wintering areas. They tend to linger along their inland route on their return north and are accessible to hunters in late winter. Breeding is Prairie Pothole Region and Salt Lake and scattered in concentrations occur throughout the West in the United States and in a wide area across Canada, stretching to the Northwest Territories. Wintering is western and southern United States and Mexico.

Habitat and diet: Winter habitat is lakes and tidal bays and estuaries with areas of shallow water. Winter feed is aquatic plants.

Hunting techniques and arrangements: Hunting techniques are over lines of diver decoys with diver calls.

Ruddy Duck

Ruddy duck drake. Credit: Alan Schmierer.

Identification at distance and in flight: This is a small, chunky diver, even as divers go. Coffee-table books illustrate the drake with a dark-russet body, black head with white cheeks, and a bright-blue bill. In fall and winter it changes to a dark brown, matching the hen. Tail feathers stick up like a brush.

Range, distribution, and migration patterns: Breeding is in the interior of the western United States and Canada and the Great Lakes. Wintering is along East and West Coasts and across the Gulf states and Mexico.

Habitat and diet: Preferred habitat is marshes and shallow lakes. Primary diet is pondweeds, wigeon grass, bulrush seeds. Larval insects are a secondary food source.

Mergansers (Fish Duck, Sawbills)

Mergansers are ducks like no others. Two species, the common merganser and the hooded merganser, are widely distributed and are placed with the freshwater divers in our discussion, and are commonly encountered across North America. Fish eaters, they have more in common with the sea ducks than with the dabblers or distant cousin divers that share their habitat. Ranging even into the mountains, dedicated trout fishing enthusiasts hold them in low regard. But, as far as the duck hunter is concerned, they're divers. On the other hand, the red-breasted merganser is usually encountered by those hardy hunters out on the storm-lashed seas or on the Great Lakes, and are considered with the sea ducks in our discussion.

Common Merganser (American Merganser, Fish Duck, Sawbill, Goosander)

Identification at distance and in flight: The common merganser (sometimes grouped with sea ducks) is the most widely distributed and most numerous of the mergansers. They may be recognized in flight by their large size and low, fast flight with fast, shallow wingbeats. "Bat-outta-hell" comes to mind. Individuals resemble fast-moving, streamlined, rocket-propelled lawn darts if you manage to get a good look at them. Head crests are folded in flight. Flights are often small. Along with all of the mergansers, the common merganser rides

Common merganser hen. Credit: Alan Schmierer.

Common mergansers, Big Hole, Montana.

low on the water, only the head, with crest unfolded, and the back are above the water surface.

<u>Identification up close and at hand</u>: Close up and at hand, the drake has a very dark green head with no crest, and black back and gray rear. Chest, sides, and belly are white. Hen has a brown crested head and white neck, with gray body above the water surface, white below. The long pointed serrated bill for catching fish common to all mergansers can be examined. Both drake and hen have red bill, legs, and feet.

<u>Range, distribution, and migration patterns</u>: Breeding grounds extend from the eastern coast of Canada to the western coast and on into Alaska, with an extension into the US Mountain West; wintering area is distributed across the southern and middle United States. Wintering habitat is across the United States and the west coast of Canada extending to southern Alaska.

Hooded Merganser

<u>Identification at distance and in flight</u>: The hooded merganser is second only to the common merganser in distribution. Identified in flight as a small-sized duck flying fast and low over the water with rapid, shallow wingbeats, usually as a pair or very small flock. On the water, they hold to themselves, usually as one or two pairs. In flight, the crests of drake and hen are folded down. The crests unfold on the water to reveal the prominent white feathers of the drake and the wild-looking russet brush of the hen. Head movement of the drake makes the white crest appear to turn on and off. They ride very low in the water so that only the black back of the drake and the dark brown back of the hen show above the water surface.

Hooded merganser pair.
Credit: JoAnne Airhart.

<u>Range, distribution, and migration patterns</u>: Western migration is between breeding areas along the lower Alaska coast and the northwestern United States and wintering areas on the Baja Peninsula.

The Eastern migration is from breeding areas over southeast Canada and the northeastern United States. Wintering areas are along the Gulf and south Atlantic coasts. Breeding area is most dense across southeastern Canada and the northeastern United States. At less density, breeding stretches thinly across lower Canada and the upper United States. Wintering is along the east, west, and Gulf coasts and broadly across the southeastern United States.

Habitat and diet: To note during scouting: habitat preference is small sloughs, ponds, and streams with cover about.

Red-Breasted Merganser

Here, we get a jump on the discussion of sea ducks in the next section with a duck family that has members on land and sea. The red-breasted mergansers mark the transition from freshwater divers to saltwater divers. Red-breasted mergansers are the most specialized sea ducks of the merganser family.

Red-breasted merganser. Credit: Alan Schmierer.

It follows that they are far less likely to be encountered by hunters, other than the hardy souls who venture out on the big thunder waves.

Identification at distance and in flight: Identification in flight is a very shallow wing stroke that propels it fast and low in a straight line across the water. Like most mergansers, if you get a good look at all, the red-breasted merganser has the streamlined lawn dart configuration characteristic of the rest of the family: a mostly dark on top, white on the underside, feathered lawn dart.

Identification up close and at hand: In the water close up, it sits very low on the water so that the top side is the only part you see. The drake's head is a greenish black with a crest, and the back is black. The hen's head is brown and also crested. At hand, the red-tinted chest in front of a white belly with gray toward the rear and the red eyes of the drake and serrated bill are distinctive. Drake and hen have red bill, legs, and feet.

Range, distribution, and migration patterns: Breeding area is broadly across northern Canada and Alaska. Wintering is along the west coasts of Canada, the United States, and Mexico; the Great Lakes; and along the east and Gulf coasts of the United States.

Habitat and diet: Winter habitat is bays and estuaries. On rivers and lakes, food is salmon eggs, salmon fry, golden shiners, suckers, minnows, and sculpins. At sea, diet consists of herring and sculpins close to shore in brackish water, as well as sunfish, minnows, pawns, and crustaceans.

Sea Ducks

Sea ducks are grouped not as a matter of any closely shared biological traits, but for their shared habits and habitat, and to some extent, in the way we hunt them. All sea ducks are divers, but not all divers are sea ducks. They have the same habitat, they all feed on sea creatures, and we hunt them with the same techniques.

The following are sea ducks as defined by the Atlantic Sea Duck Project Chesapeake Bay Ecosystem Model: goldeneyes, the bufflehead, harlequin ducks, eiders, long-tailed ducks, scoters, and mergansers.

From the practical perspective of duck hunters, wildlife management groups sea ducks collectively in bag limits separately from other ducks, which is how we'll handle them. (Refer to references suggested at the beginning of the chapter.) We'll discuss them as individual species in some instances and as close families in others.

There's concern over current declines of some families. Researchers haven't been able to determine the reason. A big obstruction to investigations is that there's only limited information on the annual cycles of place and time of many sea duck groups. It's very difficult to do research into the exact factor, or factors, impacting population numbers.

Scoters

All scoters are hunted using the same techniques: rocky ledge edge over decoys; layout boats among decoys; camo big boat over decoys.

Black Scoter

<u>Identification at distance and in flight</u>: In flight, appears to be a black, medium-sized, two-pound duck with a twenty-inch wingspan, flying low and fast over the water.

<u>Identification up close and at hand</u>: At hand the drake is all black, except for a white patch on the head, a yellow knob on the bill, and dark gray legs and feet. Hen is whitish brown.

<u>Range, distribution, and migration patterns</u>: Breeding ground is the Boreal Forest of Canada and Alaska. Wintering area is Pacific coasts of Canada and the United States, the Atlantic and Gulf coasts of the United States, and the Great Lakes.

<u>Habitat and diet</u>: Winter habitat is coastal bays and large freshwater lakes. Feed is mollusks (blue mussels), crustaceans, insects, and aquatic plants such as pondweeds.

Black scoter. Credit: Alan Schmierer.

Hunting techniques and arrangements: Hunting techniques are shooting over decoys from the rocky ledge edges of bays; layout boats among decoys; camo big boat over decoys.

White Winged Scoter (Sea Coot)

Identification at distance and in flight: In flight, a large black duck weighing four pounds and with a twenty-three-inch wingspan, flying low and fast over the water. White speculum can be seen in flight. The drake is all black, with small, white wing patches.

Identification up close and at hand: At hand a small, white crescent can be seen over the eye. Drake has an orange bill with a dark knob at base; legs and feet are orange/red. Hen is gray with a black bill.

White-winged scoter. Credit: Alan Schmierer.

<u>Range, distribution, and migration patterns</u>: Breeding area is western Canada and interior Alaska; wintering areas are Pacific and Atlantic coasts. Migration between breeding and wintering areas is en masse. White-wings form large groups in wintering areas and mix with other sea ducks.

<u>Habitat and diet</u>: For scouting, winter habitat is open ocean, coastal bays, and large freshwater lakes. Feed is mussels, crabs, crayfish, and barnacles.

<u>Hunting techniques and arrangements</u>: Hunting techniques are the usual sea duck techniques, including a long line of decoys out into open water to draw birds into shotgun range. Black jugs will work for decoys.

<u>Additional information</u>: Poor eating; strong taste.

Surf Scoter

Surf scoter. Credit: Alan Schmierer.

<u>Identification at distance and in flight</u>: As with all the scoters, the surf scoter appears as a black duck flying fast and low over the water. The name is derived from its preference for feeding along the surf line. It's usually seen in large flocks.

<u>Identification up close and at hand</u>: In hand, the drake has black-and-white patch on the front and back of head. Bill has red top with yellow end, black spot over white either side, with a hump over middle top. Hen is whitish brown.

<u>Range, distribution, and migration patterns</u>: Wintering area is same as that of the white-wing.

<u>Habitat and diet</u>: Habitat is same as the white-wing.

<u>Hunting techniques and arrangements</u>: The surf scoter is hunted like the white-wing.

Long-tailed Duck (Oldsquaw)

Long-tailed duck. Credit: Alan Schmierer.

Identification at distance and in flight: This duck is different from any other. It's white from a distance, flying low over the water during the fall hunting season; black from a distance in summer breeding plumage. Medium-sized ducks, drakes are around two and a half pounds, hens are slightly smaller. Very noisy in flight; repertoire includes yodeling, clucking, and growling. Tail gets longer with maturity (pictured is a young drake) and progression toward overall black breeding plumage in summer.

Identification up close and at hand: In hand, the drake during fall is black with gray back from shoulders. Very long dark tail is distinctive. Head and neck are white with tan cheeks; back is black. Black bill with pink band. Hen color pattern consists of blends of whitish, light sides with darker back; face is whitish with brown crown. Both drakes and hens have white belly sides and gray legs and feet.

Range, distribution, and migration patterns: Breeding area is far northern Alaska and Canada. Seldom seen by waterfowl hunters in their breeding area north of the Arctic Circle. Wintering area is along eastern Canada and the US east coast, the Great Lakes, along the Pacific coasts of southern Alaska, the west coast of Canada, and the Gulf Coast.

Diet: Feed includes crustaceans, mollusks, fish, and insect larvae. Capable of diving deep to feed.

Hunting techniques and arrangements: Hunted by all sea duck techniques. Mature drake in fall plumage considered a trophy.

EIDERS

In flight, all of the eiders appear to be very large ducks, among the largest of all ducks. They fly with strong, rapid wingbeats low over the water, often pairs or small flights in a line formation. Overall color of all eider drakes is some combination of black and white; hens are brown. Colorful details particular to each species can be seen in detail at hand.

Hunters of eiders consider some, perhaps all, species of eiders to be trophies rather than routine table fare. Some of the eiders are lightly hunted due to habitat along the remote far northern coasts of Canada and Greenland. Spectacled and Steller's eiders (breed along Arctic coast; winter on Alaska Peninsula) are declared threatened and not hunted.

All species of eider are considered at risk or threatened. Research is underway to determine the cause of the population decline.

Common Eider (American Eider)

Identification at distance and in flight: The flight of common eiders is fast and low over the water. They're the largest of all ducks. Drakes are about twenty-six inches long, with weight around six pounds; hens are smaller, with weight around three pounds. Males appear to be generally white; hens are a

Common eider. Credit: Alan Schmierer.

"warm" brown. In flight at distance, the white of drakes and the brown of hens can be easily seen.

Identification up close and at hand: In hand, the drake's body coloring is white front and back, with black flanks, rear, and underside. Head is white front and neck, with olive nape and black crown with white streaks. Bill is long, with top blending into straight line up to the crown with dark olive color. Hen has a tan, mottled black pattern; bill is gray. Both drake and hen have gray legs and feet. They have a dense coat of down, with a thick layer of fat.

Range, distribution, and migration patterns: Breeding area is around the east and arctic coasts of Canada and north and west coasts of Alaska. Wintering area includes the coasts of Alaska, along the eastern coast of Canada and uppermost northeastern United States.

Habitat and diet: Eider habitat is rocky seacoasts. Diving deeply, eiders feed on shellfish primarily, such as mussels, crustaceans, and crabs. They also eat insects and plants near nesting area.

Hunting techniques and arrangements: Hunting technique is to set up well offshore, in a boat adequate to handle wind and sea conditions. Anchor and put out a decoy spread around the boat.

King Eider

Identification at distance and in flight: Flight is low over the water. In flight at distance, the white and black of drakes and the brown of hens is easily seen. King eiders are almost as large as common eiders at eighteen to twenty-five inches long and three pounds for hens, four pounds for drakes.

Identification up close and at hand: At hand, the drake has a white chest; rest of body is black with white trim streaks on sides and spots on flanks. Stiff feathers stick up from the back. The head crown and back of head are blue. The bill is striking, with a pattern of golden feathers along the top of bill; cheeks are white. The hen is tan to brown with dark feather tips. The hen's bill is olive gray. Both the drake and the hen have gray legs and feet overall.

King eider. Credit: Alan Schmierer.

<u>Range, distribution, and migration patterns</u>: Breeding area is the central northern coast and islands north of the Arctic Circle. Wintering areas are the rocky coasts along western Alaska and Canada and the Atlantic coasts of Canada and the north and mid-Atlantic United States.

Habitat and diet: Habitat is rocky coastlines and offshore during winter. Feed is mollusks and crustaceans obtained through deep diving.

Hunting techniques and arrangements: King eider hunters are often interested in taking drakes as a trophy. They are often assisted by experienced guides who are well equipped with boats adequate for rough offshore waters. Techniques are often to anchor well offshore and surround the boat with decoys.

Bufflehead (Butterball)

Identification at distance and in flight: Flight is typical of sea ducks, low and fast over the water. Buffleheads are small ducks: sixteen inches long, up to one and a half pounds, drakes are larger than hens. They're often seen in small groups and often mixed with other duck species. At distance, head of drakes,

Bufflehead drake in flight. Credit: Alan Schmierer.

Bufflehead on the water. Credit: Alan Schmierer.

upper wings, and back are black, trimmed with white; undersides are white. Hens are very dark on top, light gray underside.

Identification up close and at hand: On the drake at hand, the details of the shades of dark greenish blue and violet over the black head, the large white patch forming a crest on the back of the head, and white stripes on the upper wings may be seen. Legs and feet are pink. Hens have a white patch extending around the back of the eye. Legs and feet are a light gray.

Range, distribution, and migration patterns: Breeding area is the Boreal Forest across Canada and the Atlantic interior; wintering areas are the coasts, the Great Lakes, and the western interior of the United States.

Habitat and diet: Nests are in woodpecker holes and other tree cavities. Winter habitat is coastal bays and large lakes. Feed is aquatic plants, insects, mollusks, and crustaceans, supplemented by seeds.

Harlequin Duck

Identification at distance and in flight: Observed in flight at distance as a small, dark duck flying low over the water. The drake is seventeen inches long, with a very small wingspan of eight inches and a weight of one and a half pounds. The hen is sixteen inches long with wingspan of seven and one half inches and a weight of a little over one pound.

Identification up close and at hand: Has a white pattern over a blue-shaded body.

Harlequin duck drake. Credit: Alan Schmierer.

<u>Range, distribution, and migration patterns</u>: Breeding area is inland from the Atlantic and Pacific coasts of Canada; the west coast of Greenland; the south coast of Iceland. Major wintering area of populations on the west side of North America is the Aleutian Islands. Eastern population winters along the coasts of New England.

<u>Habitat and diet</u>: Habitat is fast-flowing freshwater streams. Feed is crustaceans, mollusks, insects, and fish.

Common Goldeneye (Whistler)

<u>Identification at distance and in flight</u>: Drake resembles Barrow's goldeneye, with more white in a similar pattern. As usual for a diver duck, flight is normally fast and low over the water. A large duck, drakes are twenty inches long with a weight around three pounds; hens are sixteen inches long and

Common goldeneye hen. Credit: Alan Schmierer.

weigh about half the weight of the drake. Usually seen in flight in small flocks of their own kind. Black and white drakes and brown hens can be discerned in good light; they present the outline of a large, low-flying duck in poor light.

Identification up close and at hand: At hand, the drake is distinctive with a black head that has a green sheen. Colors are a white spot below each eye, a white chest and a black back and rear. The bill is black. The species is named for the definitive golden eye. The hen has a dark-brown head with pale, yellowish-white eyes, a dark back, gray sides, and a white belly.

Range, distribution, and migration patterns: Breeding area is the boreal forest across Canada. Nesting is in tree cavities. Wintering is along the Pacific Coast of Alaska and Canada, across and along the coasts of the United States.

Diet: Feed is primarily aquatic invertebrates and fish; aquatic plants are a secondary food source.

Hunting techniques and arrangements: Hunting techniques are long strings of decoys with pass shooting from points on big water shores, and from adequate boats offshore surrounded by decoys.

Barrow's Goldeneye

Identification at distance and in flight: Closely resembles common goldeneye, but smaller. Identical in flight characteristics.

Range, distribution, and migration patterns: Breeding is the northwestern interior of the United States, and the western interior of Canada to Alaska, with a few areas in northeastern Canada. Wintering is along the Pacific coast of the northwestern United States, Canada, and southern Alaska.

Barrow's Goldeneye. Credit: Alan Schmierer.

<u>Habitat and diet</u>: Identical to common goldeneye in nesting and feeding.

<u>Hunting techniques and arrangements</u>: Hunting techniques same as common goldeneye.

GEESE

There are a number of reasons for the stability and increase in the population of all species of geese. Many use breeding grounds in the high Arctic, which has remained relatively unaffected by human endeavor. Conditions are stable compared particularly with the drought risk of the Prairie Pothole Region and some of the other major nesting ideas of ducks. Migrating and wintering geese tend to hold together in large flocks. Feeding by grazing cropland allows flocks to hold together. This translates into safety in numbers: not only are there more eyes to stand watch, but also a large group minimizes the number of individuals on the high-risk edge of the group and maximizes the number in the low-risk interior of the feeding or resting group. And finally, the conversion of land to agriculture, which decreases habitat and feed for waterfowl depending solely on natural food sources, but produces a bounty for geese (along with mallards and other ducks, mostly all dabblers) that have adapted to the feed produced by humans.

Introduction to Dark and Light Geese

Dark geese, of the Branta genus, appear dark at distance; a closer look reveals different patterns of black and gray overall or just the head and frontal area. Legs, feet, and beaks are black. "Dark goose" refers primarily to the various subspecies of Canada goose. Ask the average person what they know about "wild" geese, what do geese look like? You'll probably get a response centered around the Canada (no, not "Canadian") goose. For most of the human population, "wild goose" translates to Canada goose, just like "wild duck" means mallard. Canadas are the geese that tend to stay with the humans down south and are observed by humans. Gray geese, of the Anser genus, are normally included for game management in the dark geese group with dark markings and back, but with orange-tinged legs. The white-fronted goose represents this group.

Light geese, of the Chen genus, are white overall, except for black wing-tips, with pinkish legs and beak. They're usually seen during their migration flights that consist of huge masses—high in the air and moving fast on a tail wind—going south in the fall, north in the spring. Their migrations are very much in contrast with most of the dark geese, primarily the Canadas, that sort of graze their way in either direction, in flights of around a hundred individuals. Among all waterfowl, white geese have been spectacularly successful survivors. They've been so successful that they have begun to overwhelm their habitat. Special spring hunting seasons have been opened to control their ever-growing populations.

Identification Techniques Useful for Sorting Geese

Geese are all large and heavy relative to other waterfowl, or all birds for that matter.

All geese fly in some form of a "V" formation. They'll be the biggest birds in the air around waterfowl habitat, with fast-flapping wings. The color difference between dark geese, primarily Canada geese, and light geese, primarily snow geese, is easy to determine at any distance. And it's an important distinction to make. Snow geese can be hunted in extended seasons, and white is easy to see in any lighting condition.

Snow geese flights are usually seen in much greater numbers than Canadas; a thousand or more isn't unusual. Canadas are usually numbered in the low hundreds.

Canada Goose

Canada geese are collectively the most widespread and the most numerous goose species. Somewhere over six million are available for hunting. In the commonly used terms of *dark geese* and *light geese*, they dominate the dark population.

To all but specialists who study or hunt them, Canada geese would appear to be identical if each subspecies were to be observed separately. But subspecies

Canada goose. Credit: JoAnne Airhart.

range in size from the giant or great Canada that weighs up to around twenty pounds, with a wingspan of seventy inches, down to the clacking goose, with a weight of seven pounds, and a wingspan of forty-five inches. Side-by-side comparisons would illustrate the drastic differences in size, and also some very subtle differences in appearance. To those of us who would be considered untrained, only the clacking goose has distinguishing features. It's now considered to be a different species. Notwithstanding, we'll consider them as part of the greater Canada population. The rest of the various Canadas are designated as subspecies.

<u>Identification at distance and in flight</u>: Canadas can be recognized in flight by the wedge shape or offset single line of ever-changing patterns, composed of one to two hundred dark, high-flying individuals during migration. Local flights to feed are typically lower, with fewer individuals. Wings flap in a

deliberate cadence in a deep arc. Cruising speed is about thirty miles per hour, and around sixty miles per hour in the escape.

The spectacle of a mass of Canadas in flight in their ever-changing "V" formation ranks right up there with the best of sunrise or sunset shows. Identification of Canadas in flight is easy as . . . fill in your favorite. Even from under a wet blanket. Vocalizations are loud and distinctive, a *yeounk*, pronounced with a yodel, around middle "C" on the piano for most subspecies, an octave lower for the largest, an octave higher for the clackers.

Range, distribution, and migration patterns: There are seven recognized subspecies of Canada goose, the clacking goose now being considered as a separate species. With the exception of the midcontinent giant Canada goose, size of the different subspecies grades from largest in the East to smallest in the West, with the clacking geese in the far West. It gets more complicated. Canada geese sort themselves into different populations east to west, each with its own nesting and wintering areas connected by migration corridors. The separate populations may include up to three different subspecies. They sort themselves for breeding. There is very little hybridization. They mate for life with one of their own. The migration corridors overlap, which is no problem to the geese involved. They know where they're going. But it makes the work of experts in science and game management more interesting. Experts have currently designated fourteen separate populations, each with an arbitrary name. Individuals of the different populations return to the same nesting and the same wintering areas along the same corridors year after year. Some populations are combined for purposes of game management. One population is composed of year-round residents along the Atlantic coast and adjoining interior. In Chapter 9, we'll review major corridors between well-defined nesting and wintering areas as presented in best references. Current systems sometimes rename populations, which adds to the confusion. Our scheme is to just review the places where you might find Canada geese. After you carefully read Chapter 9, you'll be granted a much higher level of understanding than the rest of the hunters in your party.

Habitat and diet: Wintering habitat is shallow freshwater ponds, potholes, natural lakes, flooded fields and timber, creeks, sloughs, shallow-water swamps and upper ends of man-made lakes. Feed is aquatic vegetation, seeds, emerging grain sprouts, waste grain, and, lots of folks would hasten to add, their farms, lawns, and golf greens.

Hunting techniques and arrangements: Hunting techniques include pass shooting, and shooting and calling over decoys.

Additional information: The sights and sounds of Canadas are never to be forgotten. But there's another side to the coin. Canadas are widespread, and that includes where the humans live. The Canadas are here, there, and seemingly everywhere. Permanently. Lots of them. Which makes for an experience we sometimes wish we could forget. These experiences range from downing airliners to a thick carpet of goose poop on the green where the honkers had breakfast.

White-fronted Goose (Speck, Specklebelly)

Identification at distance and in flight: You can't mis-identify these birds when you look up. In flight, the heads and necks appear as very dark gray, chest lighter, belly black streaked, back dark gray. Big, solid black streaks over light-gray belly can't be missed. Vocalization sounds like *atta-hunk, atta-hunk*.

White-fronted goose. Credit: Rickard Holgersson.

The white-fronted goose is a tough little long-range flier, weighing in at about seven pounds. They migrate in small, usually family, groups, as is true of geese in general.

Personal observation of species flying south in migration is an experience not to be forgotten. Here's Tom's: "Dawn was just breaking. A couple hundred feet up, flying in a tight 'V' of about twenty individuals. They appeared to have been in flight all night. Going in a straight line with strong wing strokes, no gliding, no vocalizations. Straight as an arrow toward the Gulf. Colors and markings easily discerned by black pattern of large streaks over light gray front underside. No camera. Unforgettable sight."

Identification up close and at hand: Details can be defined at hand. The white-fronted goose has a white forehead over a pink-tinted bill. Legs and feet are orange. Heads and necks are a very dark gray; chest is lighter. Its belly is black streaked and its back is dark gray.

Range, distribution, and migration patterns: The population of 1.35 million is composed of two evenly divided populations: midcontinent and Pacific. Midcontinent nests along arctic coast and interior of Alaska and central Canada, gathers on southern corner of Saskatchewan and Alberta, then on to the lower Gulf of Texas and Mexico. A small part of this population is the tule goose, which winters on Tule Lake. The Pacific population migrates along Pacific to the Central Valley of California. Migration flight is the Arctic to the Gulf Coast with few stops.

Breeding area is coast and adjacent interior of Canada and Alaska. Wintering areas are California's Central Valley, the Texas Gulf coast, and spots in southern New Mexico and Northern Mexico.

Diet: Feed while wintering consists of bulrushes, grasses, agricultural crops, and waste of rice, wheat, and corn.

Hunting techniques and arrangements: Hunting is done over decoys with calls, with either white-fronted, snow, or Canada decoys and calls. Seen often in mixed flocks with snows and sometimes Canadas, and is therefore often taken incidental to hunting snows and Canadas.

Additional information: Pairs mate for life. Family groups stay together.

Brant

Identification at distance and in flight: Identifiers in flight are rapid wingbeat and high-speed flight; head, neck, and chest are black, with an underside that

Brant. Credit: Alan Schmierer.

looks dirty white. Brants are a small goose, around three and a half pounds. The males are slightly larger. The call is low, soft-pitched *ronk, ronk*.

Identification up close and at hand: At hand, white spots can be seen on either side of the neck.

Range, distribution, and migration patterns: The brant total population of around five hundred thousand is divided into two subspecies: on the East, the Atlantic brant; on the West, the Black brant, sometimes called the Pacific brant. Atlantic brant breed on arctic islands and on the northern coast of Greenland. Black brant breed along the arctic coast of Alaska and the Northwest Territories. Atlantic brant winter along the US Atlantic coast, from Massachusetts to North Carolina. Wintering of Pacific brant is along the Baja Peninsula.

<u>Habitat and diet</u>: Habitat is primarily estuaries, lagoons, and shallow bays, saltwater marshes, and, secondarily, adjacent farmland. Feed is eelgrass, sea lettuce, sedges, bulrushes, and recently, agricultural crops and pastures.

<u>Hunting techniques and arrangements</u>: Favored hunting techniques are pass shooting as geese come close into backwater with changes in the tide in and out of bays and lagoons. Hunting is done over decoys from low-profile sculling boats.

LIGHT GEESE

The light goose population is composed of the snow goose and Ross's goose.

Snow Goose

Snow geese. Credit: Alan Schmierer.

Light and dark phases of snow geese.

Identification at distance and in flight: Lesser snow geese have a light phase and a dark phase. White phase is white with black wingtips. The dark phase is dark gray with darker head and neck. Call is a shrill and piercing yelp.

Identification up close and at hand: In hand, bill is dark pink with black trim on the sides. Legs and feet are reddish orange. Greater snow geese have the same appearance, except they're larger.

Range, distribution, and migration patterns: Snow geese dominate the considerable numbers of light geese widely available for hunting. Population available for hunting is around seven million.

Breeding area of lesser snow geese is far northern Canada arctic coasts and islands. Wintering area is the Gulf Coast around Texas and Louisiana, the Texas panhandle, the adjacent area in New Mexico, and into Mexico. They are scattered over the southwest states and California. Migration is from across the Arctic down all four natural flyways. Pattern for most of the central Canada population is to gather in particular areas of Canadian prairies late into fall, then fly nonstop to the Gulf Coast. A small part of the prairie population delays along the route to feed on waste grain. In the West, migration is to the Central Valley of California.

Wintering area for lesser snow geese is the Gulf Coast around Texas and Louisiana, the Texas panhandle, the adjacent area in New Mexico, and Baja, west coast of Mexico, and into the interior of Mexico. They are scattered over and into Mexico, the southwestern states, and California.

Breeding area for greater snow geese is arctic islands and Greenland. Wintering area is the central-Atlantic seaboard.

Habitat and diet: Wintering habitat for lesser snow geese is coastal bays and marshes near good feed sources. In the Arctic, feed is sedges, grasses, and cranberry. Louisiana marshes provide roots and tubers of marsh grasses. For the rest of Louisiana, Texas, and California, agricultural plants, such as waste grains, alfalfa hay, and emerging grain sprouts are the primary subsistence. Natural feed in the West consists of bulrushes, cattails, tubers, and rootstock.

Hunting techniques and arrangements: Hunting techniques are pass shooting along transit routes from sanctuary overnight areas to feeding areas, done over decoys with calls. Snow geese often travel in flocks of hundreds or thousands, so large numbers of decoys are needed. Greater snow geese travel in smaller flocks, so smaller numbers of decoys are needed.

Ross's Goose (Horned Wavy, Little Wavy)

Ross's goose. Credit: Alan Schmierer.

<u>Identification at distance and in flight</u>: Ross's goose has a light phase and, in much smaller numbers, a dark phase. They're a small goose at four pounds and with a twenty-five-inch wingspan. Ross's geese are often seen in mixed flights with snow geese, and can be distinguished by a much faster wingbeat than that of the snows. "Wavy" in "Horned Wavy" refers to the dynamics of its flight.

<u>Identification up close and at hand</u>: At hand, the bill is much shorter than the bill of the snow geese.

<u>Range, distribution, and migration patterns</u>: Breeding area is along the central arctic coast of Canada. Wintering is in pockets of California's Central Valley, smaller areas in central southern New Mexico, and the Texas Gulf coast.

<u>Habitat and diet</u>: Winter habitat is fresh or saltwater marshes in range of grasslands and/or grasses and agricultural fields.

<u>Hunting techniques and arrangements</u>: Hunting techniques include pass shooting and shooting over decoys and calls. Usually taken incidentally while hunting snow geese.

Tundra Swan (Whistling Swan)

Tundra swan. Credit: Alan Schmierer.

Identification at distance and in flight: In flight, the tundra swan is recognized by its large size, weighing eighteen pounds with a fifty-five-inch wingspan, with females slightly smaller. They are a solid white color and have a very long neck. The tundra swan is much larger than the snow goose it resembles, but it is usually seen with a thousand other snow geese. Call is a three-note honk.

Identification up close and at hand: At hand, it can be definitely recognized as a swan by size and configuration.

Range, distribution, and migration patterns: Breeding area is across the arctic coast of Canada, and continuing across the arctic and west coast of Alaska. Wintering is along the Atlantic and Pacific coasts, the Gulf Coast and interior of Texas, and widely distributed areas in the Rocky Mountain States.

Habitat and diet: Habitat in wintering area is coastal bays and fresh- and salt-water marshes a short flight from feeding areas. Tundra swans tip up to feed on aquatic plants. In fields, they feed on corn and small grains.

Hunting techniques and arrangements: Check before hunting to ensure that hunting is allowed and if any particular permits are required. Techniques of hunting are pass shooting along routes between resting and feeding areas, in fields, and over water, using goose decoys painted solid white.

WATERFOWL GAME BIRDS WITHOUT WEBBED FEET

Sandhill Cranes

Identification at distance and in flight: Flight of sandhill cranes is typical of all cranes: slow speed with deep wingbeats. Long neck and legs are distinctive in outline. They look larger than they are: weight is only twelve pounds, but length is over forty-five inches.

Sandhill crane in flight. Credit: Alan Schmierer.

Sandhill cranes standing. Credit: The National Park Service.

Identification up close and at hand: At hand, distinctive red patch on top of head stands out.

Range, distribution, and migration patterns: Breeding area is large, extending across arctic coast of Canada and Alaska to the Great Lakes. Migration is toward wintering grounds of southern California, south Texas, and into Mexico. Stopovers along shallow rivers, stream beds, and islands, and farm ponds.

Habitat and diet: Winter habitat is prairies and farm pastures. Feed is aquatic plants, insects, small grain waste, and sprouting grain crops.

Hunting techniques and arrangements: Hunting first involves a detailed check to be sure that hunting sandhill cranes is allowed in your area of interest. Shooting is often over crane decoys in feeding locations. Pass shooting can be set up between overnight location and feeding areas. Careful scouting is needed for success.

COOTS AND RAILS

Now this is a group that makes anybody feel like an expert wingshot. They kind of flop along low and slow. Also, it's good exercise pulling through the muck of the marsh or poling some kind of flat bottom over real thick water and lots of grass.

Coots

Coots are the most misunderstood of game birds. Listen up. Coots are widespread, have big bag limits, and are good eating if cooked correctly ("correctly" being defined as Cajun style—without limits, no holds barred, on the Cajun basic food groups, beginning with a can of red pepper seasoning . . .). There are any number of coot recipes. ("Anything tastes good if you're hungry enough" as some of the old guys say. Ever been real hungry?)

Coot. Credit: Alan Schmierer.

Coots are most often seen in the company of many of their own kind.

<u>Habitat and diet</u>: Coots feed as divers and seem to prefer the same depths as other freshwater divers. Shallows of lakes, marshes, sloughs, and ponds. They're usually feeding on aquatic plants and invertebrates or any other denizen of the swamp available.

<u>Hunting techniques and arrangements</u>: Stalking is the most poular method of hunting, maybe because you're out there hunting because you can't get any other action going.

Clapper Rail

<u>Hunting techniques and arrangements</u>: Clappers are hunted by stalking or pushing a flat-bottomed boat any way except with a mud motor. You usually need to get close through real thick stuff. They hold to cover.

Clapper rail. Credit: Alan Schmierer.

Moorhen (Common Gallinule)

<u>Hunting techniques and arrangements</u>: Like clappers, moorhens also hold to the thick cover, but they might flush quicker than the clappers. Same hunting techniques.

Purple Gallinule

<u>Habitat and diet</u>: Same habitat and behavior as moorhen.

<u>Hunting Technique and arrangements</u>: The purple gallinule in full color is a real showboat to the point that it appeals to some as a trophy.

Virginia Rail

<u>Hunting techniques and arrangements</u>: The Virginia rail seems to be less hunted than any of the other rails. Maybe because they're harder to see. They seem to be legal to hunt in all states, which is not the case for all rails.

Moorhen (common gallinule). Credit: Susan Young.

Purple gallinule. Credit: Alan Schmierer.

Virginia rail. Credit: Alan Schmierer.

Sora

<u>Additional information</u>: The sora is pretty much a ditto with the rest of the rails.

Snipes

<u>Identification at distance and in flight</u>: Now here's a little nonduck that can humble the best of shooters. Snipe are small and fast and very elusive. They flush and leave at about one hundred miles an hour and then make a ninety-degree turn, then maybe the other way about the time you catch up.

<u>Hunting techniques and arrangements</u>: Snipe hold in marshes that run from shallow to deep. If you can hit a few, they make a good hors d'oeuvre. A flat-bottom boat is good for carrying enough ammo to get many of them. It's a real good day when you can fill up the empty boxes.

Sora. Credit: Alan Schmierer.

Snipe. Credit: Alan Schmierer.

Snipe and mallards up. Credit: JoAnne Airhart.

It's not uncommon to see snipes in migration with mallards. This photo shows typical flooded low-ground pasture. Stepped over a levee and everything jumped out of hide or feathers except the quick-reacting JoAnne, who got the photo.

NO-SHOOT SPECIES

Introduction to the No-Shoots

Words to stay out of trouble: "If you're out hunting waterfowl and see a big white bird come over flying slowly, don't shoot." Words to stay out of trouble number two: long legs sticking out behind the tail.

So, you've been out there before daylight with no action. Maybe should have done better scouting. Looks like you might sit there all day without a single duck comin' by to check over your carefully placed decoy spread. You're about ready to take out your frustration on the first thing that comes by, outdoor ethics notwithstanding.

Here comes somethin'. A great big white bird flappin' along ever so slow. Your trigger finger starts itchin' horribly.

Don't do it, my friend. You're getting ready to turn a slow day into a very bad day. Rankin' right down there.

Remember that little pamplet that came with the state regulation booklet along with your hunting license? Toward the back, if you looked that far, is a set of very clear drawings of big birds that you may see hangin' around the marsh that are not duck, goose—not anything legal to hunt. If you read the information around the drawings, you find out that you leave them up above in the sky and let them slowly flap and glide on their way. They're the no-shoots. And the penalities for shooting one that may be on the verge of extinction are very high.

We'll not go into the details. What we will do is give you the identification information to keep you out of trouble. None of the no-shoots could be mistaken for a streamlined, fast-wingbeat, fast-movin' duck, goose, or any other legal waterfowl. The no-shoots are typically large and slow in flight, and most of them, as is obvious from the photos, will have long legs sticking out behind their tail when airborne.

Whooping Crane (Don't Shoot)

Identification: Flight is with slow and deliberate beats of very long and wide wings.

Range, distribution, and migration patterns: They may be observed from a distance in wintering areas along coasts. Species is very endangered, and they are highly protected.

Great Egret (Don't Shoot)

Identification at distance and in flight: This snow-white, regal bird is stately in flight, with long legs extending to the rear well behind the tail.

Range, distribution, and migration patterns: They may be encountered migrating between breeding and wintering areas. Breeding area is scattered over North America, concentrating inland from coasts and widely along the Mississippi north to near the Great Lakes. Wintering is along the Gulf, Atlantic, and Pacific coasts.

Habitat and diet: Often seen as it forages through open shallow water areas of marshes, coastal lagoons, and the edges of lakes. Feed is primarily fish but also catches all types of prey in shallow water.

Whooping crane. Credit: Alan Schmierer.

Great egret. Credit: Alan Schmierer.

White Pelican (Don't Shoot)

Identification at distance and in flight: The American white pelican is a very large, snowy-white bird, with a length of around six feet, and a wingspan around ten feet. It's not long and lean. The pelican's weight can be over twenty pounds. The bill is impressive, up to fifteen inches long, with a large throat sac hanging down. Male and female are identical with the exception of size. Males are larger.

White pelican. Credit: Alan Schmierer.

White pelican pair.

Flight is often observed to be soaring. On the water and in flight, the long neck folds back so that the head appears to rest on the chest. The carry of head and beak is distinctive.

Range, distribution, and migration patterns: Most of the population nests in the prairie provinces and northern regions of Canada, though a relatively small part of the population nests on islands of the Great Salt Lake. The western population is located across Idaho and adjoining states. Wintering is along the southern coast of California and the Gulf Coast. They may be seen resting in tight flocks along their migration routes. Wintering and migrating flocks of twenty birds rest in secluded backwaters. Flocks are disturbed at the approach of perceived predators.

Habitat and diet: Winter habitat is shallow, protected coastal bays and estuaries and lakes. White American pelicans feed on fish from the surface of the water rather than diving from the air after fish as do their brown relatives. Dining is a much more sedate affair for white pelicans.

Double-Crested Cormorant (Don't Shoot)

Double-crested cormorant. Credit: JoAnne Airhart.

Identification at distance and in flight: This is another big, slow-moving bird with slow, deep wing flaps, commonly seen around the water. Flight is often in lines or a "V" pattern. The double-crested cormorant has a long, snake-like neck and long bill, and can be seen wading in the water and diving for prey. Unlike ducks and geese, their feathers are not waterproof, so they're often seen on a rock or log with wings outstretched to dry. The double crests are seldom present to make definite identification. Just don't shoot them.

Range, distribution, and migration patterns: Breeding area is across southern Canada and the northern United States, west of the Great Lakes to the Rockies, and east of the Great Lakes to the Atlantic from eastern Canada. Wintering areas are the Atlantic, Pacific, and Gulf coasts.

Habitat and diet: Habitat is very generally aquatic. Feed is primarily fish, but prey includes anything in the water the cormorant can catch.

Great Blue Heron (Don't Shoot)

Identification at distance and in flight: Recognition is straightforward: it is unique with its distinct gray-blue color. Large in size, its length is up to four and a half feet and its wingspan is over six feet. It stands up to four and a half feet high and can weigh almost eight pounds. Plumed feathers on lower neck. Wingbeat is slow. Its long neck is folded in flight, extended in takeoff and landing, and "S"-shaped while standing. Usually observed in singles or pairs.

Great blue heron. Credit: Alan Schmierer.

Range, distribution, and migration patterns: Summer is spent in northern interior states of the United States and into Canada. Winter range is across the southern United States and interior from the Atlantic, Pacific, and Gulf coasts, and along the west coast of Canada.

White Ibis (Don't Shoot)

<u>Identification at distance and in flight</u>: This is a large, slow, white bird with black wingtips, seen around marshes. Its wingbeats are slow and deliberate, with intermittent glides. The medium-length neck is extended in flight, with bill turned down. Legs extend past tail in flight but are shorter than the legs of cranes. Flocks are made up of up to thirty individuals.

<u>Range, distribution, and migration patterns</u>: Wanders far to the north after breeding in summer. Wintering range is the Texas Gulf coast into western Mexico.

White ibis. Credit: Alan Schmierer.

Habitat and diet: Habitat is saltwater and brackish marshes along coasts, and freshwater inland. Feed is small aquatic prey: crustaceans, amphibians, and reptiles.

Wood Stork (Don't Shoot)

Identification at distance and in flight: A large, white bird with a bald head and black tail, wingtips, and trailing edges of wings. Slow wingbeat interrupted by glides and soaring. Bill is turned down. Wingspan is over five feet; legs extend beyond tail in flight. Usually seen as singles or in small flocks.

Range, distribution, and migration patterns: In summer, disperses far to the north. Winters in Florida to Texas and Eastern coast of Mexico.

Diet: Feed is primarily fish and other small aquatic prey.

Wood stork. Credit: Alan Schmierer.

Swans (Don't Shoot, Usually; Without a Special Permit, Never)

<u>Identification at distance and in flight</u>: Swans are a very large, and in North America, white bird. Their length is close to five feet, with a wingspan of ten feet, and they can weigh over thirty pounds. There are three species of swans in North America: mute, trumpeter, and tundra. Tundra swans are smaller with limited hunting permits issued, but, as discussed outside of this "No Shoots" section, protected in more places and at more times, than not.

Wingbeat is rapid for a bird of such large size. Long necks are fully extended in flight. Legs are short. Flights are often composed of pairs of up to ten to twelve individuals. Larger groups may use a "V" formation.

Mute Swan. Credit: Alan Schmierer.

Range, distribution, and migration patterns: In range, swans are sparsely distributed across the northern contiguous United States, Canada, and Alaska. Often permanent residents across the United States and southern Canada. Freeze-up moves them south.

Habitat and diet: Feed is primarily aquatic plants; secondary is grazing on land and some insects and small prey.

WATERFOWL AROUND THE GLOBE

Our presentation of waterfowl identification has been focused on the species of North America, and the context has been compliance with hunting regulations. We probably don't need to point out—but we will anyway—that waterfowl hunting goes on around the world. And it just might be on the bucket list or at least show up on the daydream list of some of our readers. We'll give an overview of the waterfowl species around the world to guide your Internet searches so that you'll have an idea of waterfowl species of the world. Toward the end of the book, we'll give you an idea of where to start on hunting arrangements in case you want to make those daydreams come true.

Eurasian Waterfowl

A great many ducks and geese are circumpolar. If the hunter goes abroad to Europe, most of the dabbler ducks will look just like those back home. There are some exceptions. One is the widely distributed garganey. The hen looks like a female teal. The drake looks like a teal with a white trim streak over each eye and down the back of the head and neck. Another is the falcated duck, which has a very dark green head and a white ring around the throat. The Eurasian wigeon looks like an American wigeon with a different paint job. The Eurasian teal looks like a green-wing. Dabblers unique to Asia are the spot-billed duck, the Philippine duck, the Baikal teal, which has a complex black-and-white swirl around each side of the head, the knob-billed duck, and the sunda teal.

Diving ducks are the same or slightly different versions of the divers of North America. The canvasback stays in North America, the redhead mingles with the Eurasian common pochard and red-crested pochard. The tufted duck could be taken for the ring-necked duck with a spike of feathers on the back of the head, and the ferruginous duck, which resembles a ring-necked with a dark-red paint job to go with a black back.

Sea ducks are the same, with the exception of the smew, restricted to Europe and Asia, and the hooded merganser, restricted to North America. The Chinese and scaly-sided mergansers are unique to Asia.

The North American cast of dark geese can be found across Eurasia.

South American Waterfowl

A few North American waterfowl are also found in South America. Dabblers are the mallard, blue-winged and cinnamon teal, and the American wigeon. Several South American species appear to be close relatives to North American species. Dabblers are the white-cheeked and yellow-billed pintails, the red shoveler, and the Chiloe wigeons. Species found only in South America are dabblers such as the puna, the yellow-billed, the ringed teal, the Brazilian and silver teal, the crested duck, the knob-billed duck (also found in Asia and Africa), and the bronze-winged duck. Species of flightless, or near flightless, so-called "steamer" ducks occur only in South America. These are the Falkland, Fuegian, and Flying. Diving ducks common to both Americas are the ring-necked and lesser scaup. Divers unique to South America are the rosy-billed pochard (resembles a ring-necked with a big red bill) and Southern pochard (resembles a ring-necked with a blue bill).

There are three South American species in a group by themselves. These are the screamers, named after their calls. They are the horned screamer, the crested, or northern, screamer, and the southern screamer.

Sheldgeese and Shelducks only found in South America are: the Andean goose, the ashy-headed goose, the kelp goose, the Magellan goose, the orinoco goose, the ruddy-headed goose, and the Muscovy duck (also found in Central America).

Africa

Familiar North American dabblers also found in Africa are: the mallard, the gadwall, and the northern pintail. Dabblers found in Eurasia as well as Africa are: the garganey, the red-crested, the marbled teal, and Eurasian wigeon. Dabblers unique to Africa are: the African black duck, Meller's duck, Hartlaub's duck, knob-billed duck, Madagascar teal, and the hottentot teal. A diving duck found in both Africa and North America is the greater scaup. Divers in both Africa and Eurasia include the crested duck, the red-crested pochard, the tufted duck, and the southern pochard.

Africa is also home to a series of geese that are not true geese. These are: the Cape Barron goose, the spur-winged goose, the magpie goose, and the pygmy goose, which is actually a small perching duck. African sheldgeese and shelducks are: the Egyptian goose, the South African shelduck, and the blue-winged goose.

New Zealand, Australian, and Pacific Waterfowl

Dabblers of North America also found in the far Pacific are the mallard and the northern shoveler. Dabblers unique to the region are: the Pacific black duck, the Australasian shoveler, the Australian wood duck, the freckled duck (an ancient species of duck), the Auckland teal, the Campbell Island teal, the chestnut teal, the gray teal. Diving ducks unique to the area are the white-eyed duck and the New Zealand scaup. Shelducks of the area (all of which look like birds of paradise) are: the Australian shelduck, the paradise shelduck, the Radjah shelduck, the blue duck, and Salvadori's teal. Shelgeese (also spectacular) are: the Cape Barren goose, the cotton pygmy goose, the green pygmy goose, and the magpie goose (an ancient species of goose).

Migration and Identification

Migration could be considered as a defining characteristic for nearly all waterfowl. A few species are all-year residents, but for nearly all species, insight into migration is a valuable tool of identification. Each species tends to have its particular schedule, which often depends on weather conditions, but they'll often come through your area in a particular sequence. For instance, you see a flight of small ducks darting along during the month of September. You need to run through your identification sequence, but they're probably teal. And if you're out there on the edge of the water with a shotgun and a bunch of decoys set out, they'd better be teal because it's the special teal season and if it's anything else pushing their schedule up and you bust some . . . big trouble. Lots of states have restricted seasons on some species. Know the regs, know "wutzatduck" zipping over, and check the calendar.

Chapter 2

Techniques, Methods, and the Hunting Experience

Let's move ahead now with more insight than you had back at the Introduction. Now we start to think about hunting, and successful waterfowl hunting is as complex as our quarry and its habitat.

If you get into waterfowl hunting for the duration, your destination can be found at the end of the Conclusion. This is where you get to decide your route to get there, to exceed the best of what you've seen on the Saturday outdoors channels or all of those publications. The plot of this story is up to you. How do you prefer to hunt? What methods? What techniques? Where? The quality of your waterfowl hunting experience is determined by the selection of the overall strategy that will create the most personal satisfaction. Choices will create your strategy: the setting, arrangements, methods, and techniques of the hunt; the point where nature and hunter intersect and blend; the reason that otherwise reasonable people can be found in a freezing blind in the mist and fog before daylight.

The rest of this section will give you insights into the methods and techniques of hunting in the various habitats. Don't be concerned about your lack of the skills required to execute the methods and techniques illustrated through the chapters that immediately follow. Tactical skills will be covered in the last chapters of Part I; the enablers come in Part II. We provide insight into the skills and everything required to effectively hunt in those various types of locations. Preparation for the hunt goes on year-round. Activities of learning and practicing skills will become a major part of the total experience. Finally, Part III will give insight to help you sort through the complexities of the choices that you now know are ahead.

So, the first element of your strategy selection is insight into the methods and techniques of waterfowl hunting. Turn the page and hang on, 'cause here we go!

INTRODUCTION TO HUNTING METHODS

We'll present methods generally applicable to all hunting in the sequence of practice: scouting and location, stalking, and making the kill. Stalking includes the concepts and execution of the specialized tactics of waterfowling in general and (widely used terms): driving (jump shooting), and ambushing, either by posting on a likely route (pass shooting) or luring into ambush (decoying and calling). Making the kill requires mastery of the art and science of wingshooting. The sequence is loose, and many methods, or phases of methods, are skipped by experienced hunters. Concerning location, they'll know in July where they'll need to be before first light next October, next November, and next December.

Experienced hunters usually have developed instincts that enable them to be better waterfowlers. Instinct allows them to react quickly and make decisions without deliberation. Much of this is learned from the school of hard knocks.

Now we'll introduce you to a broader perspective on tactics, to give some context to the activities involved in duck and goose hunting, to explain why we use some hunting methods and not others, and to show why some methods are either illegal or unethical. We'll try to indicate where the lines are, assuming you want to color between the lines. As a bonus, if you ever take young hunters afield with you, you can answer at least a few of their questions.

Historical Background

Why don't we normally hunt with a muzzleloading cannon loaded with grape-shot? Or with full auto rifles? Why don't we hunt all night long with full autos fitted with night scopes, or hunt out of high-powered boats or aircraft, and take all of the geese and/or ducks that we want to? Well, all of these "hunting" methods have been used, but are not anymore, for a variety of reasons.

Originally, hunters were out for subsistence. They took prey animals (the term *game* is a recent invention in relative terms) by any and all means that they could come up with. Our ancestors ran prey down and made the kill using handheld weapons. Wildfowl would seem to have been immune to overhunting by these primitive methods for the most part; they've been using water as a barrier to terrestrial predators for a long time before humans showed up. However, modern humans are thought to have been the first to make a variety of missiles, including throwing sticks, sling-propelled rocks, spears, atlatl-propelled darts, and arrows propelled by bows. These are believed to be the first stand-off weapons—and potential wildfowl takers. Traps and thrown nets were also used. Somewhere along the line, ducks and geese were domesticated and used as the first, and, no doubt, very effective decoys. Crafted artificial decoys of various constructions have been discovered. As falconry was developed by the ancients, it most likely became the most effective hunting strategy and hunting method until the development of firearms. Falconry currently has designated hunting seasons.

The evolvement of firearms, to be outlined in Part II, resulted in shotguns that were absolutely effective implements for the taking of waterfowl. And these guns coincided with the time of maximum exploitation of the natural resources of North America. Species of wildlife that existed in seemingly limitless numbers were practically eradicated within a single decade by market hunting. Conservationists, often led by outdoor enthusiasts, acted to rein in the market-driven madness. Game management (the terms *game* and *sport* had meanwhile originated in Europe with recreational hunting and fishing pastimes of the upper classes) brought rules and regulations to control hunting and fishing. Just in time for most waterfowl species.

Many bucked and kicked at such controls. But this curtailment of some individual prerogatives did keep the ducks and geese from going the way of the passenger pigeon. Migratory waterfowl regulations are made available every year with explicit instructions as to what's allowed, and what's not.

In addition to federal- and state-enforced regulations based on law, a tradition of ethical behavior has developed based partially on good sportsmanship and, in some cases, on ethical de facto game management. These practices aren't written down anywhere to our knowledge and seem not to be uniform or at least universally enforced. Some are still argued one way or another. For most, an example of sportsmanship would be that the hunter refrain from shooting waterfowl not on the wing. What if the hunter can't make a shot, but lures a swimming duck into the decoy spread by calling? Examples of ethical practices would be going beyond regulation requirements of bag limits of two mallard hens and refraining from taking any "Suzie's" due to the high mortality of nesting hens. But sometimes the hen comes straight down through the trees with the drake, so that if you shoot, you take them both. Competent wingshots also practice shooting ducks in the front of the body using adequate leads or taking care in arranging setups to take incoming ducks with frontal shots. Shot patterns in the front of the body have a high percentage to take out wings, head, or lungs so that the bird goes down immediately when shot within range. Shot striking the rear of the body will penetrate at considerable range, and result in gut shots that don't bring the bird down, but will result in a lingering death at a great distance, never to be recovered.

Geese are big and tough. Shots should be for the head and within range. The so-so wingshot who thinks he or she is pretty good shoots a goose at long range so that it can't be retrieved and eventually dies hard and goes to waste. Shoot close. Shoot for the head so that it falls like a big rock. Shots taken beyond ethical range can be heard striking goose wing feathers but won't bring them down. Shot striking too far back beyond ethical range will result in gut shots. So while our hunting methods have to fit between the lines drawn up and enforced by state and federal game managers, there's still plenty of room to operate, and it's up to us to set our own standards of conduct well within the regulations.

Scouting

Pick scouting every time. There's nothing better than being where the ducks, or geese, want to be. Nothin' better. Ever. There's a well-worn piece of advice to the effect, "If you have the choice between being good, or being lucky, pick lucky every time." That's good advice. But, something you have more control over as far as waterfowl hunting goes, is, "If you have a choice between being the best wingshot, being the best caller, having the best decoys, being the most experienced decoying, having the best camo, having the best shotgun, and it goes on and on, or being an inexperienced, beginning duck or goose hunter who takes the time at every opportunity to scout around the area where you plan to hunt, where you'd like to hunt, where you'll never get to hunt, pick scouting every time." What's the magic? Just look. How do really good guides get to be really good? They've looked for a really long time. Scouting is the answer to all the really burning questions, which are:

- First, where are the ducks and/or geese?
- Second, how do we get there?
- And third, moving up rapidly in priority in lots of areas, where are all of the other hunters going to be? And, sometimes, you may have to include everybody else. Where will the nonhunters be?

Then, after answering all these questions, you must get up stupid early and do one or more of the following: win the race to that place on public land; hire a guide who's already done the scouting; ask permission to hunt on private land, early, sweetly, and close the damned gate to keep the cows in and don't drive over cropland; or, if you're in Texas, buy a lease where you or a friend saw ducks last year; if you don't have a friend who hunts, find one. But however you manage to do it, scouting to discover where the ducks or geese are located is a prerequisite for getting into shotgun range of either.

Waterfowl follow a daily schedule that starts with a flight from the place of sanctuary on water where they spent the night separated from the natural predators of the night. All species of waterfowl require plenty of feed to sustain enough energy for their high activity levels. The waterfowler attempts to accurately predict where they'll head at first light to feed. Subsequent methods are then used to entice them into shotgun range as they show up at that location. Most techniques of taking waterfowl are a variation of the ambush.

Most waterfowlers go by the not-so-innovative, but effective, first principle of location: the most likely location ducks and geese will head for tomorrow morning is where they were to be found heading to yesterday morning. This is a sound principle, unless they were disturbed yesterday morning by a bunch of hunters shooting at them.

Chapter 3

Jump Shooting and Pass Shooting

The primary activity of duck and goose hunting, with a few exceptions, amounts to decoying and calling to lure the game to within shotgun range. Those few exceptions can be a lot of fun and productive as well when practiced with good techniques.

A productive byproduct of cross-country stalking on foot is that it's the best technique to scout all of the favorite hideouts puddle ducks and sometimes geese use for loafing during the day as they take a break from working over spilled grain from recently harvested crops in the fall or tender sprouts of recently planted crops early in the winter.

Habits and habitat of different species tend to render them more or less susceptible to stalking techniques and jump shooting. Wigeon ducks often graze on tender emerging plants on open fields and pastures, which they prefer to be partially flooded or, at least, have a few puddles for landing. It's very difficult to sneak up on feeding wigeons. This contrasts with the habits of gadwall ducks. They tend to hold to banked sloughs that hide them from predators, but which also interfere with their line of sight to spot approaching danger. Gadwall ducks are very susceptible to stalking. Diver duck species are susceptible to stalking due to their inclination to dive under the water surface to escape immediate danger rather than taking flight and leaving the area as do the dabblers. Divers as a genus have more difficulty in taking flight, often running over the surface of the water as they build up sufficient speed to get airborne. Diving is quicker in evading danger and effective when they can move away from danger by swimming underwater, but when surprised by stalking humans they inefficiently take to flight. Dabblers have neither the inclination nor the capability for an effective underwater escape. They pop up from the water surface and take flight at the first hint of danger.

Tactics of Active Combined Location/Stalking: Jump Shooting

Actively finding and stalking waterfowl was widely practiced by subsistence hunters, sometimes in conjunction with the use of primitive decoys. Numerous arrowheads found around the shores of northern lakes indicate that direct stalking was a problematic technique even for the most expert bowman stalkers. The same applies to modern shotgunners.

Stalking ducks and geese as we practice it usually takes some form as the straightforward "go in after 'em" approach carried over from our youth. The only thing missing is our youth—and the stamina, misguided enthusiasm, flexibility, well-lubricated joints absent arthritic pain, and the absolute joyful willingness to slide through a few hundred yards of mud in a low crawl for the chance of a couple of quick shots as a few puddle ducks explode into flight in a panic. Picture the skinny kid Eddie, then fast-forward to the current Eddie moving in on mallards at the low crawl with his faithful Bart moving abreast, using his most stealthy doggie version of the low crawl.

Our techniques and tactics weren't especially elegant, but they were reasonably effective. We'd walk to a likely stock pond or small soil conservation lake, approaching from behind cover to keep out of sight of any ducks on the water or coming in to land on the water. That usually worked out to be crawling up the backside of the dam or embankment, then popping over the top. The ducks would be dabblers and flush straight up. The barrage wouldn't be too heavy considering we all carried single shots, but with practice, we sometimes managed to get off a couple of effective shots.

This is a good place to bring attention to an essential that was left out of our youth: ear protection. This is the second most important thing to remember after keeping the gun pointed in a safe direction. Ear plugs are the minimum, but ear covers over plugs are better. You'll not need to say, "Huh?" so many times in your maturity.

TALES OF COMBINED LOCATING AND STALKING

Gadwall hideout inaccessible.

Approach is difficult.

Sneak on gadwall in defilade.

Gadwall hideout with access.

Speed kills.

Elaborate stalking tactics.

Stalking doesn't always work.

Canada geese daytime resting hideout.

PASS SHOOTING

In pass shooting, hunters take a stand where ducks or geese are likely to pass within shotgun range. Ducks, particularly teal and gadwall, can be decoyed to make a low pass over a setup. Other instances where pass shooting can be productive is along routes between overnight sanctuaries and feeding areas, or between feeding areas and daytime loafing areas. These tactics can be blended with cross-country traverses of stalking techniques and tactics.

Detailed insight into key locations of overnight sanctuaries, feeding areas, loafing areas, and routes used by waterfowl between all three allow hunters great flexibility when a road network is available between the locations where they have access permissions. Waterways running through extensive public land or swampy or marshy areas can be accessed by shallow draft boats and airboats.

Pass Shooting Setup between Resting and Feeding Areas

Meticulous scouting and a weather forecast can turn up an effective alternative to decoying and calling geese into a feeding or resting area set.

Scouting of a hunting group is done the afternoon before the hunt planned for the following morning. Geese will have filled themselves in surrounding fields and are back on the lake for security where they'll spend the night. Geese on and around the water will number from in the hundreds up to the thousands as they congregate after migration. It's a daunting prospect to get enough decoys out to attract a flight. Big professional outfits can pull it off, but a small private group will usually find themselves better off to find a good ambush situation along routes between secure resting areas and feeding areas. You quickly develop an eye for the linear landscape forms going in the direction the birds want to go. Fencerows count as landscape on the high plains. Anything to break up the constant winds counts, for that matter. Then hope to not have a bright sunny morning when the geese fly hundreds of feet up.

In this case, as if it were planned, and it was, a warm and sunny afternoon turned to a dark and foggy winter day in the Texas Panhandle, the geese flying low out to the grain fields from their overnight water roost. A pass-shooting setup will probably be more productive than putting out the decoys in this case. Gotta love that Panhandle weather. Spin the pages under your thumb back to page 289 for a great pass shoot illustration. "How'er them oiled-up autoloaders workin' this mornin', boys?" Moral: Always have an old slide shucker along in the wintertime in the Panhandle.

Sea ducks fly very low over the water to get the energy-saving ground (water) effect boost. They'll fly along a bank and around the point rather than fly over the barrier. Pass shooting along a long breakwater along the New England coast might be the most productive setup on a dark and dreary day.

Pass shooting sea ducks.

Chapter 4

Shooting over Decoys

Decoying: Theory and Practice

We've engaged the true experts to illustrate realistic decoy spreads—experts that know exactly how ducks and geese look on the water under different situations. Our expert consultants are real ducks and geese. You're going to miss the standard set of sketches of cartoon ducks and geese you usually see when decoying is on the docket, with representations of decoy sets that look like the letter "J," "V," "W," "X," or anything else. They seem to come and go with time. You'll not even see a drawing of the spread that's worked great for some old-timer in a particular place and circumstances for the last fifty years or so. You'll never be in that place. We'll start with the ducks and geese and take it from there.

We'll present some examples using decoy setups (*sets* for short) to help you translate from the real thing into what you create as a lure for the real thing. A little context here: This chapter will emphasize the factors to get the ducks or geese within shotgun range; the next chapter concentrates on safely making an ethical shot. Part II presents detailed instructions as to the techniques of shooting and factors to consider in selecting a shotgun that suits you.

LURING OF WATERFOWL: DECOYING AND CALLING OVERVIEW

So, with the stage set by scouting on different scales and locations, the waterfowl hunter's challenge is to lure waterfowl to within shotgun range—an elaborate version of the basic ambush.

The most effective lure element usually works out to be the decoying as opposed to the calling. The beginner usually finds decoy placement easier and quicker to master than the complex repertoire of communication vocalizations of ducks and geese. The appropriate vocalizations for specific circumstances have to be executed to perfection. The slightest error in selection and execution of the vocalization will put ducks on high alert or send them veering off to another location faster and more surely than silence. Success in decoying and calling usually involves a mix of decoys and calls: experts may be good at both; the novice would probably do better to emphasize the decoys. You can get away with less than perfect execution with the decoys—up to a point.

Traditionally, advice for the new hunter has been that the order of importance is scouting, then decoying, then calling. For the experienced hunter who already knows where the ducks or geese are, and what the decoy spread for that time and place should look like, the order is calling, then decoying, then scouting. Words to live by for generations. But then change always comes.

The new game in town is motion. Traditional duck hunting techniques have always included some motion to go with those inert decoys sitting on the water, some way to cause ripples on the water. Then the motion decoys came along with mechanical wing movement to simulate ducks landing. The goose hunters for a long time have added action to the decoys: there's lots of movement in large gatherings of real geese. Some goose decoys move like wind socks. They *are* wind socks. For extra effect, hunters laying low within the decoy spread wave flags. The practice has migrated to duck hunting. It appears to be an effective supplement to calling. Some enthusiasts consider it as a calling replacement. Some say that goes too far. One thing that most agree on is that flagging is easier to pick up than calling. Our experience is that it takes some technique to get the flag waver to look like part of the decoy set. We're open to suggestions.

Decoying and Calling the Shallow Water Dabblers

The several variables controlling the configuration of the shallow water setup for dabbler, or puddle, ducks can seem to create almost unlimited forms when explanations go into requirements tailored to particular circumstances. This is an absolutely baffling puzzle to the newcomer. Experienced duck hunters seemingly never give it a thought as they walk up to a new place and start tossing decoys out before walking over to the optimum shooting position.

Here's a quick review of the small shallow-water world of the dabbler ducks: prairie potholes; sloughs; openings in flooded timber; pools in creeks and rivers; flooded pastures and crops; shallows and shorelines; freshwater swamps; and saltwater marshes characterized by shallow water with small open pools in vegetation. Dabbler ducks are adapted to obtain their subsistence by consuming a diet of predominantly aquatic plants, with lesser proportions of aquatic animals, insects, and shellfish, obtained in shallow ponds and streams. Their "trademark" method of feeding is to lower the head into the water and feed, tipping their body forward, tail up, to reach the feed more easily by extending their head deeper into the water as required. A minor fraction of their subsistence is obtained by foraging or grazing on dry ground.

This tends to restrict the dabblers to depend on shallow water for their sustainment. But, since the dominant proportion of duck populations turns out to be dabbler families, it follows that there's plenty of shallow water to be found in their extended environment, which stretches from the pond-dotted prairies of Canada to the Gulf shores and all of the shallow water along the intervening routes.

Placement of decoys has some general guidelines that leave room for individual touches. For small waters, the usual practice is to scatter six to eight decoys over shallow water used for feeding, with a separation between decoys of over ten feet. The desired effect is a scene of unafraid ducks happily feeding on a little hidden-away pond as seen from the air by passing ducks moving along at a fast clip. Note that the easily-seen-from-the-air aspect is important. Hunters should be concealed or in camouflage if cover is sparse. Expect ducks to be coming into any wind to touch down. Dabbler ducks coming into a pond completely surrounded by trees may drop straight down onto the water, seemingly flapping their wings as if flying in place. They can also leave the same way, pulling straight up with powerful strokes. Such small ponds may be hunted by one hunter, with decoys arranged so that the only clear landing area is within range of the hunter.

Larger bodies of water require more decoys to get the attention of ducks on the wing. Note ducks landing in the photo: one coming in, and two leaving ripples from landing.

You might refer back to this picture from time to time. Note that the ducks are not at all evenly spaced. Some are landing coming straight in toward ducks already on the water. They're not coming in at one big gap, or

Undisturbed ducks in prairie pothole.

Realistic decoy spread with fliers.

Late-season mallards.

Late-season decoy spread.

"V" or whatever. They're just comin' in whenever and wherever they feel like comin' in. Just like a bunch of ducks. You might as well note that, for the record, geese come in just like a bunch of geese. Here's the takeaway. You'll hear it again more than once. If you're going to fool a duck, you've got to think like a duck. Sequel: If you're going to fool a goose, you've got to think like a goose.

Wait a minute! That's a picture of the real thing in the first two photos.

When ducks are disturbed or threatened, they tend to crowd together on the water as shown in the

Ducks holding to center of stock pond, indicating a high threat.

third photo. When hunting late season for ducks that have been hard hunted all the way from Canada to Texas, decoys may be placed closer together to represent threatened ducks. The confident open spacing will look suspicious.

TECHNIQUES AND TACTICS OF SHALLOW-WATER SETUPS FOR DABBLERS

A decoy set becomes much more effective when movement is introduced. Ducks that look to have found a good feeding place often have guests dropping in.

Ducks landing with undisturbed feeders or resting is a normal sight in nature, widely mimicked by decoy spreads. Some fundamentals to remember are that ducks always land into the wind. And they never come in to land over ducks already on the water. The ducks illustrated are coming in a clear landing zone at the side of the group already on the water. Referring back to the first photo of the series photo on page 117, note that that landers are coming in at two spots: on the right side in an opening among widely spread ducks on the water; and on the left and center, as indicated by the ripples. One is still in the air.

Decoy spreads always have open landing spots in front of the shooters, and are more effective with a couple of flier decoys above the water with wings in motion (see photo on page 118) This is a good set to draw ducks across a small lake. The bigger the lake, the more ducks in flight, the more decoys. Note ducks landing to the side of ducks on the water.

Large, open bodies of water or extensive marshlands with open water are usually hunted with larger spreads of decoys, ranging into hundreds. Decoys may simulate dabblers or diving ducks, with a few coot or geese decoys to one side to attract attention and provide reassurance of security. And both are easily seen from a distance.

The photo to the right is a larger spread on a lake tucked in close to an old road. Some ducks near the bank are gathered close and feeding. Most away

Everything's out there.

from the bank are spread apart, indicating low threat level. There just happens to be a notch in the loosely gathered ducks on the water with a couple of fliers coming in. They're paying no attention to the stack of dead brush close to the water's edge.

This is about as close as we can get to a decoy version of real ducks feeding close to shore: ducks landing, low threat level, some lovable coots that reassure ducks. Geese will work, too. This spread is designed to draw ducks from across the lake from any direction. Boat is set so that ducks come around into the wind straight toward the boat. Eddie refers to it as the "All out rack 'em and stack 'em spread." (Eddie gets a little carried away sometimes.) But then the game warden stopped by that morning and visited. Nobody else had anything to check. Made friends with Scout and wanted to set up a date with a nice female lab. Break's over. Back to business . . .

Memorize this formula: When you're hunting over shallow parts of a larger lake, the main objective becomes one of attracting ducks within range of your setup. Obvious enough. A spread of a couple hundred decoys or more is arranged, considering the wind and leaving a spot or two for incoming ducks to come in within shotgun range. A couple of moving wing decoys on stakes suspended just above the water surface attracts the attention of passing ducks and seeks to entice them to land on the planned spot. Ducks close together are feeding in shallows. A few coots are gathered close to look reassuring and draw attention from a distance. There are jerk lines to make some of the decoys bob and create realistic ripples as would be produced by swimming ducks. There's also an upended tail decoy that squirts water to create ripples. Sounds far fetched, but it's surprisingly effective.

As illustrated on the left, decoy spreads can and should be designed to fit particular spots.

Tailored shallow water spread.

Small spread off a point.

You're always on the lookout for spots that may be no good today, but if the wind swings around on another day, you know where to be. Eddie had noticed this location and, on a morning when the wind had shifted enough to upset the original plan, this place looked really good. The original plan called for a large spread of dekes—too many for this spot, however. So, he set out what seemed to be enough decoys to fit the shallow water and dead stuff. Extra decoys were tucked in behind the boat. The spread is very loose and invites ducks to come in to the water in big holes, in some cases dropping in over decoys on the water. Ducks are fatally attracted to a spread with a different look.

Ducks come from any direction depending on the wind and land outside of decoy spread this page. This old blind has been in position for years and is considered part of the landscape by ducks.

Take note of the ducks tightly centered middle of pond page 119. If hunting a small body of water late season, most of us tend to place decoys around the edge. That's where the dabblers feed. Right? Well, looks like maybe sometimes we're outsmarting ourselves. These are holding in a tight little knot right in the center. Appear to be staying out of shotgun range just in case. Very unhandy, but might be worth it to get the decoys tight in the center with the idea that some more with the willies might tend to join.

Dabblers feeding in shallows usually create ripples, and sometimes splashes. An old technique used before motorized decoys, and still effective, is to put still water into motion. Ripples can be created with a boot in the edge of the water, or mud balls pitched into the water when ducks are approaching. A step up is to use segments of cord to rig a number of decoys into a line to resemble ducks swimming in line, which is a normal thing. One end is anchored some distance out in the water, the other end is pulled with the end string, which stretches to the hidden hunters, where it is jerked, as it's termed, to create ripples. Moving up a notch, decoys are available to go beyond simply indicating feeding with decoy configuration of head under water or tail tipped up. Tipped-up tails can be motorized to bob, or squirt water to cause water motion. We'd like to have the patent on whatever it takes to simulate the action in the following photo, of a canvasback feeding in shallow water.

Decoying the big freshwater divers. Canvasbacks (page 126) tend to collect and move across the water in a regal manner. It takes a little rigging to keep the decoys all facing in the same direction in order to be taken for these real Cans.

The photo on page 126 shows lots of ducks with several Canadas on a mountain river. "There's a lot of ducks in them thar' hills." Duck decoys simulating the ducks in this photo can be dropped in still pools with the usual rigging. Ducks rest on rocks in the rapids looking for the next hatch. Secure standing decoys to rocks any which way you can. Ducks or geese in line in the swift water can be simulated by rigging on a single line with a heavy anchor on the upstream end. More decoys are usually needed to draw ducks on rivers of this size. Always use caution, for the safety of both

Water flying as canvasback feeds in shallows. This photo is always good for a grin. The big freshwater diver canvasback is designed to feed by diving. In very shallow water, however, they can't make the roll-over nose dive to get those big rear-mounted feet engaged. They just kick up water. All of the little dabbler ducks in the vicinity are backing off to give that big boy plenty of room.

the hunter and the retriever, when working swift water. It's best to work the still pools. Most rivers you'll ever work will have less velocity than this one.

Decoying technique involves a lot more than numbers and fancy decoys. Sometimes your favorite layout just isn't working. As illustrated on page 127 Eddie had his usual small, spread-out, happy-duck set on a cold morning, intent on bringing ducks in off a small lake into a favorite tree-lined pocket. It's not always easy. Decoying decoy-shy mallards from an open lake to a shallows decoy spread is tricky, and we were having no action. We ultimately concluded that we needed a reset of the dekes on ice illustrated page 128.

The photo on the bottom of page 128 shows decoying for wood ducks. Woodies are drawn to their natural habitat of flooded timber. An effective technique is to deploy decoys (the most effective are wood duck decoys) in front of well-concealed hunters in the trees. Attention of the incoming ducks

Ducks resting near geese. This illustrates a good addition to your decoy spread. Ducks are less threatened when they're in the presence of geese. This photo shows ducks mixed with geese along the edge of a glacier-formed lake in northeastern South Dakota. If the geese think the spot is okay, then the ducks will think it's okay. This is a realistic-looking decoy set of ducks and geese. Wait a minute! This bunch is real. This can be used as a model to decoy skittish late-season ducks. A couple of Canada decoys with a small duck decoy spread is often more effective than the duck decoys alone.

Freshwater divers in deep water with dabblers on shallow edge. This shot is all-out sneaky. Only other ducks would notice that divers and dabblers are where they should be. It's got to be okay down there. This set brings in both divers and dabblers.

Predawn canvasbacks on parade.

Ducks with Canadas on river.

Usual happy-duck spread in the trees with no action. Time to rearrange the furniture. Maybe a little closer arrangement in a line out from under the trees might look more realistic to spooked decoy-shy mallards.

Changed the decoy spread. A few yards away, decoys in a line and more open. Floating empty indicates action picked up.

Decoy set for wood ducks in flooded standing trees.

is drawn to the decoys. Decoys are intended to look like ducks in hiding. Confusing, but effective. Be ready for shots at fast-moving targets. A few minutes before this photo was made, a pair of wood ducks had come diving around the tree and brush at over sixty miles per hour within a couple of feet from Ken and Maggy the retriever. They were long gone before he could make the slightest reaction.

COASTAL BAY DECOY SPREADS FOR DIVERS AND SEA DUCKS

Coastal hunts usually begin with a boat ride as part of the experience. (Note the opening of Chapter 11.) In the Gulf, massed redheads provide a lot of the action. Bay boats that can be pushed back into the forage are the normal transport. Big, open-water, sea-rated boats and open-water boat handling skills are key elements for safety and success when hunting the group of divers commonly known as sea ducks along the northern coasts. It's nice to have a good captain (in this case, Capt. Reilly McCue) to keep a lid on when it gets down to 10 degrees below zero and the waves are high. What a way to make a livin', Captain.

Decoy spreads are arranged to entice ducks, or a few geese on a good day, to come in toward a spot on the water within range of hunters hidden in a fixed blind or a camouflaged boat. Experienced hunters who habitually shoot over big decoy spreads get enjoyment out of the elaborate, and labor intensive, preparation leading up to the crescendo of action when a sizeable flight is enticed to come in exactly as planned, descending into the designated landing spot. An obvious long run across the water for takeoff is more attractive for the divers. Other times, if the excitement wanes when a third pass is higher than the second, you'll need an expert come-back call to brings them in.

Deep freshwater lakes or open bays call for diving duck decoys, while the open ocean calls for sea duck decoys. Long strings of sea duck decoys are arranged to pick up ducks coming in and guide them to land close to

Eider sea ducks decoy spread. Credit: Kurt Crowley.

the shooters, who are often hiding on rocks at the water's edge. The term is "shooting from the ledge." And yes, the rocks are cold and hard.

Another productive sea duck option for the hardy and steady of nerve is to shoot from a small, low-profile layout boat with a tender close enough to do the retrieving of the hunter as well as the shot.

Decoying Geese

Geese usually gather with their own kind going into the fall. Some are a little late, as you've seen, loafing with ducks. But when you'll be trying to decoy them, they'll usually be with a number of friends and family—hundreds of Canada geese; thousands of snow geese along with other light geese most of the time. Goose protocol is that small flocks in flight are usually drawn to larger gatherings on the ground or the water. That makes for big sets of decoys. The goose hunter is always looking for ways to make the spread look like big numbers of geese with no shooters around. We'll demonstrate what the geese want to see, then give you some ideas of how to make the geese think your spread looks like our examples. People are still looking for the ultimate goose decoy spread: real cheap and real fast and easy to set, but mostly, a spread that really looks like geese to the geese. This is what you want it to look like.

You're always going to get a thorough inspection of every detail of your spread, usually by a feathered old-timer with an eye for detail. And all the eyes of the junior members of the flock will flick over to see what the old one thinks. Anything that looks unnatural will break the old one's lockup and those wings will start flapping again, and then all the rest will follow. A flock on the ground or water isn't as uniform as it appears to the unpracticed eye. It's actually granular, composed of individual family units. Any successful set has to reflect that granularity.

Then there are those hunters scattered among the decoys who are definitely not going to look like pieces of grain field without some effort on their part. Camo clothing will just go so far. If there's still a lot of straw that came through the combine and it is still reasonably fluffy, then you have something you can work with. One method is to spread the straw back, dig a shallow hole (which needs to have the divot replaced), and then pull the straw back around you. In this case, your clothing ideally would blend with straw. If the straw has been bailed, try to get some of the bails to make a hide. The new ground hides work best if you can match the trash left in the field, then put some of the field trash over the hide. Think through how you're going to get into battery when you need to and get the trash out of the way as you come to battery. The best way to blend into a wintertime grain field is to hope for a dusting of snow. Be careful what you ask for, as a lot of snow is a mess. A critical point sometimes overlooked is that the spread has to comfortably accommodate a landing of a group of large heavy birds with four- to six-foot wingspans, plus a little elbow room for jostling in case of turbulence. A lot of experienced goose hunters believe that geese prefer to land among the masses if there's plenty of room to come in with a few gusts coming through. That's maybe ten to fourteen feet apart. Other hunters go with conventional closer spreads and an open place—all within range of your shotgun, so you can put a hard hit on that big bird as it's coming in.

This leads into the biggest thing about decoying geese: everything is big about geese. Big birds. Big numbers of geese in flights. Real big numbers of decoys to bring them in to the guns. The most realistic decoys are the full body ones, floating or standing. An embellishment is oversized goose decoys big enough to hide a hunter. These of course mean spending more money, finding more haul space, and getting less sleep in order to start early enough to set them all out. An alternative is to use a wind sock that sort of looks like a goose, with a goose head attached on a wire stand. Or maybe you use about several hundred flags about the size of geese, either light or dark, and hope for wind. You can also use several hundred plastic bags, either light or dark, scattered across the ground. In this case, hope for no wind. Or maybe the best solution is none of the above, all of the above, or something in between. One of the three of us has been involved with all of these solutions except the coffin shaped like a goose. That's going too far.

With the points common to all geese covered, we begin to address the big divide: light or dark?

Canadas on bank of irrigation pond.

The dark goose population is made up of the Canada goose, the clacking goose, the speckled-belly goose, and the brant. The Canada goose has the largest population of the dark geese species.

From the decoying perspective, flights of Canada geese tend to be in the hundreds during migration and wintering. Shooting may be over water or field. Canada geese, and therefore, Canada geese decoys, are often seen loafing along a shore, with geese coming in to the water and swimming to the shore.

The total light goose population is made up of the snow goose and the Ross's goose. The snow goose has the largest population of light geese. Both species tend to migrate and feed together. The illustration conveys the massive numbers of light geese that migrate and winter together. From the decoying perspective, flights of light geese tend to be in the thousands during migration and wintering. Their normal habit is to rest and overnight on relatively large waters undisturbed by hunters. That usually amounts to a sanctuary, with entry controlled by government regulation or property rights. Without official sanctuary, thousands and thousands of eyes would put the flock on the alert. If the threat stays or recurs, they move on to a more secure place. Light geese may leave the sanctuary to feed throughout the day. They may be hunted with pass shooting along their routes to feeding areas per the previous chapter. Success usually depends on poor weather

Snows on large power-plant impoundment.

conditions to force flights down to near ground level. The most common, and usually most productive, method is field spreads of decoys in feeding areas.

Decoy Spreads for Canada Geese

Real geese loafing on the water naturally string out to suggest a couple of small trotline setups of decoys. Geese are moving in very distinct family groups. This structure can be duplicated with several short strings on individual sinkers. A small gathering of decoys without family structure is an indicator to geese that this bunch can't be trusted.

Family groups appear to be mingled, but dynamics indicate that the family groups are moving as units. Water sets of decoys need to draw landing birds into one zone. Setting out a decoy spread big enough to draw geese on open water is sort of a science project that goes on and on. More geese, more trotlines. Big water spreads can be a big project for moving and rearranging. Note that family groups can still be distinguished in larger gatherings.

Small gathering with strings of family groups.

Large gathering with family groups mingled.

Take note of any geese in flight to get a count of the number moving together. You need to have out more decoys than the groups on the wing. A hundred decoys can easily draw in a few geese. Bringing in a big flight takes a lot of decoys and a certain amount of finesse that comes from experience.

Decoy Spreads at Water's Edge and in the Field for Canada Geese

Field spreads are often set up along shorelines, and this setting is not particularly unusual.

A string heading for the shore.

An embellishment to the standers on shore is a string coming across the water.

Just like ducks, geese are attracted to agricultural operations. That's often, normally actually, the best game in town. You think with all of this irrigation apparatus that there might be a hayfield around here somewhere? You bet.

In this case, geese simply walk from the edge of the water lightly feeding on the sparse, picked-over sprouts adjacent to the irrigation pond. They fall in with the active feeders moving along the best hay close to the edge of the field. We've also seen them feeding on irrigated alfalfa hay dispersed across a large field, appearing as gray dots across a sea of green.

FIELD SPREADS FOR LIGHT GEESE (SNOWS AND ROSS'S)

Very large flock on ground, grazing on new-growth wheat. Part of a cast of thousands. There is a pattern to the dynamics of feeding. The feeding flock stretches out in a long line as they land, then proceeds to feed in the direction of the line. Movement very dynamic with one element flying up and low over those on ground, skipping low over the grazers, and then landing along leading edge of progression onto new grazing. A continuing progression of groups

Snows on a wheat field.

Fliers from end of the line to the front.

Fliers coming over the line.

Snow goose decoy spread. Credit: Kurt Crowley.

of individuals lifts up and begins to fly from the back end of the line along the feeders to the front end of the line.

Line jumpers gliding in to front of line.

New jumpers joining.

Photo above illustrates a professional spread, about as good as it gets. Lots of decoys. There can't be too many snow goose decoys. Note the simulated fliers on poles at either end of the spread. Effectively mimics fliers in the air moving from the rear of the long string of feeders to the front of the line.

Inside the decoy spread.

Close, ground-level view of goose decoy spread. Note landing zone within shotgun range. This professional spread is made up of full body goose decoys in alert, others head down in feeding poise; wind sock goose decoys, some with heads, some without, that are less realistic but add motion. Sometimes two-dimensional flat panel goose decoys are added in order to put out a decoy spread with enough decoys to attract the real birds. Two-dimensional decoys are arranged at all angles so that some will be seen from any angle. The moral of this story is that it's difficult to illustrate a decoy pattern from ground level.

Coastal Decoy Spreads for Geese

Brant are often hunted along with sea ducks along northern coasts. Brant decoy strings are set to bring incoming birds to shooters set up on the ledge.

Brant decoys along the ledge. Credit: Kurt Crowley.

A tender boat sets the decoys out and picks up birds downed. Layout boats are sometimes used to shoot some distance away from the shore when conditions allow.

Goose Decoy Notes Quick Check

Canada goose decoys will bring in Canada, speckled-belly, snow, and Ross's geese. Decoys for a big goose spread are always a trade-off. It's generally accepted that full-body decoys, actual mounted geese, are the ultimate. They're expensive and you want to avoid getting them soaked. Setting them out can also take forever. Full bodies made in a factory are all you'll ever see in the real world. In the field, you'll usually see a progression of goose decoy authenticity from 2-Ds down to scattered plastic bags. Friends from the Texas Panhandle in years past would wrap themselves in sheets and took snow geese back when they were a rarity. Flags can also be used to coax geese in. It's generally considered that flagging is easier and quicker to master than calling.

Setups: Theory and Practice

After all of the planning and effort to get the decoy spread out just right to pull the birds within shotgun range, there's still one critical step to be made: making the shot. Better make it count.

Heads up! Down actually. First thing, don't keep that shot from happening.

"Comin' around, lookin' good, one more pass."

"Okay, who looked up?"

Theory of the Set

We've narrowed the waterfowl hunting orchestration down to the final crescendo: Making the shot. A lot of moving parts are involved. Mindset focus is making a safe, ethical shot, shooting in the context of the hunt, and taking into consideration the retrieval of the kill.

A landing zone in front of the decoys is left open for ducks to land without flying over other ducks, at least most of the time. If a spread is very loose with ducks scattered widely to feed, ducks will drop into big holes over a duck on the near side of the hole. They'll also land downwind if that's the easiest way to get into a hole. Sometimes a spread that breaks, or bends, the rules is the most effective into the season and the ducks have patterned the way humans make spreads. (Sorry, but . . . to fool a duck, or goose, you gotta' think like a . . .)

For the setup to be effective, the shooters should be positioned to make effective and ethical shots on game without endangering other members of the hunting party. That's under all circumstances, no matter how how crazy the action is. And remember that hearing protection advice.

Shooting will be instinctive after you've internalized everything covered in Chapter 5 Situational awareness developed during practice with shotguns should be second nature. Don't even think about going afield without full command of the gun. This means knowing how to load it; keep it pointed in a safe direction; hold and handle it; shoot it; make it safe before and after shooting it; and unload it. Successful wingshots combine insight into waterfowl characteristics and behavior, with instinctive shooting developed through constant practice. Situational awareness and predictive intuition determine range and lead of the shot. All of this will be covered in Part II.

The first step to ethical shooting is a healthy dose of honest self-appraisal. You'll notice that most of the setups illustrated will have the shooters arranged to get straight-in, minimal lead shots. That's also the shot into the front of the duck, or the head of the goose, for an instant, ethical kill. It's the best setup when new hunters are in the party. We'll present setups designed to get passing shots requiring full leads and/or exquisite technique and timing for the more skilled and experienced. It's not a good idea to over estimate your skill level, as that's a good way to be stuck with an unflattering nickname. You might prefer to hunt alone or with a nontalkative close friend until you get better.

Another consideration to be internalized is perspective. Ethical shots that instantly bring game down and are recovered should always be the goal. In the case of ducks, and even more so geese, that translates to shot load into the head and wing area. The optimum perspective for this shot is a frontal shot. Passing shots should be directed at the front and wing, quartering front and side. Shots quartering from the rear are from a perspective with a high probability that shot load will impact gut and legs. The gut shot is lethal, but won't incapacitate quickly enough to allow recovery. Geese can't survive without full capacity of both legs to feed on land and take off from water. Making shots on geese amounts to more than just hitting them. Geese are big and tough and possess a certain vitality that matches their size.

Experienced and practiced shooters develop ethical shooting techniques and shots, based on insight into flying characteristics of various species of ducks and geese under different circumstances. Flight characteristics of different species can be associated with speeds of flight, which are essential for estimating distance and direction of leads. You'll have to consider that some ducks tend to fly with dips and dives, while others plow straight through the air in a predictable way. It all depends on what duck you're going after. Remember Chapter 1?

Boat load of gear.

Practice of the Set

A certain element of discipline and coordination. And some situational awareness helps a lot.

There are lots of advantages to boat sets that take advantage of the wind and shore contours. But they do come at a logistics price. For example, it takes some technique to stow a couple hundred decoys organized as to type, make the spread, and then pick it up later without the whole thing turning to a tangled mess.

Any theory of designing the decoy spread and executing calling and making the shot doesn't get off the ground, or water, without the stuff to make it happen.

Boat setup overhead view.

This angle doesn't do much from the standpoint of bringing the ducks in, but it illustrates for the hunter a spread that brought in the only limits on the lake that day.

Duck is traveling downwind when the set catches its eye. Hunters pick up the ducks. At this point, hunters look with their eyes instead of turning their faces up toward the ducks.

The usual location of shooters is close abreast, firing in sectors to the

Duck's eye view comin' straight in.

front and sides. Sectors may overlap. Safety is the top consideration. You'll note in Chapter 5 that we practice taking turns down a line of shooters. Everybody gets a turn at getting a shot off in sequence of location along the line. This gets any uneasiness out of the system before getting into a boat or setting along a bench.

The set on the right is duck's eye view our big mouth set. Design is to have most of the decoys away from the bank in order to push newcomers over close to the water's edge. Where the old blind is on right side of the photo. This duck is looking down-wind. Ducks coming in from across the lake behind us will swing around and come in along the channel to land upwind. This shot shows the old blind with the landing zone in front, with decoy fliers and large group of decoys out in the channel crowding the incoming ducks toward shore.

This relatively small stock pond is a good hunt with the wind from any direction. Just locate the decoys on the side that gives the incoming ducks a landing zone ahead as they come in over the water in to the wind. Ducks will always come in over water if they can. Our hunters, Eddie and Ivy Marie, are concealed straight across the pond.

Sector division of shooters in boat. Note extra decoys hidden behind boat not used for this small spot.

Big mouth set, duck's eye view.

Small pond behind the house.

A slightly larger stock pond with a few more decoys than the spread in the backyard. There is a gap in the spread, with fliers pulling incoming ducks straight in to the hunter concealed in brush. The straight-in frontal shot is always the best, but it's also the shot where the incoming ducks are looking straight at the hunter. No twitching before the gun comes up and you can blaze away.

Small spread simulating feeding in shallows.

Ducks will keep an eye on those decoys on that always-smooth water and not notice or recognize the invisible clumps flat on the ground as illustrated below. Ducks don't seem to notice low profiles as long as they don't see a fresh face turn to look at them head on. Note that this set requires the

Duck's eye view. Comin' in low to mossy stock pond.

full ninety-degree lead for the usual wind, which is either straight north or south. But dabblers usually hang around ten feet above the water for less than a second before they backstroke down. In that instant, you have a zero-lead required. We note in Chapter 5 that eye-trigger-finger coordination is key, rather than eye-hand coordination, as in baseball or basketball. Physical requirements of this set are real good pop-ups, so you might do a few sit-ups the week before you set up.

A lot of experience around this spot brought to mind a tactic we've used every now and then. Sometimes a broken morning's hunt can be saved if it's obvious that the first location just isn't going to be productive. Decide quickly to pick up and leave, then get the dekes back in as soon as possible. Eddie trains his dogs to retrieve decoys. He can clear out of a spot fast as the pups

Sea ducks set off the ledge. Credit: Kurt Crowley.

can get 'em in. Make the move, pitch 'em out, set up the setup, and you're in business. There are different schools of thought regarding use of retrievers to bring decoys in after the hunt. Some say it ruins the decoys, some say it ruins the dogs. We'll save that discussion for Part II.

As illustrated on the preceding page, boat is retrieving shots. Hunters are set up among big rocks along the shoreline. Sea ducks don't require as much stealth on the part of the hunter as the skittish dabblers.

Most tactics of making shots on geese call for close arrangement of shooters in an eighteenth-century infantry line, only in a low, reclining profile, ready to pop up on signal. Shooter technique of a big goose set is to lay back on a layout while you try to hide under a decoy flag and look like whatever's

Snow goose set. Credit: Kurt Crowley.

Canada goose set.

under you (dirt, snow, or green sprouting wheat—in this case, a harvested cornfield) as you recover from setting out the decoys.

More deluxe ground blinds arranged along the trail of straw thrown out by the combine as it harvested the grain can be very effective. Worked for these hunters.

Duck Calling and Goose Calling

Calling ducks and geese is one thing we don't feel we can write about effectively. And we, for the life of us, absolutely cannot get a good picture to illustrate how to call. Here's our take: Begin with recorded instructions. Get duck call and goose call apps on your phone so that you can share with friends anywhere except church. Concentrate on a small repertoire until you get the hang of it. Avoid overcalling. Repeat until you're old.

Fire Discipline

Shooting is controlled by the signal of a designated shooter, usually the most experienced hunter in the party. Each party of hunters has a particular vocal signal, such as "Take 'em," "Shoot," "Cut 'em," and the universal "OK." You'll note in Chapter 5 the shotgun games we play to practice the concept of shooting discipline and familiarization with shooting in close proximity to other shooters.

Aspects of the Experience

The moment of making the shot is the pinnacle for most new hunters. The experience is poorly conveyed by written word, although every writer makes the effort. Ours can be found at the beginning of Chapter 11, which attempts to convey the sensations of the moment by word and illustration.

PART II

Overview of Gear and Equipment

INTRODUCTION TO PART II

Equipment, Skillsets, Gear, and Insight

This part of the book is all about the equipment needed to make the shot, the skillsets that enable you to hunt using your chosen strategy, and the gear that rounds out your outfit. You'll find that hunters, and those in the business of selling them stuff, generally define all stuff as falling into one of two classes: (1) gear, which includes boots, clothing of all types, GPS units, packs, knives, and everything else, except for (2) equipment, the implements to "reduce to possession" in legal terms, to "take" in polite terms, to "make the shot" in waterfowler terms—in plain terms, to kill.

PROCUREMENT OF EQUIPMENT AND GEAR IN THE CONTEXT OF MASTERY OF SKILLS TO USE IT

The emphasis of this book is on doing. Equipment and gear procurement is discussed in terms of using—of doing. Skill levels always trump quality of equipment in this endeavor. Quality should be at a sufficient level to avoid compromise of skills. That's usually attained fairly economically for most of us. The biggest factor driving skill levels is practice. The biggest factor driving level of practice is having fun at it.

SOURCES OF GEAR AND EQUIPMENT

Throughout this section, I'll be presenting information pertaining to the use of specialized gear and equipment. Before I jump into the details of each of the various types of gear and equipment, a few general comments regarding sources of supply will be convenient for reference. Online and catalog outfitters are almost universal sources of outdoor equipment. I'll abbreviate reference to one of the biggest as simply *Cabela's*. For ordering, the full information is: Cabela's, One Cabela Drive, Sidney, Nebraska 69160-9555. You can search online by going to www.cabelas.com, or call toll-free at 1-800-237-4444. Another outdoor equipment outfitter that carries an extensive stock of waterfowl hunting gear is *Outdoor World Bass Pro Shops*, 2500 E. Kearney, Springfield, Missouri 65898-0123 (1-800-227-7776). A specialty duck and goose hunting supplier that carries top-grade gear is *Mack's Prairie Wings*, Stuttgart, Arkansas, 1-877-MACKSPW (1-877-622-5779).

A Rational Progression of Equipment and Gear Acquisition . . . or Not

Your authors sometimes share a quick little trip back to where we started in our outdoor sports participation. One of our recurring topics of marvel pertains to all the stuff involved with waterfowling, usually how much of it there is, and how much stuff is involved now in comparison to earlier times. These trips back to our beginnings as waterfowlers are a good starting point for defining the minimum requirements of the stuff of goose and duck hunting. Much of this dates back to when the tactics and techniques of hunting were driven by the means available. The quick overview that follows outlines the progression of acquisition of the typical beginning waterfowler.

Waterfowling Minimum Equipment and Gear with Associated Techniques

Minimum equipment, gear, and credentials:

- Hunting license with federal migratory waterfowl stamps
- Training credentials in hunter safety required by many states
- Shotgun and shells
- Warm, dark clothing, wool socks, and boots

Hunting techniques appropriate for outfit:

- Stalking or ambush of waterfowl on small ponds, streams
- Retrieves by hunter of clean kills and falls (birds hit and unable to fly but can escape by swimming or running and hiding on the bank may require wading and hunter run-down)

Essential skills:

- Firearms safety
- Wingshooting using low angle of passing shots
- Ambush setups to get low angle of passing shots (straightway escape)
- Identification of waterfowl on the wing and in hand (to stay within legal bag limits of all species)

Minimal Outfit Plus Concealment and Basic Comfort

Equipment and gear additions:

- Camo clothing
- Waders

Hunting techniques appropriate for outfit:

- Same as for basic, but without requirement to quit after getting wet

Essential skills:

- Same as for basic

Basic Equipment and Comfort plus Attraction of Waterfowl

Equipment and gear additions:

- Decoys and calls

Hunting techniques appropriate for outfit:

- Same as basic with comfort, but much improved success

Essential skills:

- Basic calling
- Decoy sets
- Camo and techniques of concealment

Basic Equipment and Comfort, Attraction of Waterfowl, and a Retriever: The Complete Basic Outfit

Additions:

- Retriever

Hunting techniques appropriate for outfit:

- Shoreline of any body of water, retriever use results in no losses of cripples
- Your best hunting pal and devoted family member, if you accept the commitment to do the training; a reliable hired staff member if you hire a professional to do the training

Essential Skills:

- Retriever selection and care
- Retriever training by hunter or selection of professional trainer

Complete Basic Outfit with a Boat

Additions:

- Dedicated waterfowling boat, or kit modified fishing boat

Hunting techniques appropriate for outfit:

- Any body of water appropriate for boat

Essential Skills:

- Boat handling and navigation

Complete Basic Outfit with Specialized Goose Outfit Land Decoy Spread

Additions:

- Land-based decoy spread and hides

Hunting techniques appropriate for outfit:

- Attraction and ambush of flocks of geese in feeding areas and along routes

Essential skills:

- Large decoy sets
- Long-range passing shots using heavy loads

Complete Basic Outfit with Specialized Goose Outfit Water Decoy Spread

Additions:

- Boat- and water-based decoy spread and hides

Hunting techniques appropriate for outfit:

- Attraction and ambush of flocks of geese in resting areas of large bodies of water

Essential skills:

- Large decoy sets
- Long-range passing shots using heavy loads

Chapter 5

Skillset and Equipment to Make the Shot

This chapter covers the shooting skills that are required to hunt waterfowl. The fact that these are beginning requirements shouldn't be taken to mean that they're simple and easy to master. You'll still be trying to master some of them after fifty years.

SHOTGUNS AND WINGSHOOTING

Your level of skill with a shotgun will be the biggest factor contributing to your success in duck and goose hunting. First, a brief review of shotguns.

Summary of Shotguns

Firearms first evolved as smoothbores, with no rifling. Shotguns were considered the area-weapon version of the smoothbore musket. They were handy for short-range combat and for the taking of wildfowl for subsistence, which normally involved shooting wildfowl on the water. The blast was directed (pointed) into a raft of stationary waterfowl, across the surface and in a direction calculated to incapacitate the most ducks with that one shot. Fast-moving targets were beyond the realm of the practical shooter, considering the ignition time involved in applying match to powder.

Development of improved ignition systems were paced by illegal wild-fowlers who poached on shooting grounds reserved for the gentry. And nothing could attract the attention of gamekeepers and guards more than a burning match in the night. This situation eventually lead to the invention of the wheel lock and versions of the flint-striking steel arrangements, until rendered obsolete by the invention of the ignition cap. The cap's speed of ignition finally made wingshooting a possibility. Shot-filled shells ignited by primers quickly made breech-loading shotguns the standard. This neat little progression happened over a span of four or five hundred years.

The musket version of the smoothbores became the standard version of fire-arms used for military applications. Stabilizing the fired slug by imparting a spin to it came much later and was developed for high accuracy when shooting game at long range. It fired a large round slug aimed into the mass of an approaching infantry formation at over fifty yards or so. It was aimed with one eye looking down the barrel, using a single bead on the muzzle as a sight. It could be aimed at an individual at fairly close distances, but the emphasis was on efficiency and speed of reloading. Lines of infantry practiced to get off three massed volleys in the time it took an advancing formation to approach bayonet range. Bayonets wielded by survivors of the massed volleys decided the outcome of the engagement.

Rifles had long since been developed by the time massed infantry charges were standard tactics, but the reliably firing smoothbore flintlock musket remained the military standard since it could be recharged faster. Bullets that expanded to fill rifling grooves and could be quickly reloaded, coupled with reliable ignition of percussion caps, finally led the way to modern firearms. Breechloaders firing primer-ignited cartridges became the standard.

MODERN ERA OF FIREARMS

New waterfowlers may not catch the inside joke of the almost napping shot-gun accessory in the picture. This makes us all better wingshots, particularly with those 16-gauges. They'll always come around when the shotguns come out just in case anything interesting develops. When action gets slow, time for a nap.

As smokeless powder became available in quantity at commercial prices, the firearms manufacturers in the late nineteenth and early twentieth centuries scrambled to develop new designs for sporting rifles and shotguns. All of the new designs introduced or adapted from black-power designs were some form of mechanism now referred to as the action.

Some designs stuck with tradition for a few years—note

Shotguns.

the Remington double-barreled shotgun on the left side of the photo with "mule ear" hammers patterned after percussion-cap-ignited black powder shotguns of a few years earlier. But the barrels were made of poured steel to withstand higher pressures than the Damascus barrels used with black-powder firearms. The clean lines of the Winchester Model 37 single-shot next to it quickly became the pattern of the first shotgun carried to the field by an army of young hunters. These shotguns use break-open actions. A lever is pushed to unlock and tip the barrel(s) to remove the empty shells. The barrels are single, side-by-side, or over-under, with double or single triggers. Single triggers of modern design fire one barrel, then spring back ready to fire the other. Note the over-under right end. Two fast shots, but care has to be made to put the action back on safe if only one barrel is fired. A single-barrel, break-open action was the first shotgun for most of us.

The center of the photo shows three of the most popular actions of the early 1900s. These are the slide-action repeater Model 97 in 16-gauge, a hammer-less (actually enclosed hammer) Winchester Model 12, and the long-barreled full-choke Remington Model 870 Wingmaster. The 870, Tom's favorite, is still a top seller. The pump action is driven by the shooter. The forearm is pulled to the rear to eject the empty shell and cock the hammer, then pushed forward to chamber the shell and lock the action. Manual control allows the shooter to control the force used to work the action to jack in another shell through sleet and snow and whatever else is coming down when the geese are on the wing. The matte-finish, change-out choked (usually modified) 870 next to it better accommodates steel shot.

The most popular action going into this century is the automatic action. JoAnne has a long-time preference for automatics, including the recoil-operated Sweet 16 Browning Auto 5 in 16 gauge and the gas-operated Weatherby SA-08, which has hardly a nudge of recoil even in 12 gauge. She's also good with her Stevens-Savage over and under in 20 gauge, which makes the most of her natural shooting swing.

JoAnne's fast-handling, fast-shooting Weatherby SA-08 has been her everyday shotgun for a while. Eddie's favorite is the Browning Maximus auto, which allows the hunter to flip a shell into the chamber of an empty shotgun to pick up that last flight that always drops in out of nowhere. Tom has now joined Eddie with a Maximus fitted with a Pachmayr slipover recoil pad/stock extender for those of us who don't want to have a expensive custom-fitted shotgun bumping around in the truck.

Your Personal Shotgun

A shotgun is more of a personal thing than any other type of firearm. The prospective wingshot needs to approach buying one as if he or she were trying on clothes. Before you head for the store, read over the following sections pertaining to wingshooting If you're new to the game, we also recommend that you buy your first shotgun at a place where you can get some assistance from somebody who knows what he or she is talking about. You can always find a gun store with capable sales associates and a gunsmith in a town of any size. Cabella's and Bass Pro have big retail stores in most metropolitan areas and are good places to consider as a baseline. Wherever you go, consider your shotgun salesperson more like a tailor than a hardware person. A short discussion of various actions and shotgun fit follows this section. Check them out for feel and function at a well-stocked place. Develop your own opinions, maybe making multiple trips to the stores, before making a decision. A little conversation will tell if the person showing you the guns knows what it's about. Only an expert can give you an expert opinion.

Shotgun fit, as you'll see in the following sections, is a matter of your master eye being aligned with the shotgun barrel as you bring the gun to your shoulder. It's a combination of your neck and face, arms, and general body configuration with the length and drop of the stock below the plane of the barrel at the point where your cheek and stock contact.. The idea is to stand there as if you were looking down the road, both eyes open, head and neck in a relaxed, upright posture, waiting for an approaching duck or goose to come along. When the winged projectile comes along, approaching at thirty to fifty miles per hour, your shotgun will spring to your shoulder as you stand with left foot (right handers) slightly forward. Without bending your neck or tilting your head, you'll be looking down the barrel (without being conscious that you're looking down the barrel) at the approaching large bird that you'll shoot as soon as you're sure that it's a mallard drake and not a federally protected bald eagle, goshawk, or whatever. (They don't look or fly the same way a duck or goose flies, as you've noted in Part I, remember?)

The new shotgunner will find that experienced hunters may have preferences of one type of shotgun over another for reasons other than fit and function. Some pertain to safety, as shotguns are extremely deadly at short range. When Eddie was starting out, he was under instructions to carry his break-open single shot broken open while hunting. If a duck approached, he dropped a shell into the chamber, closed the action, and cocked the hammer as the gun came to shoulder. Eddie got fast at it. And to this day, during any after-action conversation, the gun is always broken open, practice or hunting, unless a shot's coming up within the next few seconds. One reason he carries a Browning Maximus is that it can be unloaded, with the action open, yet he can quickly pop a shell into the magazine. It's automatically chambered, and before you know it Eddie has another duck on the water and Bart has another job.

JoAnne likes an over and under. When she drops a couple of shells down the tubes, they stay right there until she takes them out again, fired or unfired. She doesn't like the idea of shells flying around from magazine to chamber, moving faster than you can see. For safety's sake, the shotguns of some families always had an external hammer that the shooter could keep an eye on. Winchester Model 97s were the gun of choice long afer the Model 12 became the favorite of most wingshooters. After all, there would always be another young Airhart coming down the pike needing a hammer to keep reminded of. . . .

Now that we're up to speed on the shotguns, let's move on to putting shot into a place where we want it to be. And that starts with the pattern of the shot.

Shotgun Actions, Chokes, Shotgun Pellets (Shot), Cartridges (Shells), and Fit

The shotgun action is the mechanism that fires the shell to send the shot down the barrel, extracts and casts away the empty shell from the chamber, loads a fresh cartridge, and secures it in place in the chamber. Types of actions include lever actions, bolt actions, slide actions, and automatic actions. It's all about the need for speed, as the hand motion required to work lever actions and bolt actions is slow compared to the alternatives. Slide-action shotguns that require little motion are the fastest hand-operated mechanisms, and are favored by many due to their reliability under adverse conditions such as cold and ice. The fastest actions are the automatics. The mechanism may be activated by the energy of recoil or controlled diversion of expanding gas. It kicks the spent shell out and slams a new one into the chamber, ready for another shot before the shooter can react. That last part can sometimes be cause for concern.

Terminology of Shotguns and Shotgun Shooting

The terms used to define the various elements of selecting and shooting a shotgun make absolutely no sense if you haven't come of age with one in your hand. Following is a very cryptic introduction.

Shot is the common term for shotgun pellets. Different shot sizes are selected for greatest effect: small-diameter light shot for small birds at close range; large-diameter heavy shot for geese at longer range.

Shotgun shells are the common name for shotgun cartridges. Diameter of the shell (gauge) is the measure of the inside diameter of the shotgun barrel.

A larger diameter holds more powder, a larger shot load, and greater power of the gun. That's a good thing, up to a point. That point is reached when the greater recoil, the shove, actually a hard kick, to the rear in reaction to the load going out the front becomes painful to the shooter, even with soft pads in place to attenuate the shock.

Gauge

Size of gauge is measured by the weight of lead ball that fits the inside diameter of the barrel measured in fraction of a pound, for example, 10-gauge size is defined as 1/10 of a pound. Other gauges are as follows:

- 12 gauge = 1/12, .729 inches
- 16 gauge = 1/16, .662 inches
- 20 gauge = 1/20, .614 inches

A ringer is the 410, just straight up .410-inch diameter.

Don't try too hard to make sense of it—hasn't made sense since the fifteenth century or so. It's stamped on the barrel and labeled on the box of shells. Just match those numbers and you'll be okay.

Shotgun Shot

Size of shot is designated by a numerical identifier that corresponds to diameter of the round shot. Shot designations and shot size are as follows:

- #2 = .150 in
- #4 = .130 in
- #6 = .110 in
- #8 = .090 in

Shotgun Choke

The term *choke* refers to the constriction of the shotgun barrel at the muzzle, which shapes the size of the shot pattern on the way to the target. The constriction may be formed by permanent deformation of the barrel or with a screw-in insert at the muzzle.

A measure of the constriction is designated by a name that suggests the level of effect.

Constriction in Inches	Designation
.000	Cylinder (No constriction)
.005	Skeet
.010	Improved Cylinder
.020	Modified
.035	Full
.050	Super Full

Barrel Length

Different barrel lengths have evolved for different types of shooting. Don't fret too much about it. Skill overrides such niceties.

Short range: Skeet at the Range/Upland Bird, Fast, Straightaway Shot	24–28 inches
Long Range: Trap/Waterfowl, Wide Swinging Pass Shot	28–36 inches

Patterning Your Shotgun (Shotgun Pattern)

To pattern your shotgun, the usual practice is to shoot at a bed sheet and see where the holes are. A good pattern is uniform, with dense pellet holes, but our interest is to have a lethal cloud of pellets covering approximately a pie-plate-sized ten-inch circle. The circle has to be over the target, and the best chance for this to happen is to have the target directly in front of the barrel. The means to that end is to precisely shoot the top edge of the pie plate. The target is covered by the barrel so that the image is obliterated to the master eye.

The photos illustrate the dense pattern on the centered target. Aiming (one eye shut and the master eye carefully holding the bead on the target, usually the bottom of the target because that's the way we see it most clearly) invariably results in setting the target on the bead, as demonstrated by the upper plates over the target-centered plates. The pellet hole patterns surrounding the plates can be seen on the field archery targets. Routine patterning used to check out different loads on different shotguns as shown by target top of page 166 doesn't use an expensive archery target, for obvious reasons.

Setup for checking patterns.

Plate intended to have most dense pattern is placed over the center of an archery field target. Plate above centered target demonstrates less dense pattern.

The pattern on the target top of page 164 illustrates the effect on a large duck at typical range using steel #4 shot at thirty yards, pointed precisely at centered plate.

The next pattern top of page 165 shows the hit on a goose using steel BB shot at forty yards, same technique. By chance, we also note the pattern that steel shot makes when the pellets hold together. General notion holds that steel shot tends to make these patterns more often than lead. Also a good reason for any miss.

The ten-inch circle is the area that the wingshooter needs to cover with a lethal density of pellets. That covers the head, lungs, and major wing bones of a goose or mallard-sized duck, encapsulates a small duck at a range of around thirty yards, and gets a goose a few more yards out. The shooter swings the projection of that ten-inch circle ahead of the moving bird so that the flight of the shot pattern and bird intersect at a point ahead of the bird's position.

Large duck at typical range.

Goose at typical range.

Normal setup for checking pattern.

The ten inches also coincides roughly with one foot, which is the standard unit used in discussions of leads. Photo top of page is our usual target for pattern with bead carefully over top of plate, even if you don't see it that way with both eyes open.

Techniques for Precision of the Pattern

As pointed out in the discussion of patterns, the desired shot pattern is most dense precisely in front of the barrel. In order to get a good measure of pattern, the bead is on the top of the lower plate, which is close to being centered on the target. Shooting precisely at the top of the centered ten-inch diameter target covers the intended target with the barrel. Focus of the shooter's eye should be on the target, which should be sharply defined. The master eye is looking along the barrel with focus on the target so that the barrel is slightly out of focus. Both eyes follow the target.

Now for the Pointing . . . (Shotgun Pointing)

Pointing is done instinctively, deliberately, or with a combination of the two. This is a simple statement that has been debated in duck and goose camps for years. We'll try to be instructive, impartial, and succinct.

Pointing Defined

Pointing is defined as both eyes open with the master eye looking down the barrel. The target is in focus and the barrel is blurred. With training and

Gun coming to battery with barrel and target both in focus.

experience, the shooter will become more focused on target and less conscious of the barrel and bead.

The image on page 167 is not the image to make the shot. This is the image as you bring the gun to battery, when the width of the rib appears to coincide with the ten-inch pie plate about thirty yards downrange. Thirty yards is about right if you're using heavy shot. This image should last about 200 milliseconds. With a little practice, you'll go through it instinctively.

Some shooters use this instant to estimate distance to the target. A little practice and it becomes instinctive. Here's a quick look at measurements useful for stadia range estimates as measured on a Weatherby SA-08. We suggest practice looking at a ten-inch plate at a range of thirty yards. At this range, the rib fits the ten-inch plate, while the barrel almost fits at about forty yards. Read duck and goose.

As the gun comes to shoulder, the eye momentarily sees the end of the barrel. At this instant, the target should be coming into focus, with the end of the barrel defined before turning to a blur as complete focus turns to the target. The image of the rib, or complete barrel as preferred by some, can be seen by the dominant eye. As discussed in the preceding paragraph, at thirty yards the rib and ten-inch target match. It's not too far to make a shot. This image goes away as the barrel covers the target and the off-eye estimates lead.

For aimers, the dominant eye, operating without benefit of the shut off-eye, estimates the lead holding the bead on or under the target, with usual results illustrated by the patterns of our centered and over-centered pointing exercise. "Blinded in one eye, don't see too good out of the other," as the old refrain goes. Meanwhile, our two-eyed shooter, with good feedback of lead from the completely operative off-eye, makes a fine shot.

As illustrated, the eye is slightly above the actual position for pointing along the rib and bead as if the gun is coming up.

The image top of page 169 is intended to visually recap what you should see with correct technique. The image of the plate is obliterated by the barrel. The target is sharp, barrel is fuzzy. The image on page 170 becomes the normal with practice.

Clear focus on target as barrel becomes fuzzy.

Correct focus to make a shot.

WINGSHOOTING DONE RIGHT PER CLASSIC INSTRUCTIONS (WITH A FEW ADDED DETAILS)

If you want to become a good wingshooter, proper form is critical. Start by holding the stock firmly into your strong side shoulder. Stand at a forty-five-degree angle to the target, with your left (weak side) foot forward for the right-hander. Your feet should be eighteen to twenty-four inches apart (depending on your height and size), with fourteen to twenty-two inches between your heels. Start with the gun held low, then bring it to battery in one smooth motion while you look at the target. Swing it forward enough so that it clears whatever you'll be wearing when you're hunting in a twenty-five-mile-per-hour wind with freezing drizzle. Both eyes should be open and you should still be looking at the target, head up. Pull the stock into your shoulder and you should be looking down the barrel with the side of your face against the stock if the gun fits correctly. Both eyes should be open but you're only pointing the barrel at the target with your right eye. Practice bringing the gun to your shoulder with your right eye aligned with the barrel until you can do it automatically. Now, with the stock held tightly into the shoulder, head upright with the comb of the stock against the face, right elbow up, both eyes open with the master eye looking down the barrel, lock up like a steel gun mount from the waist up. Shift your feet and body around until you feel settled in. To move, turn to swing the gun barrel horizontal to the ground by swiveling your hips. With a good stance, your legs will know what to do. Gun support should be rigid. Swing the barrel straight up and down with rotation around your shoulder socket, elbows still locked. Your face and eyes will follow the barrel. You can follow a flying clay target as it passes in any direction using a combination of horizontal rotation or swivel around the hips and vertical rotation about the shoulder sockets. Get out to the range and start practicing on clay pigeons.

The Next Step(s)

As the standing shooting position—turning at the hip, changing elevation with the arms—becomes automatic, it's time to add to your repertoire. Try it from a kneeling position. Take a seat on a bucket. Lie on the ground. Lay flat on your back holding your shotgun across your chest and do a sit-up as the clay is launched. This is really turning into fun, right? Did I mention that you'll need to make some shooting connections other than your friendly local shooting club before you get into the real techniques of practical shooting for hunting?

The End of Classic Wingshooting Instructions

Standard classic instructions end with an admonishment to pick a technique and practice it until you can hit the target consistently. And that's about it for classic instructions. Just keep on bustin' shells until you usually hit the clays. Good luck!

We're not going to leave it at that. You need to be aware that it's a big world out there in the realm of outdoor shooting sports, and it's just full of aimers. They routinely make ethical, aimed shots at moving game, large and small—sneaking, walking, and running. There are also beginning instructions for young people that are a takeoff on the country kid progression that your authors used to learn the basics. We'll go into the analytical approach to leads on moving game, with an emphasis, of course, on ducks and geese. The instruction provided will allow you to translate a wide range of experience to wingshooting, and that's the way to get really good at it.

OVERVIEW OF WINGSHOOTING TECHNIQUES

There are four generally recognized techniques of wingshooting: *snap shooting*, also referred to as point 'n shoot, with the barrel stationary; *constant lead*, in which the barrel moves at a constant arc (swing) speed ahead of the target, with follow-through after the shot; *wing through*, also referred to as the English method, in which the barrel swings from behind the moving target through to a point a short distance ahead of the target (speed of arc swing is faster for fast target, slower for slow target). This latter method uses the momentum of the gun and the shooter's swinging body to carry the lead a sufficient distance ahead of target; and a *combined technique* of constant hold on the target to establish speed and direction with a swing ahead just before the trigger is touched off.

A very important aspect of leads that is often overlooked is that they have to be adjusted not only for the flight speed of the target, but also for the range. Simply put, it takes longer for the shot load to get to a target that's farther out. Note that point 'n shoot requires instinctive movement and quick reactions. It's widely used on jump shooting of closely flushed birds. Grouse hunters also employ it to make shots on birds flying through timber. They select an opening ahead of the bird and make the shot to coincide with the bird clearing cover.

The constant lead technique is widely used by deliberate shooters. Constant lead requires smooth coordination and accommodates shooter reaction time and ignition time of the shotgun during the course of the swing. It depends less on intrinsic natural skills but requires the shooter to be able to estimate ranges and speed of targets in real time. Practitioners of this technique familiarize themselves with the flight speed and distance to the birds being hunted.

The swing-through technique depends on the ability to make a repeatable smooth swing at all angles. It requires precise timing of the swing and trigger pull with the sight picture just in front of the target in order to create the required lead for targets flying at different speeds. This is the most widely used technique among instinctive wingshots.

The hold-on-target with swing-ahead technique works well for some shooters. The hold-on target establishes the arc swing, which is increased at the final instant before the shot is fired. This tends to accommodate passing shots at different ranges with abrupt changes in flight speed, such as when dabblers flare above the landing zone for a drop straight down.

A Word from Aimers Anonymous

My name is Tom, and I'm an aimer . . . I've always been an aimer. I aimed my Daisy Red Ryder BB gun using the sights like you're supposed to. Then I aimed my single-shot .22 Winchester Model 27 rifle, which, incidentally, is surprising accurate. Then, naturally, I went on to aim the family utility shotgun, a Winchester Model 37 single-shot 12-gauge with a full choke. It replaced Dad's Model 97 12-gauge, slide action lost in a house fire. Aiming the Model 37 seemed like a reasonable technique. Its pattern at forty-five yards or so was about the size of a straw hat.

Then I went off to college and saw a series of military rifles for the next several years: issue .22s for closed tactical exercises; M-1s for parade and

ROTC summer camp training and basic entering officer school; and early issue M-14s in Europe. Aiming with a military aperture sight was easy compared to a squinty small-notch open V. I got reasonably good at it. I still have the lighter with the badge mounted on the side awarded by the battalion. With all that time on my hands that came with being out of grad school, I had a chance to catch up on the whitetail hunting I'd been missing. My favorite gun for that was a Winchester 94 30-30. Then I heard the bull elk calling every fall from Idaho, Colorado, and points west. I set about getting better at aiming. Coursing coyotes on foot with a slung Remington 700 bull barrel encouraged me to develop techniques to bring a heavy-barreled rifle to battery quickly. I really got good at aiming. Fast.

I also hunted with a bow, and I aimed that too—along the arrow with a recurve, and with a series of sights on the compounds.

JoAnne, hunting and target practicing around me, is a natural at shooting, and also became a devout aimer.

When I started hanging around with Eddie and Kent and the rest of the local duck hunting bunch, I quickly realized that being a good aimer is not a good thing in the duck hunting. Eddie taught me, and JoAnne, about pointing shotguns. And JoAnne, being a natural and coordinated everything, picked up pointing quickly. But I sort of stayed an aimer. . . . so Eddie taught me some more about pointing a shotgun and not aiming the shotgun. Seems he and a lot of others have the same ideas—even teachers of both rifle and shotgun techniques. Jack O'Conner comes to mind. So, I now point the shotgun, too. Nearly always.

One of the many detriments of pointing is that the shooter tends to put the bead, which is clearly seen by the master eye with the second squinted shut, on the bottom of the target. The center of the pattern is somewhere below that ten-inch plate as demonstrated by the patterns leading off this chapter.

To be effective, the target should be obliterated by the barrel as you keep up with the target with the wide-open second eye. You'll be holding a fixed lead or swinging through the moving target with the target obliterated to the master eye.

Wingshooting, Beginning with the Basics

For those who bothered to read my walk through misty memories of growing up in the country, you might have noted that the sequence of equipment of choices (actually, what we were allowed to shoot without adult supervision) began with a BB gun. That's actually a good place to begin for anybody at any age. Before you spring for the $3,000 autoloader or double-barreled whiz-bang, here's a plan that'll make you a wingshot with a minimum of time and expense.

Step 1. Stationary targets: Start with a BB gun that'll reliably shoot about thirty feet with reasonable accuracy and with low enough velocity to safely use in the backyard with a soft backstop to catch BBs behind the targets. (Safety first. Wear safety glasses in case of direct comebacks or any other surprises in case any kids get involved.)

Set up some sort of generously large target with a three-inch diameter spot in the center. Go to work holding the stock firmly into your shoulder, as you will your shotgun.

If the BB gun stock doesn't fit your face so that you're looking down the barrel, build up the stock with some solid padding and duck gun duct tape, and aren't you glad you don't have a $3,000 shotgun that'll never fit you! Back to business. If you find yourself looking at the sights with your left eye squinting shut, put some black tape over the back sight and use the front sight like a bead on a shotgun. Practice bringing the gun to your shoulder with your right eye aligned with the barrel until it's automatic. Then start shooting: both eyes open, master eye looking down the barrel. You'll be putting every BB into that generously sized target. Don't try to get any more precise, because that would take aiming.

Step 2. Moving targets: Set up a swinging can arrangement with some sort of support that allows the can to swing like a pendulum. Learn how to touch off the trigger just as the can swings to a stop before changing direction to swing back; then, through trial and error (mostly error), learn to swing ahead of the swinging can as it swings fast at mid-swing. Modern city dwellers go on to the clay target. We country kids, surrounded by empty Texas space, would go out to the edge of a field and take turns throwing a tin can over the head of the shooter. Swing ahead of the creative angles of the throwers before time for evening chores. We'd have time to get in plenty of practice waiting until the old folks would turn us loose with a .22 rifle.

Step 3. To the range: Back to our current time, jump to shotguns on thrown clays. Put on the ear protection. Out where we make up our own range rules, the new shooter first stands close to the clay thrower and shoots directly at the dead-away departing clay. No lead required. You hit it every time as soon as it becomes natural to pull the trigger when the clay looks right. (The tendency is to wait too long.) As the shooter gets into the ('cuse me) swing of it, move around to get more angle (and thus the need for more lead). The new shooter quickly picks up the idea. With more practice, and some coaching, it begins to become natural.

Analytical Aspects of Wingshooting Leads

The warm-up for this section is recalling and thoroughly absorbing the definition of lead. Lead is the distance ahead of a moving target along its flight path sufficient to place a projectile so that it intercepts the target.

An imprecise nomenclature has developed around leads. I'll apply a little redundancy to pick up most of the terms you'll hear. An animal or bird moving across in front of you broadside, right to left or left to right as you face forward, would be taken with a full lead. The direction of travel of the target relative to your intersecting shot results in maximum movement across your line of sight and the path of the pellets.

This compares with a bird flying, either straight at you or straight away from you. There's no displacement of the shot location relative to the flight of the pellets regardless of the speed of the animal. No lead is required. All other angles, either toward you or away from you, require from very small lead to full lead, proportional to zero degrees to ninety degrees relative to your line of sight. An angle of around forty-five degrees toward or away from your position is referred to as a quartering angle and requires about half of a full lead.

So, the fundamentals of leads for shots on moving birds involve two relative speeds: the speed of the bird and the speed of the projectile. Complications set in immediately, as ducks and geese fly with a range of speeds.

ESTIMATING SPEED OF DUCKS IN FLIGHT

The series of steps involved in understanding the analytical aspects of shots at moving birds begins with establishing some speeds of the moving bodies involved.

How Fast? How Far?

Full Leads for Ducks and Geese at Different Flight Speeds

Table I: (1,300 Ft/s Load)

Range (yd)	Muzzle	10 yds	20 yds	30 yds	40 yds
Shot vel f/s (Avg)	1300	1030 (1165)	850 (940)	720 (785)	440 (580)
Calculations time to target(s)		.0258	.0258 + .0319 = .0577	.0577 + .0382 = .0959	.0959 + .0517 = .1476
Lead in Ft/ Bird vel f/s		Ft	Ft	Ft	Ft
Mallard @ 65 mph–96		2.5	5.5	9.2	14.0
Canvasback @ 70 mph–103		2.7	6.0	9.9	15.0
Canada @ 50 mph–74		2.0	4.5	7.0	11.0
Slow pass @ 30 mph–44		1.0	2.5	4.2	6.5
Jump/Land @10 mph–15		.5	1.0	1.5	2.0
Clay pigeon close to launcher 50 mph–74 ft/s		2.0	4.5	7.0	11.0
Clay pigeon slowing after travel from launcher 30 mph–44 ft/s		1.0	2.8	4.0	6.5

Note: The surprising amount of lead required for a crossing shot to connect with a mallard or canvasback at speed. These calculations use average velocities of the shot load across the ranges considered as if they were a linear decrease in velocity. They're actually nonlinear, but results are easier to make sense of if they're kept simple.

The next table is furnished to give an indication of leads required for the different loads.

Full Leads for Ducks and Geese at Different Flight Speeds

Table II: (1,600 Ft/s Load)

Range (yd)	Muzzle	10 yd	20 yd	30 yd	40 yd
Shot vel f/s (Avg)	1600	1270 (1450)	1050 (1160)	870 (960)	520 (700)
Calculations time to target(s)		.0207	.0207 + .0260 = .0467	.0467 + .0316 = .0780	.0780 + .0430 = .1210
Lead in Ft/Bird vel @mph and f/s		Ft	Ft	Ft	Ft
Mallard @ 65 mph–96		2.0	4.5	7.5	12.0
Canvasback @ 70 mph–103		2.0	4.8	8.0	12.5
Canada @ 50 mph–75		1.5	3.5	6.0	9.0
Slow pass @ 30 mph–44		1.0	2.0	3.5	5.5
Jump/Land @ 10 mph–15		.3	.7	1.2	2.0
Clay pigeon close to launcher 50 mph–74		1.5	3.5	6.0	9.0
Clay pigeon slowing launcher 30 mph–44		.9	2.0	3.5	5.5

Note: That data for high-velocity loads indicates little effect on leads at normal shooting ranges.

Calculations

Leads can be understood using straightforward calculations if the speeds of the moving birds (rough estimates from observation) and shot (precise manufacturer's measurements) have been determined. The intention is to work incremental distances for more accuracy without the mystery of calculus.

Some calculations are involved to get units of measure; both bird and shot speed is measured in feet per second. We'll also consider leads in feet:

5,280 feet/mile/divided by 60×60 sec/hour = one mile in an hour, or mph

or

1.47 ft/sec = one mph converted to feet per second

At a range of thirty yards, or ninety feet, a particular hot shot load moving at an average speed about 800 ft/sec takes 90/800, or .113 sec to go the thirty yards.

So, while the shot goes 90 feet, or 30 yards, the birds moving at 70 fps goes 70 fps $\times$ .113 sec = 7.91 ft.

Three interval average speeds were used to make the tables. It's best to make a fine grid computer solution, but this gets the idea across.

HUNTING AND SHOOTING MOVING GAME AND THROWN CLAY TARGETS YEAR-ROUND

The best, some would say the only, way to become an expert wingshot is to do lots of wingshooting—not only during duck and goose season, but all the year through, hunting other birds during the appropriate open seasons. Upland bird hunting and shooting most closely approximates the speeds and ranges encountered in duck and goose hunting. You can also practice wingshooting through lots of thrown clays so that you can make shots on moving birds instinctively. Trapshooting can simulate waterfowl hunting, while skeet is good for the other fast and maneuverable fliers.

If no bird seasons are open, you can still go hunting for the squirrels and rabbits. They are about the same size but are usually closer, and along the ground, with cover for more of a challenge. The shotgun serves to accommodate those minor errors in lead. The sporting clays range simulates wingshooting and shooting at running small game moving fast along the ground.

But considering how good you'll be getting with all that practice, you're ready to take the next step. And make your own calculations.

Shotgun Leads for Other Game Compared to Waterfowl

Table III: (1,300 Ft/s Load)

Range (yd)	Muzzle	10 yd 30 ft	20 yd 60 ft	30 yd 90 ft	40 yd 120 ft
Shot vel f/s (Avg)	1300	1030 (1165)	850 (940)	720 (785)	440 (580)
Calculations time to target(s)		.0258	.0258 + .0319 = .0577	.0577 + .0382) = .0959	.0959 + .0517 = .1476
Same as Table I. Lead in Ft / Bird vel @mph and f/s means Lead goes across rows/Bird velocity reads down Column		Ft	Ft	Ft	Ft
Clay pigeon close to launcher 50 mph–74 ft/s		2.0	4.0	7.0	11.0
Clay pigeon slowing launcher 30 mph–44 ft/s		1.0	2.5	4.0	6.5
Pheasant 40 mph–59		1.5	3.5	5.5	8.5
Cottontail 35 mph–51.5		1.3	3.0	5.0	7.5
Jackrabbit 45 mph–66.1		1.7	4.0	6.5	10.0
Tree squirrel 12 mph–17.6		.5	1.0	2.0	2.5
Dove 60 mph–133		3.5	8.0	13.0	20.0
Quail 45 mph–66		1.7	4.0	6.5	10.0

SHOOTING PRACTICE PRELIMINARIES

Considering the inconvenience of trips to a gun range and the baggage of a club, we decided we'd just make a backyard skeet range part of the homestead. Our get-togethers with friends and family often gets around to topics of guns and shooting and archery and fishing, so we might as well work some of it off.

Among the several selections the duck hunter has available (and is actually required to make in a practical sense) is the type of equipment selected to make the shot. And that means, first and foremost, selecting a shotgun that is right for you.

No amount of talking, thinking, looking at pictures of shotguns, looking at shotguns down at the store, and sorting through the advice from friends, family, and guys down at the gun store can replace pointing real shotguns at real flying clays under the watchful eye of a really good wingshot. JoAnne started with an autoloader, then Eddie loaned her that over-under. A quick trip back to the store next day resulted in an early birthday present!

"Pull!" Bill sends the clay. Eddie observes. Note that they start out with the clay flying dead away so there is hardly any lead. The shooter doesn't realize that it's all about getting the eye and trigger-finger synced. Then they'll open up that lead a little bit at a time.

JoAnne takes a crash course in wingshooting.

Eddie, Barrel, JoAnne, Shot String on the way, and clay all aligned.

Clay and shot.

Remember the last chapter, on getting dead-away shots or shooting just as the ducks come almost to a full stop before they backstroke down that last ten feet or so? Eye-trigger sync.

Yes, that really is the shot string on the way. It can be seen low and to the left of the low branch aligned with gun and clay. One point to be made by this photo, which actually shows the shot string, is that a pattern doesn't cover a washtub. It needs to be centered on that pie plate to be effective. There are other points to be made from a more detailed look at this photo. The main point might be the quality of the coaching. An experienced and sharp-eyed wingshot can align eye, barrel, and clay, and then watch the shot fly to the target. A good coach observes and recommends if correction is required. The shooter makes any correction, if required, before the next clay comes out of the slinger (before the shooter has too much time to think about it). The reload quickly becomes second nature. The dead away is moving toward full lead.

Experts Made Young and Experts at Birth

Early start theory: Ivy quickly picked up wingshooting. An expert with the .410, she is working on getting a 20-gauge autoloader as this is being written. She's covering her sector at the back of the boat page 143 with her retriever pal Scout ready to go.

The best start is early.

The natural.

The previous page shows Ivy at a very young age on a clay with BB gun. About this age, any kid can learn any skill, any language.

Above, Ike shoots a shotgun for the first time after Eddie's instruction. The first shot hits the clay, then another and another. Eddie took all the credit. He said that the hold was perfect.

Eddie and young ones form up for a shoot-around next page, Eddie is good but Ike is better! Tom was more than happy to record the whole thing. I won't let Eddie forget that one.

Young Tom joins in, as seen below, and the younger ones make him look bad as well. We concluded that Ike gets his shooting skills from his mother. It certainly can't be his father, Tom, or his grandfather, Tom.

These are just a few photos to show that getting good with a shotgun can be a lot of fun.

Eddie gets beat by Ike for rest of afternoon.

Young guns first shoot-around.

Old big guys shoot-around: Bob, Nekoda, Tom, Eddie. Credit: JoAnne Airhart.

Approaches to Getting That Practice, Practice, Practice . . . Without the Rest of Your Life Getting Away

Make practice a part of your life. The fact is that the shooting practice it takes to internalize the sight picture and finger coordination may lose its fascination over a period of time. An option is to try the family-sized version. All that practice seems to go better if you surround yourself with similarly minded folks. You can also make connections at the public shooting range or join a shooting club. Before long, you'll be out there all the time with friends and family having a great time while you knock off hundreds of shots a month. Shooting sporting clays, which involves thrown clays at all angles, is probably the best training for all-round shooting skills at moving targets.

Field practice.

When we're hunting ducks or geese on private land, we'll sling out a few clays at odd actions and angles after the morning flights have passed. It's usually good for a few shooting jokes if nothing else. Keeps everybody humble.

Kick off the boots and put the earmuffs on over the ear plugs. Eddie and Scout sling a few out for Tom after the morning flights.

Wingshooting Before Waterfowl Season

Most hunters of anything with feathers manage to make the most of dove season early in the fall. Fast, small, high-flying game birds taken by pass shooting are a challenge to any shooter after the predictable clays of the summer. It's somewhat similar to shooting at fast, high-flying ducks and geese, and probably the best way for the new shooter to get wired in to leading real game birds in the field.

Chapter 6

Skillset of Retriever Training and Handling

What would waterfowling be without the retriever? Some hunters with deep wrinkles at the outside corners of their eyes and stiff dog hair on their pants would answer in a blink, "Hellofalot less complicated is what it would be, that's what." Then, after a pause to flash back through visions of exasperation, admiration, pleasure, pain, memories of episodes both ridiculous and poignant, dogs of days past, with a glisten from the inside corner of an eye, they add, "I'd have quit years ago without 'em."

Another hunter would think of trying to retrieve floating ducks from muck-bottomed ponds, or maddening chases after cripples through a marsh featuring downed timber. "They're the biggest factor to achieving better conservation, ethics, and total enjoyment of the sport of waterfowling." Welcome to the world of the web-footed dogs.

HUNTER TRAINING OF RETRIEVERS FOR WATERFOWLING

A reality check before the considerable commitment: the alternatives and consideration of the Lab (hint as to the preferred breed for us) as a member of the family, assuming the family has the time and space required for a four-footed member (keeping in mind considerations such as whether both parents need to be in the workforce when the kids go off to college within the next couple of years).

Here you encounter probably the biggest "or" of all. Buy a trained retriever or buy an untrained pup from a good breeder, and dedicate a significant part of your life to making it the best working dog that ever snagged a duck.

If you're contemplating getting in on this facet of the game, we recommend that you do what you're going to do anyway: Buy a copy of every last how-to book, DVD, article, and everything else you can get your hands on to cover every last detail of retriever training for all the details. Don't overlook YouTube, of course. Knowledge is just one of the many things you'll never have enough of (or time, or patience . . . and the list goes on). Pups never come in standard models, which is what makes this project something to be remembered forever. How you remember it is up to you. Open your heart and do your best and your retriever will be *your* ultimate retriever regardless of what anybody else thinks.

You have to seriously commit a big part of your time and concentration on retriever training. It's pretty easy if it's just you and the dog. That's not the usual case, however. If you're capable of affection for your canine friend, you'll probably encounter a human to love sooner or later, and there you go. That pup will become a beloved member of the family. Retriever training will have to fit into the regular routines of life, like a job and family responsibilities.

Then there's the lifespan aspect of the human–dog relationship that most don't consider. The human is immortal as far as the dog is concerned. If we're past childhood, we'll have changed very little over the lifetime of the dog. And we're left to mourn the passing of our friend, or friends, over the course of our lifetime as a waterfowl hunter.

As far as recommendations for references on retriever training go, it turns out that the only book that each of the three of us own pertaining to the topic, *Game Dog: Second Revised Edition*, was written by the same author: Richard A. Wolters. His take on retriever training isn't the current bright new insight, as he passed away in 1993, and many of his ideas were controversial during his lifetime, but he's still widely quoted. Techniques that Eddie and Kent followed in training their dogs are based, sometimes loosely, on the Wolters approach.

Origins and Nature of Widely Used Retriever Breeds

We include a few short discussions that give general reviews of the most widely encountered waterfowl retrievers. That usually narrows the discussion down for us to which color Lab you prefer, but we'll attempt to be open minded. It's hard to beat any of the top retriever breeds with those big webbed feet when the chips, or ducks, or geese, are down.

Summary of Retriever Breeds

A lot of reference information exists pertaining to different breeds of retriever. We've found from firsthand experience that every retriever is unique, and concluded that more differences in overall performance exist within a breed than across breeds of retrievers. Basic instincts of retrievers are definitely different from breeds used to herd sheep and cattle, guard dogs, or companion dogs, but all of the retrievers are wired about the same. Characteristics all retriever breeds have in common are: trainability and inclination to please; controllability; a soft mouth to avoid damage to retrieved game; and boundless enthusiasm for jumping into icy water, on command, to go bring that bird back to the boss. A summary of widely used retriever breeds follows. Just try to imagine that our written words sound like the voice-over of the commentators at the Westminster competition.

Labrador Retriever

Labs are hell-bent retrievers. They are intelligent and quick to learn how to do anything to please their humans. They've become the most popular family dog in this country, with their friendliness toward people in general, and, for the most part, other dogs. And they are, of course, lovingly devoted to the people they've bonded with.

Labs are often exceptional in all aspects of the hunt, to include picking up the sound of incoming waterfowl and marking multiple downed birds. They're very manageable when required to retrieve on command in coordination with other retrievers in the party. We're sure they would make great wingshots if they could get those useless thumbs to work.

They're derived from the St. John's water dog and were developed as a specialized breed in England about one hundred years ago. The popularity of Labs among folks with absolutely no inclination to hunt waterfowl has led to some complications for hunters. Many breed lines have long been for show. Hunters need to be careful to check that lines of the breeder have hunting credentials. We also feel that resumes of direct ancestors should reflect excellence in hunter training followed by performance and enthusiasm for the hunt rather than for the complicated exercises of field trials.

Chesapeake Bay Retriever

The Chessie is big in size and heart. The breed was bred for market hunters of the nineteenth century. They were bred to make very large numbers of retrieves in a short time under very harsh conditions along the wintry Atlantic coast. The breed is derived from St. John's water dogs bred to working retrievers in the Chesapeake Bay area, originally by well-off local gentlemen and later by rough-and-tumble duck hunters. It's still a rough and tough, intelligent, fast learner.

They're very upbeat dogs and happy regardless of conditions and may let it be known with a vocal outburst and a big grin. They make nice family dogs when nicely socialized through puppyhood. They don't love everybody they meet, as would a Lab, and some may be strong willed in training. Consistent training every day with some playtime after work will produce good results.

Golden Retriever

Golden retrievers are most noted for their beauty of coat, conformation, and movement. The breed was originally bred from pedigreed lines in Scotland as a hunting dog, and it remains so today, but they can hold their own with any retrievers out in the swamps. Goldens are among the very top in intelligence of all breeds, and are calm, quick to learn, and have a sweet temperament. They're great family dogs and particularly patient with little kids.

Goldens are so successful in show competition that waterfowl hunters need to be very careful that their selection comes from a breed line of hunters. You can count on being available for long exercise sessions, along with training and regular, extended grooming of that beautiful coat, which sheds a ton of hair every week.

American Water Spaniel and Boykin Spaniel

These two breeds are outside of our firsthand experience, so we're trusting our few small boat connections and Internet research for this summary of the top little retrievers. They have a particular appeal to anybody who's ever been dumped by a big retriever out of a small boat and into the swamp with the 'gators.

The American water spaniel (AWS) originated in Wisconsin a couple hundred years ago. They filled the need for a very general retriever, upland and water, birds and furbearers that could work cold waters from small boats. Ancestors were a mix of spaniels and retrievers. Needless to say, folks in that time and place didn't have time to make extensive records of breed lines. Bloodlines are considered to vary in temperament. Prospective buyers should make a detailed effort to determine if their selection will get along with kids if he or she is going to be a family dog. Population of the breed was never large or particularly popular.

The nearly identical and much more numerous Boykin spaniel seems to have largely replaced the AWS as the small hunting dog. The Boykin originated in the South about one hundred years ago. Origins make for some interesting stories, but most dog people think the AWS must have been a major part of the mix. Enough locals were involved to instill acclimation to hot weather. Some sweethearts in the gene pool instilled a very nice temperament in the breed. The Boykin loves everybody it meets, including the kids, and makes a great family dog. Boykins seem to be born wired to retrieve on land or water and make a good flusher upland. Training is usually easy, as long as you don't go into the very complicated stuff. They're inclined to inherit a list of ailments, so new buyers need to get educated and make an in-depth check of their selection's bloodlines.

German Shorthaired Pointer

This is another breed outside of our wheelhouse, but you can get a load of free info fast from owners and breeders. It seems that to know them is to love them. They have a reputation of being quite a package. Originating in Germany as implied by the first part of the name, and not restricted to retrieving per the last part of the name, this is a dog that excels in the double duty of pointer and retriever for hunters who want a dog for pointing upland birds and retrieving both upland birds and waterfowl. They'll also go after large dangerous game. The German Shorthaired Pointer is a member of the web-footed club that can also handle rough terrain. They're very high energy and athletic. They need lots and lots of exercise and training, plus room to roam. Thank goodness they're very intelligent and trainable, as well as obedient and great family dogs. Just keep them engaged. They are always looking for a job, and if not provided one, they're independent and fully capable of finding one on their own. They'll go after birds, deer, wild hogs, bears . . . and the list goes on. In common with the other large retrievers, they need a lot of food and water. Also in common is their tendency to get fat with age as their activity levels edge down.

Eddie's First Retriever—Guess What?

The thing you notice about cold and ducks and water all going together in our old-time version of duck hunting was that we usually came back home with frozen, icy pants. No dogs to jump in the cold water to retrieve the ducks. Finally, by a combination of imagination, hard work, and good fortune, Eddie became the only kid in the Blue Ridge Texas School District with a genuine retriever. He was envied by all of his duck huntin' buddies. His retriever didn't look like the retrievers on the *Field & Stream* magazine covers (more on this later). The story on the rest of our retrievers, or actually nonretrievers, illustrates our limited span of knowledge concerning dog breeds and the concept of breeding specific dog breeds. Whenever we got an idea in our collective heads, we acted with the resources we had at hand. So, when we decided we wanted to go hunting, we'd turn to the family dog at hand—cow dog, squirrel dog, coonhound, you name it. It always worked out to the same results, too: completely frustrated kids, confused and annoyed dogs. Most of the dogs around the farms ran to breeds (usually mixed breeds) more inclined to herd cows, chase rabbits, find squirrels, or tree raccoons than retrieve birds. All except Eddie's. His dog immediately took right to retrieving a ball thrown from the stock pond/swimming pool diving board, and skipped right on to serious stuff like birds, ducks, and doing all the rest of a retriever's repertoire, including sniffing around in circles to zero in on downed quarry of any kind. The kicker is that Eddie's dog was a poodle that somehow turned up in Blue Ridge, Texas. So here was this pedigreed poodle that somehow turned out to be a hunting dog true to its long-ago ancestors in Russia, somehow circumventing the fate of those distant cousins who were transplanted to France and then to Hollywood.

Waterfowling and the Retriever

Here are three reasons why retrievers are such an integral part of waterfowl hunting:

- Efficiency: Hunting with a retriever beats running after a duck through the muck in a pair of waders.
- Ethics: Taking advantage of the natural talents of a retriever allows retrieval of downed waterfowl that would otherwise be wasted.
- Enjoyment: The enthusiastic and good-natured companionship of a retriever enhances enjoyment of the waterfowling experience.

Retrievers are born with the inclination to retrieve, but they have to be trained. In other words, they come with some assembly required. Training retrievers can be a touchy subject, as almost every private dog owner prefers training using gentle techniques. Lots of professional trainers, however, use aggressive techniques with extensive negative reinforcement ("force fetch") to efficiently maintain schedule. Not all dogs respond favorably to these methods, and a dog returned to its owner may be ruined. The odds of this happening are slim, but it's still a bad outcome for the unfortunate dog and owners. The hunter-turned-trainer may not end up with the best retriever in the world, but he will still end up with a dog that is a true buddy for life.

Considerations in the Different Approaches to Dog Training

There's a lot of good information on training—and a lot of not-so-good information. You can read one thousand books, have fun with one thousand "new" approaches to dog training, but all of them boil down to either of two approaches:

The first approach is retriever training using gentle methods, with firm instruction but without negative reinforcement. This is the preferred, and usual, approach of the owner/trainer. Trainer's the boss, with lavish phrase and pleasurable physical affection given to the dog—read body hugs and pats with your body at the same level as the dog, but no treats. The dog is performing to please you, to feel your appreciation with physical affection at appropriate intervals, not to get the taste of a treat. Praise and physical affection are better than you running out of treats with a fat dog spoiled by too-frequent treats.

The gentle approach can produce a superior retriever that's also a hunting pal and member of the family. As mentioned previously, the best reference for details on this approach is authored by Wolters. Results are totally dependent on the commitment on the part of the trainer combined with patience, skills, and tough love. It's almost as difficult as bringing up a kid, though dogs are definitely faster. The satisfaction from successfully training your own retriever ranks right up there with the most important things you'll ever enjoy in your life.

However, you can also fall flat on your face using this approach, resulting in an ineffective retriever and a less spontaneous, fun-loving, goofy pet than if you had never attempted training. Some will go on to double down on failure, and send an older, ill-prepared dog to a professional trainer and expect a well-trained retriever with the same personality to be returned.

Some professional trainers are so good and devoted to all dogs under their care that they can perform such wonders. Some can't. Many professional trainers faced with a problem, and many as a matter of routine, resort to the second approach, what's termed as "force fetch" techniques. This approach relies on negative reinforcement, such as inflecting pain by pinches to the dog's ear, a loop of string around a toe, or a hard-applied shock collar to reinforce instructions. This method is often used by professional trainers to save time, and when done in a measured way, it's efficient, humane, and effective in training a well-performing dog, but ineptly applied, it will ruin a dog, completely breaking its spirit.

Another objection to professional training is the argument that, in the opinion of many hunters who consider the dog as an integral part of the hunting experience, turning your dog over to a pro is tantamount to giving away your pup. It becomes the pro's dog, bonding with the professional trainer. You're the dog's second bond, if anything.

Setting the Stage for Training

Hunting is a business relationship centered on mutual interest; this waterfowling business is truly a partnership between human and dog. Here are precautions, protocol, and points of emphasis to be observed, beginning with early training for a puppy intended to be trained as a working retriever:

- No tug-of-war games with the pup.
- Introduce small harmless explosions that grow into small gunshots and finally shotgun shots.
- Introduce the pup to feathers on toys and training dummies, then expand to dead birds taken in hunting. First retrieves are easy to handle doves, then ducks to include some downed but not dead, and finally geese that can have a lot of fight left.
- Introduce the pup to natural bodies of water, duck blinds, boats, and boating separate from hunting, then throw hunting into the mix.

Selecting the Pup

Seven weeks old is the widely accepted age to take a pup from the litter—long enough in the litter to learn how to fit into dog society, and to know it's a dog, but not too long so that pup becomes part of the ranking order. Dominant pups can become hard to handle, while submissive pups may lack confidence.

Selecting that particular pup to share your life is often a sweet agony. We've seen our share of print on how to pick the perfect pup. Forget it. Just like all of the loves of your life, you'll love your retriever just the way they are.

The "Think I'm Just Gonna' Give 'im to Ya" Retriever

Bart came from a breeder, Mr. Price, who was way more interested in breeding good working Labrador retrievers than making a maximum profit from his efforts—sort of a rarity in this twenty-first century. His pups were good, very good, and they commanded top prices. His one great frustration was that many of his high-potential retrievers turned out to be pets rather than the top working dogs they were born to be. Many went to pro trainers and still turned out to be less than they could have been, in his opinion.

He'd decided to let Bart's parents have another litter. Most of the males had been spoken for at a high price. His reputation as breeder was that good. And thus was set the improbable tale that began the relationship of Eddie and Bart. Eddie would visit and look at the dogs and he would talk with Mr. Price, who knew that Eddie was an avid hunter, and would train the dog himself. Eddie would talk to his beloved Dana about the dogs, then he'd visit and talk to Mr. Price and they'd look at the dogs and talk some more. Finally, Eddie let him know that he'd really like to have one if he could afford it. Mr. Price was sort of noncommittal and continued to put Eddie off as the pups approached the enchanted age of seven weeks, that age when the pup leaves the litter and its mother, and a dog and its human can create a rare bonding for life.

Finally, as the pups were in their seventh week, Mr. Price gave Eddie a call. Eddie was excited, but apprehensive. He was aware that Mr. Price's dogs went for high dollars, but he didn't know how high and he wasn't flush with cash at the time. Dana went with him. This would have to be a major family decision, one made with a measure of reason and objectivity.

There was just one male pup left. Making maximum use of that PhD in human psychology that all Labs are born with, it walked right over to Dana and looked up at her. She melted and picked it up. So much for reason and objectivity. Dana was reduced to an unspoken plea, "Please don't let this be a five-figure thing." They visited and talked about things in general and dogs in particular in sort of an oblique way. It was getting late. Finally, Mr. Price allowed as how that one particular pup was sort of a runt, but he was bright and gave an air of confidence that might verge on being hard to handle.

"You know Eddie, you might just make him amount to somethin' . . . think I'm just gonna' give 'im to ya'."

Eddie hit one of his rare speechless gaps. He looked hard at the pup. Looked full sized to him. Maybe the best-looking yellow Labrador retriever pup he'd ever seen. And there was something beyond the looks, the physical configuration. Now Eddie was beyond a loss for words. A problem sort of cropped up toward the back of his throat that physically prevented him from saying anything. He mismanaged an awkward "Thank you" that conveyed an appreciation beyond eloquence. Cuddled in Dana's lap, Bart took the first of many truck rides home with Eddie.

Since that time, Mr. Price has made many duck hunts with Bart and Eddie. He never bothers to bring a shotgun along, as he doesn't want shooting to interfere with watching Bart's performance. Far and away, Bart's the best working retriever he's ever seen . . . and he's seen quite a few.

The Training of Bart—and Eddie, Too

What follows is a summary of an intense, fun time never to be forgotten. We'll do it with a fast forward, which is the way you'll look back at it. This is how you spell commitment.

Week Seven or Eight

Early puppyhood away from the litter begins, which includes socialization of the pup and its humans. Bart learns how to fit into human society and bond with humans. Early puppyhood is when the strongest bonds with humans are made; a favorite human takes the place of Mom. For the owner/trainer, love 'em while you train 'em is permitted. It has to be a business relationship, however. Don't show your love with a stream of treats. Provide a private place in the home for the pup, if that's where he or she will stay. It should be a secure and safe sanctuary where the dog is undisturbed. Bart had a place in the house. He also spent some time in the chicken pen so that he wouldn't kill chickens. Burt actually became a playmate of the chickens. The rooster, of course, didn't care to play.

Training from the first day, rules and guidelines:

- NO is the first command and commands must be followed; they're not optional.
- No peeing or pooping on the floor of the house.
- No feeding from the table.
- Make sure the pup isn't the center of attention all of the time.
- Start teaching the concepts of SIT, STAY, and COME (instructions for the trainer follow). These are the basics of control that need to be hardwired.
- Don't play games that lead to trouble, like "chase" or "keep away" with any object in dog's mouth. No pulling against the pup with anything. No chewing on any of the training equipment (but it's OK for your boots and waders to be at risk).
- Fetch is the name of the game, so let's play it all the time. Retrievers have fetch bred into them, so enjoy it with them until it's completely ingrained. Keep it fun while the dog is young—pups have a short attention span.
- Just got home from work? Then relax playing fetch with a ball; the pup's been waiting all day for this.

Week Nine

Throw a stick in water for Bart to retrieve; shoot gun in opposite direction. Training starts to get serious. Bart's program of structured training starts to take shape. But still, play is never over during training. Phasing into the ten- to twelve-weeks-old structure and continuing through one year old and beyond—and it's still all about fun.

Weeks Ten to Twelve

At this age, Bart fetched different things like quarters and so on. One such quarry was a quail wing, dragged through pasture, so that Bart could track and find feathers. A fishing pole was used so that Bart wasn't following Eddie's scent trail (the same fishing pole Eddie used to get ducks to the bank before he got Bart).

It's important to make training fun and include lots of variation, all concurrent with SIT and HEEL commands with hand signals and whistle. Here's a fun game to include in your training. It's called Doggie Baseball.

Set up stakes in the shape of a big baseball diamond with about seventy-five yards between the stakes. Put several softballs or tennis balls around each stake. Retriever and coach stand on home plate. From HEEL, direct the dog's attention to the stake you are looking toward, using a hand signal to direct dog's gaze if required. Make the command of BACK with an outstretched hand and step in the direction of the balls around the stake. If all goes well, the dog will run out and come back with a ball. A variation on this is to throw the ball out to be retrieved.

After innumerable reps, Eddie stands on home plate and Bart goes out to the pitcher's mound. (SIT and STAY, learned after fetching, are key here.) Eddie now uses hand signals to direct Bart to retrieve balls from 1st or 3rd base, then 2nd base, all the while using the BACK command.

With the baseball game still running, introduce the STOP command, using a whistle with hand up. Make an interruption of the usual routine, then redirect Bart to another base.

The game goes on, but with the introduction of a dummy launcher powered by cartridges. Make a bigger diamond. Retrieves should be done with dummies and wings whenever the ball game gets to be same old, same old. Eddie and Bart continued to work hand signals moving into the field trial league. Then came Bart's first duck season.

Eddie was anxious to see Bart's first performance using directed signals to find a shot fall. It never came up. Turned out that Bart was the best fall marker of anybody in the party, dog or human. It took Eddie a few times of attempting to get Bart directed to figure out that Bart was always right. Bart would follow Eddie's direction until Eddie came out to help. While Eddie was on the way, Bart would run over and pick up the fall, or chase it down, as required. Dogs can detect the odor of a duck, or anything else, better than humans. They eased up on the field work after that.

An important detail is to train a dog to KENNEL or KENNEL UP, into their bed or travel case on command. That's loading up in the back of a truck—a tall four-wheel-drive pickup—over the lowered tailgate. (Note: Don't ever help the dog get in with a lift from you.) Start with the wheels in a ditch or a cooler for an assist—it's basic training and starts with a run for everybody into the truck. Old dogs use the cooler, younger ones may or may not.

Postgrad, Orientation, Conditioning, New Experiences

Kennel up and take some short rides to fun destinations, then take some longer ones. Let your dog be around other people and around strange dogs. As far as other dogs are concerned, it's best to start with opposite sex (but not in heat) in the case of fully equipped males. Sometimes the boys don't get along and you don't want your young dog to get a complex. Take precautions around mature hunting dogs that might have a territorial thing regarding their people, hunting gear, and their "pack" if they hunt together. And don't let your pup get caught in the middle of another dog's retrieve. If they're inclined to be on the "hot" side, they might need to be on a leash until it's time to retrieve.

Be sure to introduce your dog to fences of all types and give them practice negotiating them every which way: going under fences, going over fences, going through fences, and running along a fence to find a hole in it.

If you're going to hunt from a boat, you and the dog should do some boating before duck season. All the games and practice done on land can also be done on the water. The dog gets trained in such details as to where the ladder or landing pad is for getting back into the boat. The same applies for blinds on the water.

Along the way, introduce unexpected noises: little noises when the dog is a pup and working up through toy cap guns (if you can find one); shooting in combat games (back off if it's too much); starter pistol far off and then closer; then the same drill but with real guns.

Ongoing Hunting Experience

Bart started dove hunting at six or seven months, whenever the season opened, and continued from dummies and wings as if there was no interruption.

Make a point to not let the dog retrieve every dove. Occasionally, make them stay while you retrieve the bird (every once in a while) so that the dog knows that the retrieve is on command rather than automatic. This little point will save you a lot of confusion for the dog when duck season rolls around. It eliminates the impulse to jump in and get 'em when another flight is in sight and coming in.

When duck season came along, Bart awakened to his calling. A natural. Retrieves from water as expected, at a hand signal, at Eddie's direction, runs around the small water to save all of that swimming, spots four falls at once, always stays outside the blind so that he can spot the falls. He's lots better at it than any of the humans. Can make a perfect spot a thousand yards out.

Some Family Snaps of Bart's Post-Grad Training

Bart and Eddie made a trip out to the Texas Panhandle for Bart's first goose hunt. You have to see it from Bart's perspective. A lot of dove retrieves. "This is easy." A good many duck retrieves. "This is fun, jumpin' into the water." Then way out here in a foreign land, Eddie knocks down a snow goose. So Bart goes after this big thing, and it's quite a tussle. Eddie has presence of mind to get his phone out as Bart starts back across the road.

Gotta' get this thing under control.

Bart accepting accolades from fans.

Following are several very blurred shots with goose wings flapping and excited dog tail wagging. Bart just dispatches the thing and finishes the retrieve. Like any good dog trainer, Eddie heaps lavish praise on Bart.

Along with all of the things retrievers are trained to do, such as retrieving and spotting, he's also very good at duck forecasting. He's always looking and listening, but mostly downwind. He picks up wing noise several hundred yards out.

Bart has gone to great effort to teach his understudy Scout everything he knows. But Scout's a hot dog, always ready to go before instructed. Bart has always loved to recover the dekes and has passed it on to Scout. So he and

Guess which direction the ducks came from? Bingo. Bart was the only one of the bunch to get the memo.

Eddie have worked overtime after the hunt to train Scout to pay attention and go on command. The photo illustrates a dog paying attention and ready to go on command.

Scout enjoying a little remedial training.

Chapter 7

Gear

Skillset of Selection and Use of Calls and Decoys

It's easy to sort out the dedicated duck and goose hunters by their vehicles, shotguns, gear, and their decoys. The truck will usually have mud and grease on it, and that's just on the seat cushion. Who knows what's on the bottom layer of the bed, especially up at the front, under the toolbox?

The key to recognition of a real waterfowler will be the decoys: They're going to look good. Two schools of thought exist in regard to decoys: They'll either be of the highest quality, or they'll come from various sources, with lots of refurb and custom modification. In either case, for the serious hunter who enjoys hunting various waters, there will be lots of them. And they'll be spotless, with all the rigging fixed just right, in a special way known only to the owner.

By the time the hunter gets to this fringe area where only the dedicated hang around, he'll have specialized in either ducks or geese. And everybody who knows anything knows that there's no such thing as a dirty duck decoy or a grungy goose decoy.

By the high-dollar approach, most of the decoys will be new and ordered from a specialty duck and/or goose hunter supplier. And they'll all be up to date. Forget about the hand-carved versions that the collectors fight over. The current models all have intricate feather patterns, tones, and textures that present a precise sheen over the body, head, and wings. Goose decoy heads and necks are designed for typical poses seen in the field: sleeping, feeding, a few looking around to spot danger. When you buy them in a package, duck decoy sets include more males than females, as is typically seen in the field due to the higher mortality of nesting females.

Refurbishing, Maintaining, and Embellishing Decoys

Keeping decoys up to standard is a labor of love for the successful hunters. Ivy Marie and Eddie take it a step above, adding embellishments of extra white and details to make the decoys look interesting to those jaded late-season mallards that have been looking at decoys and getting shot at for months and hundreds of miles.

The embellishing part is where things get interesting. Many hunters make a point of having decoys with a lot of white or lot of black. Ivy Marie, the brains of our outfit, concluded in an instant that if we were going to repaint

Santa's workshop on the shop porch. Credit: JoAnne Airhart.

the old decoys, we could just make them have more white than the originals. Then she went on to say that we could add some glitter and purple and really make them show up. Eddie thought that was creativity gone too wild, but they now have mallards with more white on their behinds than we've ever seen before.

Where's that paint I just bought today? Everybody uses Texas Rigs because you can pick up that mess on the ground and it untangles on its own.

Ivy added a few details to give her decoys a little more character.

Needs a little touch-up and may come out a little whiter.

Bring 'em in, hook 'em up, and we're out of here.

A sprig can get a lot of white and still look like a real pintail.

Eddie's on board with the white. Looks like that mallard Ivy's working on is about to get some interesting details.

Before and after. Credit: JoAnne Airhart.

Texas rigged and into the shop. Credit: JoAnne Airhart.

Texas rig in the field.

Lots of white on that pintail. Credit: JoAnne Airhart.

More white on those mallards. Credit: JoAnne Airhart.

Hunting Gear

This part of the book will give a quick overflight of gear in general. We'll hit the high notes on some particular items.

Blinds

Modern, professionally operated, high-dollar equivalents of the classic hunting clubs and preserves have permanent duck hunting blinds with accommodations ranging from basic to all the amenities.

Homemade blinds take on limitless forms on both land and water. Internet searches on duck hunting blinds will set you on course to find the best design for the particular location you have in mind. In so doing, you'll also become acquainted with folks with all sorts of experience that you can take advantage of. If you're going to the trouble of making your own blind, pick out a good spot for it, according to water and prevailing wind. Don't forget to check with whatever form of land management that controls that perfect spot you've picked, unless you own it fee simple. The best blinds are usually the ones with little expense and a lot of imagination. One of our favorites consisted of some pallets that came into the plant with the last equipment delivery, some fence posts driven into the mud, and netting from the local farm store.

Beginning with the see-through stage. Wire fencing supports brush of choice.

Final touch is cedar that everybody wants cleared from pasture anyway. It's the "Easy Blind" with sitting hunters out of sight.

The Raymers' "easy blind."

Taking shape.

Standing hunter.

Ground Hides

This collective term describes a wide range of means used for concealment by hunters, using shallow depressions made in the ground. Natural materials or loose refuse left after farming operations have traditionally been used to cover or obscure the fresh digging and hunters. A range of synthetic materials in different patterns and textures and colors and tones is now available from manufacturers such Avery.

Personal Camouflage

This is where the clothes and other covers merge into a seamless blob of invisibility—with a shotgun sticking out from under it.

Dog camo in these small sizes is hard to find.

Colors and tones of late fall around a little impoundment in north-central Texas.

Everybody camoed up.

A wading outfit in transport mode.

Matching camo and surroundings.

Layout Blinds

Layout blinds are the smallest enclosures that a hunter can hide in. They're widely used for goose hunting in open fields, with hunters situated among large decoy spread setups. A range of models from Avery and GHG is carried by Mack's and other suppliers.

Color to match is best choice.

Illinois goose hunt. Credit: Kurt Crowley.

Early-season green in north Texas.

Waterfowl Hunting Boats

Many waterfowlers consider boats as part of the equation. Boats can be used in a wide variety of applications. For example, permanent blinds are often constructed in productive duck hunting areas, in the shallows of large lakes, swamps, and coastal marshes. These locations may be far from the jump-off point where the access road ends, and a sizeable fast boat may be the only practical way to get on location by shooting light. The key is to get to your blind early, deploy the dekes, pull the boat into the camouflaged blind, disembark, and take up your shooting positions. The ducks will hopefully show about the time you're finished your first cup of coffee. This sweet setup may be constructed and maintained by a group of hunting buddies who share the expense and effort to maintain it.

An option is to use a frame or some other contrivance to support a camouflage covering. You'll find a range of setups around this theme limited only by the range of your imagination. Our friendly suppliers are ready as ever to come to our assistance. You can begin with a camo-finished, dedicated waterfowl hunting boat. Usually powered by an outboard motor, such boats range in size from large models capable of handling big lakes, reservoirs, and coastal marshes with open bay runs down to small lakes, watercourses, and freshwater swamps. Kits are available to refinish your existing boat in camo. Mack's and other suppliers carry Avery products, which include a range of blind systems for larger boats all the way down to one-person layout boats. Various camo patterns allow you to match the vegetation around the favorite honey hole.

All You Could Want to Know about Boats

There's an almost unlimited offering of specialized boats available for any kind of waterfowl hunting. We'll just list a few and assign the research as homework for the type of hunting you might want to try. There's a progression of duck hunting boats from offshore boats down to small personal watercraft that can be carried along with all the other gear.

A quick list includes: big water-open boats in the twenty-five-foot range; bass boats with camo; open boats in the sixteen-foot range; jon boats; skiff boats; sneak boats; layout boats; pirogues; kayaks; canoes; inflatables, and more. Outboard motors come in an equally large variety, from motors that work equally well on fishing boats, mud motors that have the prop on an extended shaft that pushes through both mud and water, and air boats that scoot across water, marsh grass, and short traverses of mud.

Once you've picked out a boat, always remember that safety comes first. Get enough boat. Don't go out across a big lake with a long run for waves in a little flat-bottomed boat. You're just asking for trouble. The wind may come up and you may not make it back. Better to take a "V" or semi-V-bottomed sixteen-foot boat (at minimum) that will cut waves. Wear your life jackets, and always pay attention to the weather.

Custom Modified Boats

Trading a little time for money. Buy a good used fishing boat and make a folding screen in front of shooters. Shown is Eddie's creation. Some just

Folding boat screen on the water.

Northern Atlantic big-water boat. Credit: Kurt Crowley.

make do with a camo net to cover boat, gear, and most of the hunters. Get a boat big enough for the waters you plan to hunt and keep the load balanced. Make sure you have a good way for a tired retriever to get out of the water.

A specialized boat in waters for the experienced. Speaking as middle-of-the country guys, our friend Captain Reilly McCue ensures that our sea-duck hunts don't devolve into life-threatening adventures.

The bicycle boat. Credit: Kurt Crowley.

This really is a tale to tell: Kurt's excellent Salt Lake marsh trip. A friend of ours, Kurt Crowley, was invited out to Salt Lake City by a friend of his, Don Avery, to try hunting the marshes around the lake. It's one of those public land situations where you need to get way out to get a good hunting spot. Kurt took him up on the invitation. They took off early. Kurt noticed there were bicycles in the boat, and figured they must be for weekend outings. When they reached the access ramp, they put the boat in the water and headed across the lake, loaded with the bikes and an unbelievable amount of gear. When they got to a landing spot, they loaded all of the guns, gear, and decoys onto some makeshift sleds, then went on a long bike ride through the marsh. They dragged the gear on the sleds for a considerable distance through the mud and deployed. One thing for sure, nobody moved in on them. Then came the ducks. In a short time they had their limits. Time to go back. Run the whole thing in reverse. Kurt got the photos. As you can see, duck hunters will go to extremes to get to good hunting spots.

This tale is the perfect lead-in to our next topic.

MOBILITY OVER FIELD AND WATER

This one is really wide and deep. A big element of successful waterfowl hunting involves getting out to a good place safely and early, usually in absolute darkness and over treacherous, boggy terrain or rough water that's cold enough to kill you with maybe a riptide that can drag you out into the high seas. This is starting to really sound like a lot of fun.

Staying on top of the situation under all conditions amounts to having good equipment appropriate for what you intend to do, but, more important, having the skills to operate that equipment and the physical and mental conditioning to follow through. You'll also need backup gear in case your top-of-the-line stuff craters at exactly the worst time. If it can, it will someday.

To seriously play the waterfowl hunting game, we need to be set up to handle rough waters frequented by the most hell-bent fishermen. We do have the prerogative to decide if we want to go play by land or by sea. The amphibious scope of Kurt's Salt Lake marsh trip doesn't come around very often.

Physical and Mental Conditioning

Most waterfowl hunting can be handled by anyone in good health. A few tactics require a fair amount of stamina, however. Green timber hunting is the classic. Wading a considerable distance through boggy mud loaded with gear will take your measure. So will walking over dry fields or wading through heavy mud, flooded timber, marshes, or swamps, or boating across streams, rivers, flooded timber or big waters, all in pitch-black darkness. To get the job done, it pays to be in reasonable shape. Having the right frame of mind, having the resolve to do it right, will make it all go easier.

Map and Compass

Being able to use a map and compass requires some practice, but it's a skill every outdoorsman should master. No matter if you're on flat ground, with no landmarks, or in thick trees and brush, the ability to use and trust your compass will always give you peace of mind, because you'll never get lost.

Global Positioning Systems (GPS) and Navigation Equipment

GPS systems have brought about a revolution in finding your way into and out of any mess out in the swamps, lakes, and marshes. The handheld units are easy to operate, so anyone can feel confident using them. The same applies to your boat. Get the best navigation equipment you can afford, learn how to use it, and you can go anywhere, all the while knowing that you can get back home at the end of the day without getting lost.

Sources of Maps and Charts

If by land, United States Geological Survey (USGS) 7.5-minute or 1:24,000 scale topographic (topo) quadrant maps are the standard. They also show all waterways in detail. Each map is named for a population center or major landform. USGS 1:100,000 scale Bureau of Land Management (BLM) version maps show land ownership along with the usual features covered on a map. This info can really come in handy when you're hunting public land.

If by sea, coastal maps and coastal charts are available from government agencies. The National Weather Service (NWS) and National Oceanic and Atmospheric Administration (NOAA) publish forecasts of rip currents and surf conditions along with charts.

Game management area maps are available from the state fish and game departments of each state. You can usually get them when you order your license and tags.

WADERS

Waders can be the death of you if you're loaded with ammo and all the other gear you need. If you don't have a good float cinch, and if you go in over your wader tops, you can be in serious trouble. Especially if you're hunting an unfamiliar spot, take your time, go slowly. If it takes an extra five minutes to get where you want to go, so be it. The alternative isn't worth it.

WATERS

One aspect of waterfowl hunting that seems to be taken for granted or ignored is water. Everbody assumes that water is just water. Water provides a barrier from most terrestrial predators, and feed for most waterfowl. Many species use deep water for security through the night, and as a safe base to come back to after feeding in another, more hazardous area. But the hunter has to be aware that waters have currents, waves, underwater obstacles, fog, ice, floods, and any number of surprises.

Small Waters

Duck and goose habitat includes a wide variety of small waters, including streams, sloughs, creeks, ponds for stock and irrigation, flooded farmland and timber, plus glacier-formed northern prairie potholes.

Swamps, Marshes, and Flooded Green Timber

Swamps and marshes are large, sometimes permanent, sometimes cyclic, bodies of shallow water. Depending on where they're located, they can be covered with woody plants, cypress, saltmarsh grasses, reeds, or trees. In contrast, flooded green timber is flooded annually, usually in the fall and winter. These large waters are best hunted as small waters.

Lakes and Reservoirs

Lakes are naturally occurring bodies of water. Reservoirs are man-made impoundments, built either to supply power or drinking water.

Creeks and Rivers

Much waterfowl hunting is done from the banks of running waters. Stalking techniques are usually employed, though hunters with boats often drift with the current.

Saltwater Sand Dune and Ledge Shorelines, Estuaries, Bays, and Offshore

Open shorelines occur along the ocean beach and brackish shallow bays behind the dunes of the beachfront. Flow of tidal water between the backwater and open ocean is usually unobstructed. These features predominate along the Gulf Coast of the southern United States and Mexico, where tides are low. Sheltered shores of the bays are covered with vegetation up to the edge of the water.

Saltwater Estuaries and Points

Estuaries are bodies of brackish water behind the ocean shoreline barrier, supplied with fresh water from a river source. The rising ocean tide pours through the constricted access in a strong current. It reverses with the ebb. Regions in northern latitudes with high tides experience drastic changes with ebb and flow of the tides. Locations with flat terrain may have large areas that cycle between flood and exposure to the air.

PART III

This Final Part Considers the Experience of the Hunt

Your Waterfowl Hunting Experience

The reader is now aware of the essentials of waterfowl hunting, and should appreciate the enormity of it. This is an outdoor sport that's as big as the waters and shores of all the earth, but also as small as a little pond with a dozen decoys set out and your best pal of another species there to share the experience. It's all just waiting for you to get out and hunt.

But before you do, you might take a moment here to flip back through the previous chapters on waterfowl, habitat, and how to hunt. The images that accompany the text, each one worth a thousand words, leave you with impressions of being there.

In this section, we will look at: strategy; selection of the experience; personal preferences of what, where, how, who with, action and, after the action, ultimately, the "why" of waterfowling. We will talk about personal sensations and how to make it all a reality in a practical way.

Here, we cite again references for ducks and geese and add hunting locations. We've updated material from a wide range of current data, including the very comprehensive reference for all aspects of all species of ducks and geese and swans: *Ducks, Geese, and Swans of North America*, by Kortright/ Bellrose. This is a classic, decades-long study supported by the Wildlife Management Institute and Illinois Natural History Survey and was published by Stackpole Books, 1942 through 1976. We've updated information pertaining to populations of different species and effects of habitat change since 1976. The following reference was also used for hunting locations: *Hunting across North America* by Byron Dalrymple and published in 1970, also updated with current information.

Overview of Elements That Make Up the Experience

This part of the book links back to the strategy you choose before you take to the field. That strategy generally defines your preferred duck or goose hunting experience. Part III is designed to assist you in defining the particulars of your preferred hunt(s) and how to make dreams become a reality. The nature of the game may be sorted according to two big divisions: ducks or geese. Within each will exist some variation according to species type, but, for the most part, preference for hunting either ducks or geese defines the great divide of waterfowling. Lots of hunters freely cross the divide; many of the most experienced will prefer to exclusively hunt one or the other. Habitat types define the setting, the situation of the hunt, and therefore the tactics, techniques, skills, and equipment required to make a successful hunt in one of the several habitat types. A particular habitat type may take on a different appearance across the continental range of ducks and geese.

Chapter 8

Habitat and Migration

CONTINENTAL SCALE

All successful species have optimally adapted to their habitat. In the case of migratory waterfowl, habitat becomes a series of habitats, occupied in a sequence driven by the changing seasons. And this string of habitats extends across the continents. We'll present details of our own North American continent, but the general patterns here extend around the globe.

The continental scale can be captured only from the perspective of satellites. We use the North America Satellite Orthographic Projection. The image in the book is adequate to follow our text, but you can have a better illustration of fine points with a high-resolution computer image available on the Internet in public domain, which can be enlarged to illustrate features useful for identifying regions of different types of waterfowl habitat.

Here, a general orientation of North America and its major features comes first, for the benefit of folks who haven't spent much time with natural science or geography. It's easy to pick up on the frozen white that covers most of Greenland. To the west (left) are the Arctic Islands of Canada with a dusting of white. The northern (upper) coast of Canada runs roughly east and west. Alaska is located in the upper western corner of North America. Toward the eastern side of Canada's Arctic Coast is a large notch of the ocean that extends south (down) into the center of Canada. Straight south it may be noted the five Great Lakes that form a natural boundary between the United States and Canada

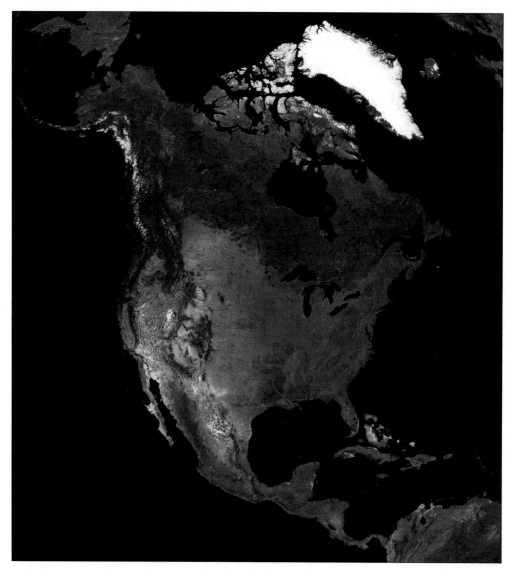

Satellite orthographic image of North America.

across the eastern side of the continent. The sharply defined Rocky Mountains trace north and south along the western interior. The lower and less well-defined Appalachian Mountains of the east also run north and south. Florida extends from the southeast corner of the United States toward the islands of the Caribbean to enclose the Gulf of Mexico. The long narrow Baja California

Peninsula delineates the corner of Mexico adjacent to California. The Atlantic Coast to the east and the Pacific Coast to the west encapsulate it all.

Definition of Regions

We define regions by vegetation color and natural features. Close observation of the tints of slate gray, green, and brown will define regions according to vegetation cover and specific landforms. Shades of brown indicate regions of low rainfall.

The slate gray of tundra covers northern Canada halfway down both shores of the Hudson Bay, on the east to the Atlantic shore, and trends northwest to the shores of the Arctic south of the western Arctic Islands. This is the Arctic region. Along the western Arctic Coast of Canada and just east of Alaska, the Mackenzie Delta penetrates deep into the Boreal Forest. Across Canada south of the tundra, the dark-green tint of the Boreal Forest Region swings around Hudson Bay from the Atlantic side of Labrador on the east to the western coast of Alaska. It surrounds the string of large lakes across western Canada and countless smaller waters visible with high-resolution magnification. Some of the shallow lakes appear as blue-green in the image.

A close look at the area just west of the Great Lakes reveals a north-south string of smaller lakes through Minnesota headwaters of the Mississippi River. Just west of the string of lakes is a very bright green area trending to the northwest adjacent to the Boreal Forest all the way to the edge of the Rocky Mountains. This area is the Prairie Pothole Region, famous as the "duck factory" of North America. It's one of the few places on earth that consists of plains densely covered by lakes. This region is actually part of the larger Great Plains Region of North America that extends broadly along the eastern front of the Rocky Mountains. Extending south from the lakes are lines of drainage trending to the southeast. This is the Upper Mississippi region. To the east of the plains, the Lower Mississippi Region continues south from the upper Mississippi, emptying into the Gulf of Mexico through its easily recognized by its extended delta. Both the upper and lower regions of the Mississippi are more of a linear feature rather than a region of broad area. An extensive deep-green area to the west of the lower Mississippi is covered by forests that run north from the coast, extending along the east side of the Great Plains. It's marked by two large reservoirs on our image. On to the west, as shown by the color change of the terrain from green to brown, the climate becomes progressively more arid toward the west to the southern extensions of the Rocky Mountains. This is the **T**ransition **Ex**tending **A**cross the **S**outh to the western North America region. We'll just refer to it as "Texas" for short. To the south and west, North America narrows into a very narrow connection with South America.

For orientation around the western Gulf of Mexico, the coast and coastal plain of Texas begins along the bend to the southwest just west of the Mississippi Delta and continues past the turn to the south and on to the eastern coast of Mexico. To the west of Texas and north of Mexico, all the way into Canada, is the Intermountain Region of the western United States, which includes the important Great Salt Lake area with salt flats highly visible in bright white. Further to the west is the Pacific Coast and the Western Interior Valleys of California. The valleys are easily recognized as the light-green areas extending north and south between the dark-green mountain forests on either side of California. On the north is the Central Valley, on the south is the Imperial Valley. The interior valleys are geographically part of the Intermountain Region, but many fowl migrations come down the coast and pull over and travel the length of the valleys. Some populations migrating down the center of the continent turn to the west and mingle with those from along the coast.

The Great Lakes and surrounding conifer forest form a region, and their drainage, which can be noted on the image, to the northeast divides the Canadian East Region and the Atlantic Maritime Region on the north and the Northeast United States Region on the south. These two regions appear to be identical, but Canada is much colder, which makes it a nesting area; the US side is for wintering. The Atlantic Coast and Piedmont Region extends to the south around Florida to join the Gulf Coast and Coastal Plains region that extends around the Gulf of Mexico.

We'll be forced to depart from the pure nature of the regions of North America and project political boundaries of a map over the regions. Colors generally represent those on the image.

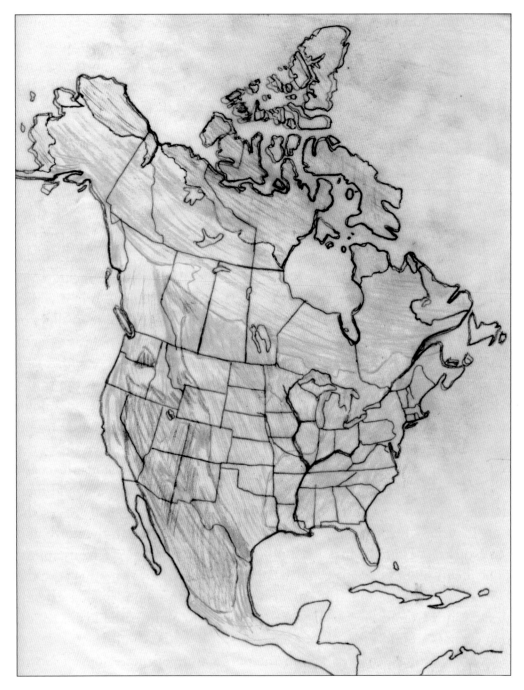

Map of states and providences over natural regions.

Migration across Regions

Most waterfowl of North America nest and molt across the northern half of North America during summer. During the harsh northern winter, most will move to the south. Nearly all species gather together for the long flight, so that the flight characteristics of all of the flight match. Migration departures are sequenced from north to south. Different species and populations of species travel along their individual established corridors, which combine with those of other species to form an extremely complex integrated network. The image next page shows a very rough and general representation of how the migration flows. The discussions elaborate just how complex the migration actually is.

Geese, with the notable exception of Canada geese, nest across the Arctic Region along coasts of all of the Arctic Islands and the continental mainland. Distributed nesting populations gather each year in particular locations spotted east to west. They head south in large flocks in a sequence of departures. Small populations may travel all together. Large populations often stage in multiple sequences of departures of large flights, then travel along the same corridor. Series of corridors spread across the north that terminate at locations across the South. Coastal destinations are along the Atlantic, Gulf, and Pacific Coasts. Interior destinations are northwest Texas, central Mexico, the southern Mississippi region, and valleys of the southern Rockies. Subspecies of Canada geese nest across the Arctic, Boreal Forest, northern Intermountain and Great Plains, Canadian East and Atlantic Maritime Region, and the Great Lakes. They will leisurely move south with the onset of cold weather. How far south they travel depends on how cold the weather turns.

Ducks disperse widely to nest across the Arctic and Boreal Forest, and in greater concentrations in the Prairie Pothole Region and adjacent parklands of the Boreal. Migration is most highly concentrated along corridors south over the Great Plains, east Texas, and the Upper and Lower Mississippi Regions. Some move on to Central and South America.

Other corridors of importance are those followed by several species of sea ducks that nest across the western Boreal Forest and migrate east to the shorelines of the Great Lakes, Canadian East and Atlantic Maritime regions, the northeastern United States, and the Atlantic Region. Populations of ducks

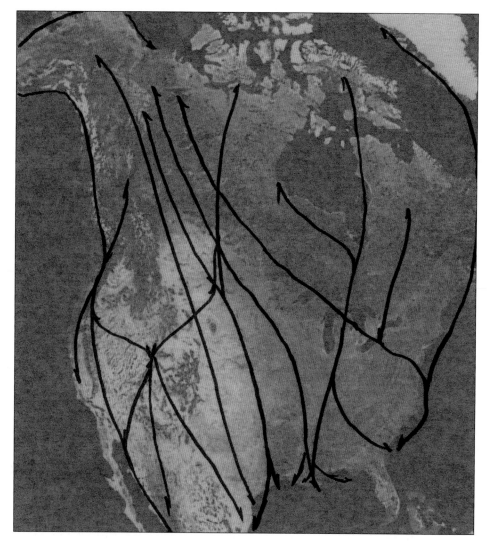

National migration routes.

that nest across the western Arctic, Boreal Forest, and northern Intermountain regions migrate along the west coast all the way along the coast of Mexico, or to California's Central Valley and the Pacific, and south to and through the marshes of the Great Salt Lake and on to interior Mexico, southeastern Intermountain, and western Texas and the Gulf.

Migration corridors of different species may gather and overlap into collections of high density along some routes, but may be widely dispersed along others. Natural flyways are composed of collections of corridors used by different species on their way to particular wintering and nesting areas defined by habitat. Boundaries of natural flyways are defined by major landforms extending generally north to south.

Natural flyways east to west are the Atlantic Flyway, the Mississippi Flyway, the Central Flyway, and the Pacific Flyway. The Atlantic Flyway is defined on the east by the coastline; on the west it begins on the southern shore of James Bay on the north, around the eastern Great Lakes, then south along the eastern mountains to the Gulf. The Western boundary of the Mississippi Flyway begins on the major islands hard by the Arctic shoreline and runs almost due south to just west of the four lakes that run north-southwest of the Great Lakes Region, then along the eastern run of the Great Plains Region on to the Gulf along the western edge of the Lower Mississippi Region where the coastline turns to the south. The western boundary of the Central Flyway begins where the Arctic coastline corners toward the north, along the Alaska coast where the Mackenzie Delta sharply projects into the Boreal Forest Region. It runs south along the backbone of the western mountains until they play out in the arid central of Mexico, then continues straight south to the Pacific coastline even with the southern end of Baja.

Some examples of the migrations of major species along the natural flyways using well-known locations should help to define migration in the context of natural flyways, and sometimes when they ignore the north-south running flyways.

Snow geese nest in famously large numbers in several areas across the Arctic. Along the Atlantic Flyway, populations nesting along the northernmost shores of Greenland and Baffin Island collect and travel south to gather on the north side of the St. Lawrence, where it narrows into the river. They travel on to Chesapeake Bay and then head south, along the coast of the Carolinas. Down the Mississippi Flyway, some populations around Hudson Bay gather on James Bay and stage out to the south down the Ohio and along the eastern Mississippi Delta to the Gulf Coast east of the river outlet and along the shores of the state of Mississippi. Other populations around the west side of Hudson Bay and northward to the shores between northern Baffin Island and Victoria Island gather around the west shore of Hudson Bay, then move to gather south of Lake Winnipeg before staging out along the boundary between the Mississippi and Central Flyways south to the border of Texas and Louisiana, then spread along the Gulf. Populations around the Mackenzie Delta merge with some of the populations east of Victoria Island and gather in great numbers in particular areas in southern Alberta and Saskatchewan. Some will fly south along the eastern side of the Rockies to southern New Mexico and the interior of Mexico, others from the western staging areas cross into the Pacific Flyway. They use passages through either the central Rockies plus the Great Salt Lake area, then down along the western coast of Mexico, or the northern Rockies and on to the Central Valley of California. Populations from eastern Siberia go south across Alaska and along the Pacific shoreline to Puget Sound and the Central Valley of California.

Migration corridors of the many species of sea ducks that nest across the Boreal Forest and Arctic of Alaska and Canada run generally east and west toward the shores and offshore of the Atlantic, Pacific, and Great Lakes.

Administrative flyways are defined in detail by state boundaries, as opposed to natural boundaries of major landform features, and serve as guidance to states in establishing seasons and bag limits (sometimes important to hunters interested in hunting a particular species). But we'll put that off while we illustrate the beauty of the habitat and the nature of things pertaining to waterfowl. It won't all be esoteric. For instance, you'll learn that agricultural operations have become the favored, actually essential, feed source for many species of currently burgeoning numbers. And we'll discuss the best arrangements to get out where you are planning to hunt.

TOURS DOWN THE FLYWAYS

We'll begin with the concentration of ducks that have nested in the central provinces of Canada and geese that have arrived from the north and have gathered in locations that are used year after year. Ducks will feed on the waste grain of Canadian fields and move south with the harvests over the Dakotas. Some geese will join, while others will go straight south along the Central Flyway.

Concentrations of geese that have staged around the more westerly shores of Hudson Bay bear straight south along the Mississippi Flyway. Many along the boundary between the Central Flyway and Mississippi Flyway to East Texas and Louisiana. Others from the James Bay gathering areas go south along the Mississippi River toward the Gulf coast of Alabama. Large populations of ducks also travel in a southeasterly direction down the Mississippi River to feed on natural food sources of flooded deltas and the high-quality grain of flooded rice fields.

Populations of ducks and geese nesting across eastern Canada move straight south into the northeastern United States. Geese from western Greenland move along the Atlantic coastlines of Canada and the United States.

Sea ducks from nesting areas across the Boreal Forest move east or west toward the Atlantic or Pacific Flyways and spread along the shores of the Great Lakes and both coasts. Many of the populations on the western side of the Prairies move southwest through the mountain ranges into the Pacific Flyway toward the moderate climates of the Pacific Northwest and valleys of California or the marshes of the Great Salt Lake.

Insight into Migration

Migrations are a major element of the nature of duck and goose species. Seasonal migration, which results in drastically improved habitat on a year-round basis, is an effective survival strategy. Migration comes with a price in that it requires exertion without resting or feeding for an extended time and distance traveled, with unfamiliar hazards encountered along the way. Each species has a characteristic approach to the annual migration.

The impetus to start each migration appears to begin with an internalized impulsive nervousness that can be observed in flock behavior leading up to a trigger: normally the onset of cold weather to start south in the fall. Warm breezes coming off the Gulf trigger the impulse to start north in spring. These triggers often coincide with an energy-conserving tailwind going in the right direction in either case.

OVERVIEW OF MIGRATION

Different waterfowl species have varied strategies to cope with the rigors of migration. Examples include weight loss from the exertions of migrations and times required for recuperation. Each species uses a different approach to recovery. Some make the trip in long stretches, followed by several days of feeding and resting; others travel in steady, short stretches, feeding and resting as they go. The sense of urgency that compels flocks to make long passages before resting and feeding for recovery varies by species. All species seem to be influenced by the weather. Cold drives them south in the fall; warmth invites them back north again in the spring. Occasionally, a major, even severe, weather event drives all flocks of all species before it. The term for this occurrence is a grand passage. It may drive individual members of the migration to exhaustion. Some species will suffer more than others. Other years may see mild weather with gradual cooling, with unseasonably warm weather throughout the entire winter. Both ducks and geese will cut the trip short if they find sufficiently moderate weather and feed available along the way. Mild winters are the cause of different waterfowl wintering as far north as the Midwestern states, but some duck hunting devotees on the Gulf Coast suggest that sanctuaries with artificial feeding along migration routes are a factor in holding populations north of the coast.

Wheres and Whens of North to South: Fall Through Winter

It's next to impossible to grasp the enormity of waterfowl hunting around the globe—there just so much information. But you can come close to grasping its extent over North America.

Here's how understanding came to one human once upon a time. Achieving profound insight seems to work best if you're leaning against a pickup.

The place was a few steps away from the front door of the Main Street Café in Estelline, South Dakota, located in the northeast corner of the state where North and South Dakota and Minnesota come together. Its landscape was formed eons ago by the ocean of ice extending across North America as it flowed under its own weight across the ground during the most recent of several cycles of glaciation. Then the climate changed to a warmer phase, the glaciers thawed and their water ran off to form different bodies.

And so it was that the particular human referred to was leaning against a pickup tailgate talking to a local farmer, who's also a hunter. It was early fall. We'd just finished lunch and walked out at the same time. I was in midst of a side trip that found me in Estelline, South Dakota, a little diversion for some waterfowl scouting.

At that time, local ducks were beginning to look like drakes and hens again after the molt. Great flocks of ducks were gathering across Canada. Geese were beginning to stir far to the north around the shores of the Arctic. And the farmer, leaning against the pickup, began to speak. He spoke from the perspective of one who's spent his entire life in the area, most of it out on the land every day.

Our conversation centered on North-Central Texas perspective of green crops of soybeans and corn still growing green. These crops had long since matured, withered, and been harvested back down in the South. In northern South Dakota, wheat had been harvested, but corn and soybeans were still green and the bean crop was still maturing and adding weight.

The first freeze is usually around the end of September. When crops freeze in the fields, plant growth and crop development cease immediately. An early freeze may cost 15 percent in weight of beans and corn. Beans and corn are harvested, either early or late, after the first freeze kills plants and grain (corn and soybeans), and the crop dries.

Hunting season starts before harvest. The first ducks taken are residents still in first plumage that follows the molt. Toward the end of September, weather changes begin to move ducks, then geese, down into the Dakotas from Manitoba just to the north, venturing into South Dakota typically as the season goes from September into early October. Geese and ducks in preparation for the migration south load up on highly nutritious wasted grain not picked up by the grain combines. This is about the time of the start of prime waterfowl hunting in northern South Dakota.

Our focus is on the dynamics of fall and winter rolling south over the progression of waterfowl habitats along their migration routes. Weather drives the migration timing of different species across particular areas as the seasons of any particular year progress—early fall and frost, into winter and freeze-up. Hunting conditions are driven by the seasons, but hunting seasons are regulated by writ and access to hunting spots is controlled by land ownership and management. The successful waterfowl hunter has learned to integrate these interactions to be out there at the right place at the right time.

Places and Time

We'll follow the regions from the perspective of our map with defined regions.

The Flyways

The term "flyways" originally described the various corridors used by different species in migration between nesting and wintering areas. Its discovery was an unexpected effect of radar observations of migrating birds. The term was adopted to designate administrative division for game management of migratory waterfowl into four districts across the United States from east to west.

Flyways extend from Canada in the north, down to the Gulf Coast. Like everybody else, we'll use it to describe the routes taken by waterfowl between nesting areas to wintering areas and back, and the administrative divisions interchangeably. Use context. Most routes do go generally north to south, but many go east to west and back for at least part of the trip. Flyways shouldn't be thought of as great common pathways through the air. You should think of them as almost countless little trails taken by different species or groups of species or even different groups of the same species that nest in different locations. Individuals gather in their nesting areas as the molt ends. Ducks are in post-molt plumage. Some drakes are in drab eclipse and just beginning the long transition to specular breeding plumage.

Small gatherings consolidate into larger and larger flocks in particular gathering areas used for the purpose year after year. Several species may use the same area. Depending on the species, or restless whims of agitated groups within the species, groups begin to leave the gathering area on their way to their wintering locations. Some species may travel together when their flight pace, endurance, internal flight patterns, and urgency to evacuate ahead of a winter storm are compatible.

Around Estelline and to the east, most migrating waterfowl follow routes that tighten to follow the Mississippi. This tight group of migration routes of many species is referred to as the Mississippi Flyway. A short distance to the west, short in terms of the distance cross North America, most of the migration south moves broadly across the central United States in a flow wide enough to cover Texas east to west. This is the Central Flyway.

Further to the west, along the eastern side of the great Rocky Mountain, runs another corridor, the Pacific Flyway. Most of the population diverts to the west, south of the rugged Bitterroot Ranges toward the Central Valley of California. Many keep moving south to Mexico. A fair amount migrates along the Pacific Coast, west of the major ranges. A big fraction of the population moving along the eastern slopes of the Rockies continues on south to the Great Salt Lake and the extensive marshes that surround it. Many join the year-round residents to stay for the winter. Others keep moving south by dispersed routes. Most will veer to the east through gaps in the southern Rockies and blend into the Central Flyway; some will bear straight south to disperse along routes that traverse Mexico north to south.

Far to the east of Estelline in southeastern Canada and the northeast United States, the local population of ducks and Canada geese are mingled with the newcomers coming in on the north winds. Heavy migrations of divers have followed the glacier-formed lakes that stretch across Northern-Central Canada. They've finally crossed across Lake Erie on their way to Atlantic coast offshore waters for the sea ducks and longshore wintering areas for the rest of the divers. Many have dropped off across the Great Lakes where they'll winter over. Puddle ducks have begun to gather across the area on small glacier-formed waters that stretch across the northeast United States and southeast Canada and head south along the Atlantic seaboard. Collectively, this route is called the Atlantic Flyway.

Winter Rolls South

Winter and waterfowl migration rolls over Estelline until the hard freeze leaves the little lakes and potholes frozen hard. The almost exact scenario has been going on over miles to the east, and about the same distance to the west across the prairies and Intermountain West. The high arctic geese drive over the North American interior going to coastal areas of the south. Some Canada geese linger on into, sometimes through, winter on waters still open.

Far to the west of Estelline, early fall sees the same basic processes go on over all of western Montana into the winter. Early fall in the Big Hole Country in southwest Montana, hay is being brought into storage for cattle that will be rounded up and brought in from the high country where they've spent the summer.

In the local North-Central Texas area along the wide Central Flyway that we call home, ducks predominate around Blue Ridge, Texas. Geese predominate thirty to forty miles to the east around Commerce, Texas. The southernmost termination of migration will vary by species according to tolerance of cold and ice. Mallards, for instance, are often the species to linger just in front of the freeze-up. This is completely opposite from the early-escaping teal that often do not stop until they reach Mexico, Central America, or South America. Migration will be reviewed under the major nesting area for each species. Then we cover the normal passage schedule for each through regions to the south.

You'll see in the reviews of different regions the schedules of migration for the various waterfowl species. The schedules presented correspond to the average conditions according to climate. Climate is defined as the normal conditions expected at that time and place. This is not to be confused with weather. Weather is the conditions that are actually happening outside at the moment. Climate is what you make long range plans around. Weather, actually the short term forecast for dark-thirty tomorrow morning, is what you use to plan what you dig out to wear tomorrow morning. Early. Now, here's where we're going. Weather is the main impetus of migration patterns. In a complete analogue of the weather forecast, you can get a migration forecast. This information can be found easily online.

Understanding and Hunting the Migration

The explication of migration of individual species across all of the regions follow the same format. Each species will be introduced in the predominant region of nesting. At the introduction of each species, their complete migration routes across the continent will be presented. That gives you the total migration of each species in one place. Then, under the heading of each region, all species that migrate across that region are presented with the normal time they come through and with the estimated number of that species coming across. So, you can see in one place the when and how many of each species you can expect on the average. You'll have in front of you the collective numbers of all species to expect and when they will be there. On average. You'll have an idea of how to hit the peak of the total surge. On average. And, yes, there are a lot of moving parts to this thing called migration. As many as all of the waterfowl across North America.

Note that estimates of arctic nesting populations can vary widely depending on breeding conditions and other unknown variables, such as unusual climate. More resources are going into research to better understand the elements that impact survival of these species.

Chapter 9

Hunting a Particular Species across North America

The three regions presented in this chapter are nesting areas. Each species is introduced in the region where it nests. For introduction, the entire migration of that species is reviewed. For the hunter interested in hunting a specific species, say mallard duck or giant Canada goose, the entire migration can be reviewed to see where, when, and how many of that species can be expected at any particular time.

A specialist hunter will know where and when, on average, their favorite quarry can be found and in what numbers. Knowing the schedule, which is actually fairly consistent, and detailed current information on weather and migration forecasts to narrow that average window, our hunter has a pretty good scouting report.

Just to make you aware of the marvelous things to come in the next chapter, those regions are migratory and wintering areas, and what, where, and when, on average, all species will be there. You can do some back-of-the-envelope computations and know the timing, on average, of the max surge across that region.

Arctic Region (Alaska; Yukon; Northwest Territories; Nunavut; Quebec; Labrador)

By the first week of September, movement is already starting across Western Alaska, Canadian Arctic Coast and Islands, and adjacent Tundra Interior. Most waterfowl have cleared out of the Arctic by early October. This wide region crosses the top of the North American continent. Works out to include parts of one state and six providences.

The Arctic Region as we've defined it includes the far northern parts of the Arctic Coasts, Islands, and adjacent tundra-covered area extending into the interior. Waterfowl return to the arctic habitat late in May and have to get out of there by mid-September. Geese and ducks are on a tight schedule to nest and hatch and protect the young through the hatchling phase. During this time, they undergo molt for a complete change of feathers, which leaves them flightless through the same time that the young are developing their first feathers. And all the while, goose and duck parents must obtain enough nutrition to overcome depletion from the exertion. Rations are short upon arrival just as the snow clears and the frozen ground thaws to form a water-logged flat that may extend for a swath hundreds of miles across. The arctic vegetation explodes as the long days of summer pass. Geese feed on fields of cotton-grasses, heathers, and other tundra plants in what's referred to as sedge meadows in a direct analogue to the sprouting grains they'll feed on the way back next spring.

There's a certain homogeneity to the Arctic. Another pattern is that, with the exception of Nunavut, the Canadian provinces that include tundra on their north have warmer regions with the same systems of agricultural enter-prises to their south. Feeding patterns on sedge meadows resemble those on grain fields. Only difference is that the waste grain has a much higher nutri-tional value. Off the scale compared with the buffalo grasses they've had to make do with for the last ten thousand years or so.

Hunting seasons across this region open with an unbelievable number of species. But the numbers of waterfowl hunters to match aren't out there. It's easy to understand why. Regardless of when the official hunting season closes, if you're not out there at the right time, all of those birds in flight have headed south before the arctic winter breaks. And getting out there comes with a very high cost in money and time, both limited commodities for practically all of us. And, despite the masses of waterfowl all around, you're only allowed a small bag limit. Indigenous residents get a break with higher limits because the waterfowl are essential subsistence for them rather than game.

Odds of a successful hunt/adventure are better if you look for the sea ducks that winter in the saltwater of the arctic and near arctic.

The springtime light geese season is better for most hunters. Bag limits are very high, and it's probably more likely that the weather breaks warm rather than arctic blizzard. That's probably, not absolutely.

Lesser snow goose populations have left their breeding areas by late August to early September to gather. The total population to leave the nesting areas is estimated to be around six million, up from around two million forty years ago. The Alaskan population gathers and will head first to the South coast of Alaska, then taking either a shortcut across the Pacific to the Columbia Basin, then down the Pacific flyway to Oregon or California, or, along the Alaskan coast to Puget Sound of Washington during October. The Pacific population of around 1.35 million, breeds along the western Arctic Coast, West Coast, and interior Alaska. They will migrate along the Pacific coast to the Central Valleys of California to winter beginning in late October through November.

The Western Canada Arctic Coast snow goose population of about 450,000 is centered on the Mackenzie Delta. Part of this population gathers and heads down the eastern side of the Rockies to the gathering areas of northern and central Alberta, then south to southwest Alberta and on to Freezeout Lake, Montana. Then some will fly southwest to join the Pacific population in the Central Valleys of California for the winter. The rest leave the Mackenzie to the southeast and mix with part of the population from the area around Victoria Island in the large gathering areas of northern Alberta. The migration peak through the Boreal Forest of western Canada is late September. These geese of the combined Mackenzie Delta and Victoria Island populations move south to large gathering areas in southeast Alberta and southwest Saskatchewan in late October. The combined flocks go straight south to even larger gathering areas in the Prairie Pothole Region and prepare for the long trip along the west side of the Central Plains, the east side of the Intermountain Region, and across Texas to the lower Gulf Coast and the east coast of Mexico.

The majority of this migration are supplied from the population, around 1.5 million, from Victoria Island and adjacent Arctic Coast Region of Canada. This population splits, part southwest to the gathering areas of northern Alberta mentioned above, part to the southeast. About 2.4 million travel into the Boreal Forest Region for a stopover in large gathering areas along the western and southwestern side of Hudson Bay. From this gathering area, next stops are in two directions: southeast to James Bay; or, to the southwest from southwestern Hudson Bay over Ontario, and either the large gathering area in Manitoba just north of Devils Lake, northeastern North Dakota, in the Prairie Pothole Region, or into the Great Plains to the upper reaches of the Missouri River. One route south as previously noted is on a slight westerly bearing south to the lower Texas Gulf into November. Another route with a slight easterly bearing passes to northeast Missouri on the way to Louisiana and east Texas. Surge occurs from mid-September into early October.

The huge gathering areas around James Bay in the northern edge of the Boreal Forest Region, collect from breeding populations along the west side of Hudson Bay and those passing through from the central Arctic, Arctic islands, and Baffin, amount to 1.2 million. About 2.6 million congregate in Banks and more directly from the south side of Baffin.

The very large, eastern arctic lesser snow geese population numbering about 4.2 million, has a migration surge from Baffin Island in mid- to late September. Large numbers flock over the southeast Hudson Bay and James Bay by mid-September. A major route south for this gathered population from James Bay passes through corridors across Michigan and Wisconsin general south over Illinois early October, and straight south nonstop to the Louisiana coast generally along or just east of the Lower Mississippi Region beginning in October and surging in November.

Most passages of the lesser snow goose are along the same routes south in the fall and north in the spring. A straight shot route south from James Bay across Illinois and to the Mississippi Gulf coast is an exception to the pattern. The return of the bulk of this population goes back through the agricultural areas of the Great Plains Region in the spring feeding along the way. They combine with geese in that area to create a surge of about three million moving north as the snow clears. They then journey back to James Bay. Over four million return to eastern nesting areas.

The Greater Snow goose, population estimated at 250,000, nests in a small area of northernmost Arctic Islands and northern Greenland. Departure from nesting grounds takes place at the end of August and early September. There is a stopover to gather on the St. Lawrence River at the end of September an early October. Some head south over the next month. All leave the St. Lawrence at freeze-up at the end of November. Many stop for a while on Delaware Bay before moving on to wintering grounds toward the coast of North Carolina and Back Bay Virginia.

Migrations of a large part of the total Canada goose population begin in the Arctic. Several more originate to the south in the Boreal Forest. A significant number are all-year residents that winter along the eastern US states. Migration begins with gathering and first departures of populations across the northern coasts of Alaska and Canada, around Hudson Bay and northern Labrador just before and around the first of September. By late September, movement has rolled into an extended surge across the Boreal Forest Region. Arrivals have begun across southern Canada and the northern US by the first of October, and continue to ramp until late in the month as populations begin to settle into northern wintering areas. During November, mid-continent wintering areas fill Northern California, the Texas panhandle, and the Midwest. By early December, Canadas in peak numbers settle into the southernmost wintering areas of southern California, the Lower Texas coast, and northern parts of states across the south bordering the Gulf.

To review, all Canada geese belong to a distinct population which nests, migrates, and winters in the same general locations year after year. This in complete opposition to some of the duck species that may end up in a wintering location a thousand miles from where they were last year. The geese know how to keep themselves in the same easily designated population. True to their form, over the next sections, we'll designate populations in a way that will remain constant, the structure that the geese use: where they nest, where they winter, and the route(s) they take along the way. Within this framework, each of these identifiers is somewhat fuzzy in terms of human precision. Nesting and wintering areas are distributed loosely along either end of the routes. Migration flights are smaller relative to the multiple thousands of the snows, and spread out as to timing.

Our populations are presented generally east to west. The population distributed long the northern Atlantic coast nests along the coast of Labrador, the north shore of the St. Lawrence, and Newfoundland is estimated from various sources with some extrapolations to be around seventy thousand. It's composed of Atlantic Canada subspecies. Migration is down the coast of Labrador through the Canadian Maritimes; along the coast of New England over Long Island; south along the Jersey shore, coastal Maryland, and into North Carolina. Wintering is spread along the southern part of the migration beginning thinly in Newfoundland and distributed in more significant numbers in the Maritimes and on to the south, tapering off into South Carolina.

The large Canada population of 1.2 million that nests in the tundra of the Ungava Peninsula and the adjacent Boreal Forest to the south is composed primarily of interior Canada subspecies with some Atlantics along the eastern reaches. Corridors of migration run along the eastern shore of Hudson Bay, south through central New York and eastern Pennsylvania to the eastern shores of Maryland, Virginia, and northeastern North Carolina. Wintering extends along the New England and mid-Atlantic coast and adjacent interior.

The next population to the west, estimated at one million interiors and 20,000 giants, nests on the southern shore of Hudson Bay, western shore of James Bay. Migration corridors pass along east and west side of Lake Michigan, around the east side of Lake Superior, and on to toward southern Illinois. Wintering occurs in Wisconsin, Illinois, Missouri, and along the Mississippi River valley to the northeast corner of Arkansas.

Adjacent to the west along the southwest corner of Hudson Bay is a population roughly estimated at 350,000 interior, and 60,000 giant Canada goose subspecies, referred to as magnum geese, or simply magnums down south.

For the interior population, this one migration corridor effectively covers its elongated range. It runs straight south passing the west side of Lake Superior and on to the south along the eastern prairies of our Great Plains Region to the lower Mississippi. Wintering is centered along north-central Missouri and extends sparsely to the Gulf. The migration thins as it mingles with other populations during wintering, but it sorts itself out as it reassembles on the way back north in the spring to its nesting area. Considerable numbers of giant Canada geese are to be found in eastern Oklahoma. High numbers of this subspecies in the area is a relatively recent development.

A giant Canada population nests in the Interlake district of Manitoba with a very short migration to near Rochester, Minnesota.

Moving west to the next relatively small population of around 100,000 interior Canada subspecies often combined with other populations of game management. Nesting is in the area of lakes of northern Manitoba and Saskatchewan. Migration is along the western prairies south into the Missouri River valley of the Dakotas and down the Missouri, then on south to North Central Texas. Wintering is along the migration route, heavy in southeast South Dakota, then very lightly south to Texas.

A large population of predominately lesser Canada subspecies to the west composed of a very roughly estimated number widely either side of one million ranges along the eastern Great Plains, sometimes referred to as the Tall Grass Prairies. Numbers are hard to pin down due to the many man-made waters used by migrating and wintering geese. The north end of this, the longest migration of Canada geese, is across the arctic coast west from Hudson Bay including eastern arctic islands. Most of the migration travels south across Manitoba through Devil's Lake, then goes south toward Oklahoma, where significant numbers start to drop off and winter. Most keep on south over North Central Texas toward the vicinity of Houston. Some drop out along the way around the lower Gulf coast until a few reach northeast Mexico.

Another long migration range of a half million lesser Canada subspecies lies across the western Canadian arctic coast to the Mackenzie Delta including Victoria Island. It extends south across Saskatchewan and Alberta toward the dry western Great Plains. Extensive gathering takes place in the southeast corner of Alberta, and southwest corner of Saskatchewan. These dry plains are often referred to as the Shortgrass prairie. It terminates in wintering grounds of western Nebraska, eastern Colorado, and the panhandle of Texas.

A relatively short migration range populated by an estimated 300,000 western Canada and a few giant Canada subspecies merges with the short-grass population along the High Plains adjacent the eastern of the Rocky Mountains, then pulls away to the west across New Mexico. Wintering area runs from the North Platte, southeast Wyoming, northeast Colorado, and on south through New Mexico.

The Intermountain west is populated by the western Canada goose sub-species population and is estimated roughly at 300,000. The area includes marshes and streams across the west from British Columbia to Alberta, with breeding along the Columbia, Snake, and Green Rivers, the marshes of the Great Salt Lake, and northern California. Migration is in small flocks gener-ally to the south, and usually not far. In the northwest, from the Columbia Basin to the Central Valley of California, and from the Snake River to Nevada and otherwise scattered broadly across the west to warmer locations.

The northwest coast population estimated as 400,000 is composed of Dusky and Vancouver Canada goose subspecies. Range of this popula-tion ranges narrowly along the Pacific coast from southeast Alaska south to Oregon. Breeding is along southeast coast of Alaska to British Columbia. Most of the dusky population migrates across the Gulf of Alaska, a few to Queen Charlotte and Vancouver islands, most to southwest Washington, then up the Columbia and south to winter in the Willamette Valley. Most of the Vancouver subspecies does not migrate.

Alaskan population of clacking goose species (formally subspecies of the Canada goose), lesser and Taverner's Canada subspecies is estimated at 700,000. Range is over Alaska and broadly south along the northwest Pacific coast and interior, narrowing into northeast Oregon and Central Valley of California. Around 400,000 cackling geese nest in the Yukon Delta and 300,000 Tavernier's in the interior. Migration of the entire population of cackling geese is across the Gulf of Alaska to the Columbia River and on to wintering grounds in the Central Valley of California. Taverner's mingle with brant and cross the Pacific to Skagit Bay of northwest Washington and on to the Columbia Basin to winter.

The tundra swan (whistling swan) nests along the Western coast of Alaska, Canadian Arctic coast, and islands. Begin to leave breeding grounds late September early October. First movement is West Alaskan coast population to the east along the Arctic Coast. Overall migration pattern is primarily toward the Atlantic Coast. One small population moves down the Pacific coast and another from the western Artic Coast down across Canada toward the Great Salt Lake.

The white-fronted goose (speckled-belly) nesting areas are in scattered concentrations across the central and western Arctic coast of Canada, and throughout Alaska. These geese make early departures and long migration flights. The Arctic Coast populations, around 800,000, are beginning to arrive in staging areas of Alberta and Saskatchewan by late August surging through in late September and peaking early October on their way down the Central Flyway on their way to the coast of Texas and areas in interior Mexico. They will surge through North Dakota in early October and across Texas later in October. Most will be in Mexico November through January.

Beginning in early September, the western Alaskan population of about 700,000 takes a shortcut across the Pacific to Washington state and then on to the west coast of Mexico. The main surge is throughout September. Migration surge through the Central Valley of California is during October.

The Atlantic brant nests in the Arctic in breeding grounds on Greenland's northern coast and several islands of Canada. Migration is across eastern Canada. Part of the population winters in England, part in the US. The population that migrates to the south in the US, estimated at 500,000, uses James Bay as a staging area, then winters along the New England and upper Atlantic Coast. All populations leave their breeding areas in late summer. The Greenland population departs September through October. The population going to the eastern coast of the US gathers from across the arctic into James Bay in October. They surge into Chesapeake Bay in November.

The black brant western population, roughly estimated at 300,000, nests in the western Arctic and into Siberia. They winter along the southern US coast and the Baha Peninsula of Mexico. The easterly population nests with the Atlantic Brant on the Arctic Islands, and Eastern Artic and migrates west past the Yukon Delta and on to the west around Alaska, along a western corridor around the Yukon River Delta. Migration is southeast across the Pacific to Baha. The birds gather on Izembek Bay in September, surge from Izenter Bay in early November, and surge on down the coast December through January.

Ducks of the Arctic Coast and adjacent tundra begin their move to the south in late August or early September.

Most of the long-tailed duck population starts moving out from their nesting areas along the Arctic Coast and tundra east of Hudson Bay in early September. At the same time, smaller populations to the east along the west coast of Greenland start south. Many in the western range scattered across Alaska and eastern Siberia, population estimated at 700,000, move along the Pacific coast throughout October. Most of the large eastern population, estimated at over one million, moves to the southeast overland and around the shores of Hudson Bay through October. Many will winter on the Great Lakes, many more move on overland to the upper and middle Atlantic Coast. The peak of migration is in mid-November.

Breeding of the common eider is on the northern coasts of Siberia, Alaska, the Canadian Arctic coast and islands and Hudson Bay, and the coasts of Greenland. Drakes are on the move from July, but the main surge of migration is in September and October as hens and juveniles move out. Some, estimated at 100,000, travel around the northern and western coasts to the southern coast of Alaska for the winter. The eastern population, which varies widely but has been estimated at two million at one time, travels east along the coast of Labrador and the northern Atlantic states. Surge of migration for most of the eastern Canadian population is into December. The west coast of Greenland population simply moves offshore for the winter.

King eiders nest around the Arctic Coast, islands, and Greenland, and winter from the Northern Pacific coast to Pudget Sound at sea along the coast. Western population has been estimated at one million. Eastern Canada and Maritime and New England coast, the Gulf of St. Lawrence, and off the coast of Labrador population is estimated at 200,000. They migrate in long lines a few feet above the water and go around points in a long procession. Flights can number between 10 and 10,000, usually 25 to 1,000. Drakes start south during summer with a layover for the molt along the way. Hens move from nesting area at the end of August into early September and arrive in wintering area in October. Eiders feed on mollusks and crustaceans.

The pintails have a very extensive breeding area and an even more expansive wintering range. By September, pintails are on the move across North America. The surge to the south increases broadly through October and November.

A significant population, on the order of one million, breeds across the western Arctic coasts of Canada, Alaska, and Siberia. During September, the most westerly nesters in Alaska migrate either straight across the Pacific to California, or along the Pacific coastline. Those from the western Canadian arctic and Boreal Forest migrate to the western portion of the Prairie Pothole Region and congregate with the bulk of the total population already there.

Nesting of greater scaup is concentrated in several locations spaced around the western Arctic of Canada and the western coast of Alaska and the Aleutian Islands. Total population is estimated at 500,000. Migration corridors are long across the continent of North America to the Atlantic Coast. Wintering destination of a small part of the migration, estimated at around 100,000, is along the northwest Pacific coast of the US. Destinations of the long east-west migrations are dense, estimated at over 300,000, along the northern Atlantic and the Northeastern US coasts. Corridors of smaller migrations, around 100,000, run the length of the Mississippi to the Gulf Coast and spread along the Texas coast. A few turn off of the main east-west corridors and go straight to the west coast of Florida.

Lesser scaup ducks use extensive breeding areas across the tundra and open Boreal Forests of the Northwest Territories and Alaska. Less concentrated areas stretch through the Boreal forests and northern prairies of Central Canada. Total population is around five million. Departures from far northern areas begin in early September and is finished by the end of the month. Most of the population, three million, migrate through or from southeast Saskatchewan southeast through October, then along the lower Mississippi to the Gulf Coasts of Louisiana and eastern Texas. Some will go on over the

Gulf to Central America. The next largest population of 1.5 million goes southeast to the Atlantic coast, then a large part will move south toward Florida. Most have surged into wintering areas through November. An estimated half million migrate south and winter along the Pacific coasts of the US, Mexico, and Central America.

The American wigeon is scattered across the Arctic with concentrations in the western deltas, about a million total.

Green-winged teal nest in scattered concentrations across the Alaskan and northwestern Canadian Arctic.

Nesting of the bufflehead is in tree cavities of the parklands and timber along the Boreal Forest concentrated primarily north of the prairies of south central Canada. There are smaller concentrations in interior Alaska and along the mountain ranges of western Canada. The short western migration drops through the Intermountain Region to the south and west along the Pacific coast and the west coasts of Baha and southern Mexico. The longer migration is to the east and southern wintering areas along the New England coast, and middle and southern Atlantic Coast, and the Gulf costs across the south. Between the east and west migrations, a central corridor runs straight south to the lower coast of Texas and interior Mexico. The main migration surge from nesting areas is during November. Arrivals in far southern wintering areas is through December.

The harlequin duck has populations on both sides of North America. The western part of the total population is much larger than the east. The eastern population breeds on the west coast of Greenland, Iceland, and the northern east coast of Canada. Migration for the most part is a lateral move to adjacent offshore feeding grounds during the winter. Some of the eastern population moves south from Labrador along the coastline to eastern Canada and the Northeastern US.

Distribution of the western population is from the west coast of Alaska to northern California. Nesting is through interior mountain ranges adjacent the cost. Wintering areas have some longshore migration. Notable is the concentration along the Aleutian Island chain. Migration begins in late September.

Boreal Forest Region (Alaska; Yukon; Northwest Territories; Alberta; Saskatchewan; Manitoba; Ontario; Quebec; Labrador)

Waterfowl hunting becomes a better proposition as we move a little farther south. The backdrop of the hunt is nice. Countless small waters interspersed through the forests, the big lakes that form the Great String of Pearls across western Canada, the shores of the Hudson and Prince James Bays, and on into the upper Great Lakes.

The Boreal Region is considered as primarily a nesting ground. Most of the sea duck populations nest widely across the region, then make long migrations to Atlantic, Pacific, and Great Lakes coastlines for the winter. Extensions of dabbler populations centered to the South also nest across the Boreal from the Atlantic to the Pacific and western Arctic. But the region is also a migration region for populations of primarily geese but also ducks that nest in the

Glacier-formed lake in Boreal Forest.

Arctic. Some long migrating dabblers nest far to the north across the tundra and move south in early fall to gather with those of their kind that have nested to the south.

A large area in the far northwestern corner of Alberta in the western Boreal Forest Region is a prairie. This is the Pease River country, and it's particularly important. Most of the considerable area of this prairie in the forest has been developed into grain farms. Very large populations of several species of geese and ducks stop in the Peace River Country of northern Alberta late September into October, and feed on waste grain.

The fall harvest, which comes early this far north, coincides with the arrivals of geese and ducks nesting in the central arctic of Canada. This is the first great gathering area of the season. The rich grain subsistence literally rescues populations of waterfowl depleted from nesting and protecting hatchlings on short rations from the sparse vegetation of the arctic shores, followed by the arduous migration back across the Boreal. Waterfowl hunters also have a bonanza of hunting opportunities shared with few hunters in the field from the light local agricultural-based population.

Nature of the Total Experience is the Wilderness Experience with Hot Spots that Come and Go with the Migration

Depleted lesser snow geese from the western Arctic coast have crossed tundra and forest to gather in concentrations adjacent to the high quality agricultural feed. Numbers across the prairies and parklands of the western Boreal peak around mid-October before departures to the south pick up. Hunters to the south can look for them as they clear freeze-up early November and come their way.

The Arctic Coast's white-fronted goose populations are beginning to arrive in all staging areas of Alberta and Saskatchewan by late August, surging through in late September and peaking early October.

Canada and giant Canada geese from the southwest corner of Hudson Bay pass through the Boreal Forest along its one migration corridor. The migration route predictably runs straight south passing the west side of Lake Superior and on to the south along the eastern prairies of the Great Plains

Region to the lower Mississippi. Hunters on their route to the south as far as Oklahoma will be on the lookout for reports of their progress.

Some long migrating dabblers, notably pintails, mallards, and green-winged teal nest in the tundra in the western north south in early fall to gather with those of their kind that have nested to the south. Most of a population of close to one million wigeon come across the Peace River Country.

Nesting of blue-winged teal is rather tightly centered on the Prairie Pothole Region with some extension northward into parklands and with lower density on into the Boreal Forest. Total population is around seven million. Blue-wings migrate in a long, very dispersed, continental-wide pattern. The densest corridor of migration is between the Central Prairies and the East Texas/Louisiana coast. Not far behind is the next major corridor to the east, which crosses Florida on the way to South America. Far destinations are the Pacific coast of southern Mexico, Central America, and South America.

Departures from nesting areas are late September through early November. Movement across all regions toward the south and west surges during October. Long-range migration to Central America and beyond continues through November.

Nesting area of the common goldeneye is tree cavities densely across the eastern and parklands of the central Canadian Boreal Forest, and sparsely into interior Alaska and widely scattered across the northern US. Population estimates are around one million based on difficult terrain conditions for data. Wintering is along and offshore of the Canadian west coast and the Alaskan southern coast with a few observations along all coasts of North America. Movement to wintering grounds begins to pick up during October and surges just before freeze-up.

The western population of Barrow's goldeneye nests in the mountains of interior Alaska, western Canada, and the Intermountain ranges of the western US as far south as northern California and Wyoming. Best estimates of difficult to obtain population numbers is around 150,000. Wintering is along and offshore of southern Alaska, western Canada, and as far south as central California and in open water of Intermountain areas adjacent nesting areas. Fall migration is late October, early November.

The eastern population nests in Iceland, Greenland, and shores of Eastern Canada. Wintering is, to some extent, offshore nesting locations, but largely along the shores of Maritime Canada and New England. Migration is late fall into December and later.

Range of the black duck is the eastern half of North America. Our very rough estimates based on rate of decline in the past is around 500,000. Nesting and wintering areas have considerate overlap. Northern nesting range is widely distributed across the Eastern Canada and the eastern Boreal Forest Regions from the coast of Labrador around the south of Hudson Bay. Highest Canadian concentrations are forests around the Great Lakes and Canada Maritime Regions. Nesting continues to the south to include concentrations in marshes around Chesapeake Bay area and with more widely distribution to the west. There has been encroachment on their range from the west by Mallard populations. Mixed breeding where the two co-mingle has diminished the black duck population from the west. True, full-blood black duck populations have been pushed to the east.

Wintering area extends from the Great Lakes and Northeastern US Regions along the Atlantic Coast to the Gulf Coast. Most dense is the coast of Northeastern US coast. Somewhat less around the eastern Great Lakes. A small migration down the Lower Mississippi Region and the Gulf Coast which has been diminished because of a shrinking range.

Migrations are short and leisurely. Movement into the Northeast from Canada runs through October. They're still drifting into states along the southern Atlantic coast through November and December.

The black scoter eastern population nests in the tundra and open forest south and east of Hudson Bay. Best estimates of population is around 500,000. Migration consists of a short hop over to the Atlantic Coast in late fall and on to the south. The West Coast population breeds inland from the western coast of Alaska. Migration is south along the Pacific Coast to southern California. Migration begins slowly in September and builds along the coasts through December.

The white-winged scoter breeding range is broadly across the western Boreal forest along inland lakes and rivers. Best estimates of population are roughly 600,000. Wintering area for the western population is along the Pacific coast which adjoins the breeding area in western Canada and extends from the south coast of Alaskan all the way to Mexico. The eastern population migrates overland to the east and winters along the full length of the Atlantic coastline.

The surf scoter breeding area is Boreal Forest in western Canada east toward Hudson Bay and eastward through the open Boreal to the Atlantic. Best estimates of population are around 300,000. Most migrate to the Pacific coast and spread from southern Alaska to Baha during September through December. Some of the central population migrates to the east and gathers from October on James Bay, then on to the Atlantic coast to join the small breeding population from east of Hudson Bay to cover the entire coastline by December.

The ring-necked duck Boreal Forest population is thinly scattered across this region. They migrate south to join the Prairie population in September.

The common merganser nests across most of the Boreal Forest with extensions south around the Great Lakes, New England, the Intermountain West, and upper Pacific Coast. Population estimates are around 650,000. They winter across the United States with an extension into the interior of Mexico. Migration out of Canada is delayed until just before freeze-up. Arrival along the Atlantic coast, Great Lakes, across the Great Plains, Intermountain West, and the Pacific coastline is late November.

Nesting of the hooded merganser is spaced widely across Canada with concentrations around the Great Lakes and northern Canadian Pacific Coast. Population estimates are around 70,000. Nesting area is around the Great Lakes. They winter thinly dispersed. Wintering areas are along the Pacific, Atlantic, and Gulf Coasts and adjacent areas inland. Arrives across northern states through November; arrive on wintering grounds through December.

The red-breasted merganser nests broadly across the entire Boreal Forest, venturing into the Arctic in the west. Population is estimated to be around 240,000. In the west, it winters along the Pacific coast of Canada, US, and into northern Mexico. In the east, it winters on the Great Lakes, and coasts of Northeastern United States and south along the Atlantic and Gulf Coast.

Migration arrives along Atlantic Coast through November, to the south and around the Gulf Coast into December.

Pintails move across the Boreal Forest through September and have moved on to the south well before cold weather arrives. The Artic population joins with those that nested in the western part of the Boreal, about two million at this point, and on to the south. Those of the thinly distributed nesting areas to the east move south across the eastern Boreal, south along the Great Lakes and New England coast or the interior of the eastern US.

The American widgeon and green-winged teal nest thinly across this region, and leave early to join their much larger populations in the Prairie Pothole Region.

Greater scaup migrate in small numbers across the Boreal toward the Lower Mississippi, Gulf Coast, and Texas Regions. Lesser scaup have limited nesting areas in the Boreal Forest. Most of the population migrates through or from southeast Saskatchewan, southeast through October.

Prairie Pothole Region (North Dakota; South Dakota; Saskatchewan; Manitoba; Alberta)

This region is considered to be a nesting area with dense populations of dabblers and freshwater divers. It's also a migration area in that large populations of geese and ducks from across western and central Canada past through.

Very large populations of several species of geese and ducks stop across southern Alberta and Saskatchewan, in late September into October, and feed on waste grain. Geese gather in particular gathering areas. Staging areas of southeastern Alberta and Saskatchewan are active by late August surging through in late September and early October on their way down the Central and Mississippi Flyways crossing North and South Dakota by early October. Large populations also pass through western Alberta and south through the Intermountain Region, then, for many, the Pacific Coast. Most action occurs late September through October as the migration moves through in the heaviest surge of the North American migration.

The western Arctic Region populations of lesser snow geese of have entered the grain producing Peace River country famished and come to the

Flooded soybean field. Typical of glacier-formed depressions in fields.

Prairie Pothole Region fat after feeding their way down through Alberta and Saskatchewan. Passage peaks around mid-October. This is the first encounter of young birds with hunters in numbers. One of the factors that make this region a popular destination for goose hunters.

The Arctic Coast white-fronted goose populations are beginning to arrive in all staging areas of southern Alberta and Saskatchewan, surging through late September and peaking early October.

The Canada goose interior population that nests along the southwest corner of Hudson Bay comes over the region along its one migration corridor.

Waste wheat grains distributed over one to two square inches. Geese pick up a lot of feed with little walking.

The mallard has the largest population, twelve million, and widest breeding range of any duck. Mallards are the most abundant duck around the

Geese on harvested wheat field.

Waste corn after harvest. This image illustrates typical waste grain, in this case corn. Trash thrown out by the combine covers much more feed than can be seen. Careful sifting through a series of spots indicated a kernel of corn about every two inches and complete ears of corn about three feet apart.

globe, and their greatest concentration is the middle of North America. As opposed to the distinct breeding areas of the snow geese, mallards use widely dispersed breeding areas across North America. Their greatest breeding concentration is the Prairie Pothole Region across the Prairie Providences of central Canada and spreads in all directions with decreasing density across Canada and the northern United States. Their migration is to the south of wherever they have nested toward the nearest, highest quality and most abundant feed. That has evolved toward agricultural areas where they linger along migration corridors along the Central and Mississippi Flyways as long as the feed holds out and the temperature isn't low enough for freeze up. Flooded rice fields of the deltas along the Lower Mississippi are the final destination for many. Texas and southern Louisiana are terminal destinations unless the winter is unusually warm, and many linger to the north. Joining the populations of western Canada and Alaska, some of the population on the western side of the prairies drop over into the Pacific Flyway toward Central Valleys of the West. The widely-dispersed populations of eastern Canada leisurely move south to the Chesapeake Bay area and along the southern Atlantic Coast.

The most concentrated nesting area is the northern central prairies of North America. The concentration decreases away from this area, but nesting of mallards extends to the south across the northern US states, and to the north across Alaska and all of Canada. Migration can be summarized as toward the south from wherever mallards have nested, and characterized as late. Mallards will linger in the north as long as food is available and the waters are open. Deep snow cover and only freeze up will move them on down the line. Greatest surge of migration is from the greatest density of nesting, which would be southern Saskatchewan, Alberta, and Manitoba. Major corridors to the southeast out of this area are down the upper Mississippi and along the Missouri; to the southwest toward the Columbia Basin of Washington and Oregon and to the south along the Snake to eastern Idaho, Central Valley of California, and on to Mexico.

Schedule of migration is for the Canadian population to clear the northern providences through October and by mid-November they've gone south to join the US population. Mallard migration is usually pushed out of the north by weather through October. On to wintering grounds into November and December.

The wintering region with the largest population of Mallards, six million, is along the Mississippi Flyway in the Upper and Lower Mississippi Regions along the Mississippi Delta through Iowa, Illinois, Kansas, Missouri, Arkansas, and Mississippi into southern Louisiana and the Gulf coastal marshes. Some hold out in the Great Plains of the Midwest. Another large population, three million, or more move south along the Central Flyway through Colorado, Kansas, Nebraska, East Texas, the Gulf Coast, and the Texas Panhandle. Significant numbers migrate westward across the Intermountain Region to winter in the Columbia Basin of Eastern Washington, almost one million, and, along the Snake River of southern Idaho about .6 million, and in the Central and Imperial Valleys of California about .7 million, and the western coast of Canada. A relatively small population, .5 million, migrates along the Atlantic Flyway to winter in the Chesapeake Bay and down the coast to South Carolina. And finally, there are wintering mallards to be found scattered across North America in between all of the places cited above.

The densest breeding grounds of the northern pintail is the Prairie Pothole Region. Total population is three million, drastically lower than the six million counted forty years ago. Breeding ranges are: Arctic Alaska and Canada along major river deltas, with a population of about 500,000; subarctic with a population of about 50,000; mixed prairie region of Saskatchewan, Alberta, North Dakota, South Dakota, Manitoba, with a population of about 800,000; parklands of the Boreal Forest, with a population of about 400,000; shortgrass prairies, with a population of about 400,000; Boreal Forest, with a population of about 400,000; Salt Lake and other areas of the west, with a population of about 800,000. Migration of the bulk of the population either originates here or passes through from regions to the north. Western Alaska population migrates along a corridor over the Pacific to Pudget Sound. Another corridor leads from the Alaskan Peninsula along the Pacific Coast to northern California. Most part of the western arctic population migrates from the Prairie Pothole Region across the Intermountain Region to the valleys of California. Some will winter there, while some will continue south to the western coast of Mexico.

The rest migrate from the Prairie Pothole to the Lower Mississippi, the Gulf Coast of Texas, the Texas Panhandle, and the east coast of Mexico. A significant number go on to the interior of Mexico and down the coasts of Central America. The rest of the Prairie Pothole Region population and the thinly spread population of eastern Canada go to the southern Atlantic coast, and some will move on to the Caribbean Islands.

Northern Pintail wintering areas: total California, 1.8 million; the Texas coast and Panhandle, with a population of about 700,000; Mississippi, with a population of about 400,000; and the Atlantic Flyway, with a population of about 100,000.

Nesting area of the gadwall is concentrated in the Prairie Pothole Region of the northern Great Plains and extends sparsely to the north over western

Pothole in soybeans with cover on edges. A little drama on a northeast South Dakota pothole. Illustration of how effective cover can be in the "duck factory" during nesting and the molt. South Dakota pothole in soybean field with a few ducks on the water. Then a few get nervous and the rest come out of the cover.

Lots of ducks in that cover. And suddenly the sky is filled with ducks. And you're jumping out your hide. Feed and cover in vegetation around the edge of a glacier-formed pothole surrounded by a soybean field. Cover away from water's edge for nesting and the molt.

Canada. Total population is four million, up from 1.4 million from forty years ago. Breeding ranges and populations are: mixed prairies and prairie ponds, with a population of about two million; parklands of Alberta and Manitoba, one million; shortgrass plains of Minnesota to Montana, with a population of about 400,000; sandhills of Nebraska, and marshes of western states, Salt Lake, marshes of states of the West Coast, with a population of about 175,000. The migration south across the Great Plains begins in September. The birds are out of the Dakotas and Minnesota by the end of October and moving through Michigan, Wisconsin, Iowa, and Illinois, with some lingering until late November. Some of the population moves west through the Intermountain Region and on to the interior valleys of California and the west coast of Mexico. Many move from the Great Plains to the east across the Mississippi and on toward the Atlantic Coast arriving in Chesapeake Bay during October. Heaviest concentration of migration goes south toward the Texas, Louisiana, and Mexico Gulf Coast, arriving during November. A large segment of the population moving along this corridor winters along the way in Texas. Another corridor goes south along the Lower Mississippi then along the coast to the central and eastern Gulf States, arriving throughout November. Some migrate to the southeast to South Carolina and Florida, others travel the Gulf Coast of the US to coasts of Central America.

Wintering areas: few on Atlantic Flyway, with a population of about 200,000, primarily South Carolina; very few along West Coast; three million of the population goes to Louisiana; Texas, with a population of about 700,000.

The American wigeon, total population of three and a half million, nests from the Arctic to the northern states. The northernmost high density nesting area is the western deltas where the great rivers of northwest Canada empty into the Arctic, with a population of about .2 million; with a population of about .9 million in all of the Northwest Territories; with a population of about .3 million in Alaska. They nest in wide distribution across the western Boreal and parklands, with a population of about .7 million, and in their highest concentration in the Prairie Pothole Region, at .9 million. Migration out of the northwest arctic and Boreal begins in late August through September. Relatively small populations migrate from Alaska along the Pacific Coast and Central Valleys of California. Another breeding area is the Northern US, with .4 million. The greatest migration is from the Prairie Pothole Region as populations from the north join those that nesting the region. Migration surges onto the Northern Plains in early September through October. Some of the population, about 1.3 million, migrates from the western area of the Great Plains through northern Intermountain Region to the Columbia and Snake Basins, California valleys and Mexico, but most move to the south and southeast across the Great Plains through October. Arrivals into wintering areas surge during November into the Texas panhandle and Gulf Coast with a population of about one million, and marshes of the Lower Mississippi and

Louisiana coast, with a population of about one million. Some will go on to Central America. A part of the migration out of the northern Central Plains goes east to winter along the Atlantic coast and Florida, with a population of about .2 million.

Green-winged teal nest over a very large area. They breed in concentrated areas over Alaska and on the deltas where large rivers of northwest Canada empty into the Arctic Ocean; across the western Boreal Forest; and a large part of the northern Great Plains and Western Intermountain Region. The highest concentrations is in the Prairie Pothole and adjacent parklands of the Boreal. Total population is around five million. More than half migrate through or from northwest Canada and the prairies to the south-southeast to the western Gulf Coasts of Louisiana, Texas, and interior and coast of Mexico. Most of the rest migrate to the Pacific Coast either directly or through the marshes of the Great Salt Lake. They'll winter along the Pacific coasts of the US and Mexico. A very few migrate east to the Atlantic Coast.

Migration is protracted compared to other species, from first movement out of the far north in September through the end of the year until arrival of the flights that go all the way to southern Mexico and Central America. The greatest surge of migration is out of the Prairie Pothole Region when arrivals from the Boreal to the north combine with resident populations. A small population moves down the Pacific Coast from western Alaska beginning in September. Movement out of northwest Canada is September through October before freeze-up, usually in early November. Last of the population moves through the northern part of the Great Plains ahead of freeze-up which occurs there between mid-November and mid-December. Arrivals into the Texas Panhandle start in late September. By November into December most of the migration has reached the Texas Gulf Coast; by the end of December migration is to the east coast of Mexico and Central America.

Nesting of blue-winged teal is rather tightly centered on the Prairie Pothole Region with some extension northward into parklands and with lower density on into the Boreal Forest. Total population is around seven million. Blue-wings migrate in a long, very dispersed, continental-wide, pattern. The densest corridor of migration is between the Central Prairies and the East Texas/Louisiana coast. Not far behind is the next major corridor to the east, which crosses Florida on the way to South America. Far destinations are the Pacific Coast of southern Mexico, Central America, and South America.

Departures from nesting areas are late September through early November. Movement across all regions toward the south and west surges during October. Long range migration to Central America and beyond continues through November.

Greater scaup in small migrations cross this region on their way to the Gulf.

Lesser scaup prefer aquatic feed over grain, and tend to pass through this region.

The primary nesting area for the canvasback is the Prairie Pothole Region, but other smaller areas are dotted across the parklands of the western Boreal Forest and subarctic deltas of northwest Canada. Total population is currently around 750,000. About half of the population, 350,000, winters along the Atlantic coast. Around 200,000 migrate to the Pacific, the balance is distributed across the Gulf and interior Mexico. Decreases in populations over the last several decades have required restrictions in bag limits, usually one per day.

Largest migration is from the Prairie Pothole Region to the south and east. The densest begins to the east along corridors that diverge, then unite, one across the southern Great Lakes, and another that crosses the Upper Mississippi. Both end at Chesapeake Bay. Other routes diverge to the Gulf Coast along the Lower Mississippi or the east side of the Great Plains. Two routes run the length of the Great Plains from the Prairie Pothole to the south Texas coast or the deep interior of Mexico.

Timing of this migration into the northern Great Plains begins in September and surging into October. Across the Intermountain West through the Great Salt Lake through October and on into California during November. The eastern route to the Atlantic surges across the Mississippi and Great Lakes during October and into the Chesapeake through November and December. Some linger along the eastern edge of the Great Plains through October and November, then head down the Lower Mississippi before freeze-up during middle of December. Another corridor runs straight south arriving in lower Texas in November.

The redhead duck breeds in the Prairie Pothole country and marshes of Intermountain locations throughout the west. The greatest breeding concentrations are in marshes of the Great Salt Lake, and in less dense marshes scattered throughout the Northern Intermountain ranges. Lower densities extend north into the Boreal Forest. Total population of the redhead duck is around 1.3 million. About one million of these fowls have migration destinations along the Gulf Coast, with the greatest resting along the south Texas Coast and the Pacific Coast of Mexico. There is a significant migration to the east to Lake Erie and Lake St. Clair that turns south toward Florida and the mid-Atlantic. A few winter on the lower west of Mexico.

Redheads gather in their breeding areas in beginning of September and surging to a peak mid-October. They begin arriving in wintering areas in late October and peak in November.

Primary nesting range of the northern shoveler is the Prairie Pothole Region of the northern Great Plains sparsely extending north into the Boreal Forest. Total population is four million, up from around two million forty years ago. Breeding range with populations is the mixed prairies of Saskatchewan, Alberta, Manitoba, Dakotas, with a population of about two million; Parklands, with a population of about two million; shortgrass prairies, with a population of about two million; tallgrass prairies of Nebraska, with a population of about two million and intermountain marshes, with a population of about two million.

The population of the west side of the Prairie migrates, along two main corridors from Alberta, around two million to the southwest across the norther Intermountain Region, down through the interior valleys of California, and on down the west coast of Mexico. Toward the east, around two million migrate to the south along the Great Plains and Texas; to the southeast down the Lower Mississippi to the Gulf. A small part of the population migrates to the east, to the Atlantic coast. Migration begin in September and surges through October. Arrivals at wintering destination surge through November. Wintering areas for redheads are California Central Valleys and San Francisco Bay, as well as Louisiana coastal marshes.

The ring-necked duck breeds across the Central Boreal Forest and the Prairie Pothole Region of the Northern Plains. Total population after some severe ups and downs seem to have settled around 500,000, according to our best information. The birds begin moving south through the Dakotas and upper Mississippi in September and surge during mid-October. Migration of greatest numbers heads straight south toward the lower Mississippi and Texas/Louisiana Coasts, arriving through November and into December. Passage through the Central US is at its peak during October/November. A large number turns toward the southeast to Florida, arriving November. Fewer leave to head east to final destinations along the Atlantic Coasts with arrivals peaking during November. Much smaller numbers from the western edge of the breeding range head for the Central Valley of California arriving October through November. Largest wintering concentrations are the southeast Texas coast and Louisiana coast.

Moss bed feeding area at shallow edge of pothole. Typical of natural feeding areas across the Prairie Pothole Region.

Chapter 10

Hunting the Surge

The regions presented in this chapter are primarily migratory and wintering areas. Information is presented in the form of time and numbers, on average, of each species population that crosses each region. With some practice, it's easy to match the numbers and time to get the timing, on average, of the max surge across that region. You can also, in passing, note what species dominates the total numbers of the surge. Just in case there might be a preference to a lesser extent than that of the specialists still rereading the previous chapter.

GREAT PLAINS REGIONS (MONTANA, NORTH DAKOTA, SOUTH DAKOTA, WYOMING, COLORADO, NEBRASKA, KANSAS, OKLAHOMA, TEXAS)

This is a big region, elongated from north to south, with a significantly higher rainfall along the east side. The northern part is where the action occurs, as ducks and geese come down from Canada in October. The migration rolls over or lingers depending on the weather. Freeze-up in the northern tier of the states in this area, while it closes down hunting for some dabbler ducks which don't go further south until pushed, will sometimes be the trigger that brings better hunting to areas to the south. Freeze-up usually moves even the mallards out going into December in the north, but masses of waterfowl winter over in the southern part of this region.

Waterfowl habitat has been transformed by human enterprise. Stock ponds and irrigation infrastructure provide safe areas for resting and agricultural crops have been adapted as a primary source of nutrition.

The interior and giant Canada goose population resides from along the southwestern corner of Hudson Bay along the eastern prairies of the Great Plains Region to the lower Mississippi. Wintering is centered along north-central Missouri and extends sparsely to the Gulf. The migration thins as it mingles with other populations during wintering, but it sorts itself out as it reassembles on the way back north in the spring to its nesting area. The giant Canada element of the population appear in considerable numbers in eastern Oklahoma. High numbers of this subspecies in the area is a relatively recent development.

Moving west to the next relatively small population of around 100,000, interior Canada subspecies often combined with other populations of game management. Nesting is in the area of lakes of northern Manitoba and

Stock pond with ducks. Across the South and West, small waters are typically in place for irrigation or stock water.

Saskatchewan. Migration is along the western prairies south into the Missouri River valley of the Dakotas and down the Missouri, then on south to North Central Texas. Wintering is along migration route, heavy in southeast South Dakota, then very lightly south to Texas.

The large population of predominately lesser Canada geese from across the Arctic Coast west from Hudson Bay including eastern Arctic Islands ranges along the eastern Great Plains, sometimes referred to as the Tall Grass Prairies. Exact numbers of these fowl are hard to pin down as a direct result to the many man-made waters used by migrating and wintering geese. Most of the migration travels south across Manitoba through Devil's Lake, then stops and goes south toward Oklahoma, where significant numbers start to drop off and winter. Most keep on south over North Central Texas toward the vicinity of Houston. Some drop out along the way around the lower Gulf Coast until a few reach northeast Mexico.

The lesser Canada subspecies from the western Canadian arctic coast to the Mackenzie delta including Victoria Island migrates south across Saskatchewan and Alberta toward the dry western Great Plains. These dry plains are often referred to as the Shortgrass Prairie. It terminates in wintering grounds of western Nebraska, eastern Colorado, and the Panhandle of Texas.

The population of lesser Canadas and a few giant Canada subspecies from Western Canada merges with the Shortgrass population along the High Plains adjacent the eastern edge of the Rocky Mountains, then pulls away west across New Mexico. Wintering areas string out from the North Platte of southeast Wyoming, northeast Colorado, and on south through New Mexico.

A population of about two million pintails pass through to the south on their way to inner Mexico and the Gulf Coast. Large numbers move through the Northern Plains during September, clearing out by the end of October and travel through the Southern Plains from November into December.

The mallard has a large population of three million or more that moves south along the Central Flyway through Colorado, Kansas, Nebraska, East Texas, the Gulf Coast, and the Texas Panhandle. These birds migrate south on either side of the Central Flyway through early November.

Most of the total population of four million gadwall travels across part of this region. The migration south across the Great Plains begins in September, coming out of the Dakotas and Minnesota by the end of October and moving through Michigan, Wisconsin, Iowa, and Illinois, until late November. Heaviest concentration of migration goes south toward the Texas, Louisiana, and Mexico Gulf Coast, arriving during November. A large segment of the population moves along this corridor and winters along the way in Texas. Another corridor goes south along the Lower Mississippi then along the coast to the central and eastern Gulf States, arriving throughout November. Wintering of three quarters of the population goes to Louisiana, with a population of about three million; Texas, 700,000 with a population of about three million; and a balance in Mexico.

The total population of around seven million blue-wing teal migrate in a long, very dispersed, continental-wide, pattern. The densest corridor of migration is between the Central Prairies and the East Texas/Louisiana coast. An estimated five million go across part of this region. Departures from nesting areas take place in late September through early November. Movement across all regions toward the south and west surges during October. Long range migration to Central America and beyond continues through November.

Greater scaup primarily run the length of the Mississippi to the east of this region.

Most of the population of the lesser scaup also pass to the east, but some turn up along this region on the way to Texas through October.

Combined widgeon populations of over three million from across the north surges onto the Northern Plains in early September through October. They don't linger for long and start arriving across regions to the south early October.

Most of the more than three million green-winged teal population migrates through this region toward the southeast to the western Gulf Coasts of Louisiana and Texas, and the interior and coast of Mexico. The greatest surge of migration is out of the Prairie Pothole when arrivals from the Boreal to the north combine with resident populations. The last of the population moves through the northern part of the Great Plains ahead of freeze-up, which occurs there between mid-November and mid-December. Arrivals into the Texas Panhandle start in late September. By November into December most of the migration has reached the Texas Gulf Coast; by the end of December, to the eastern edge of Mexico and Central America.

About 300,000 canvasback are distributed across the Gulf and interior Mexico. Decreases in populations over the last several decades have required restrictions in bag limits, usually one a day per individual. Two routes run the length of the Great Plains from the Pothole regions to the south Texas coast or the deep interior of Mexico. This migration occurs into the northern Great Plains beginning in September and surging into October. Some linger along the eastern edge of the Great Plains through October and November, then head down the Lower Mississippi before freeze-up during middle of December. Another corridor runs straight south arriving in lower Texas in November.

Several species come through this region just like a cool breeze: the teal in September, white-fronted geese through the month of October, and redheads on the way to south Texas in October.

Most of the total population of the ring-necked duck comes through this Region. The birds begin moving south through the Dakotas and upper Mississippi in September and surge during mid-October. Migration of the greatest numbers, about 500,000, is straight south toward the lower Mississippi and Texas/Louisiana coasts arriving through November and into December. Passage through the Central US is at the peak during October and November. Largest wintering concentrations, near 400,000, are along the southeast Texas and Louisiana Coast.

Upper Mississippi River Region (Minnesota, Wisconsin, Iowa, Illinois, Missouri)

This region along with the Lower Mississippi is more a linear geographic feature rather than a broad area. A wide expanse of wetlands was created by a series of dams and locks along the upper Mississippi River. This perfect habitat for wildlife that can be hunted along the river shoreline and islands and throughout adjacent marshes.

The species with the greatest population in this area are Canada geese, canvasback, redhead, and scaup diver ducks; mallards are the primary dabbler ducks. Lesser snow geese surge through the Midwest during late October.

The point where the Illinois, Mississippi, and Missouri Rivers come together in confluence and form a vast floodplain is famous for waterfowl hunting and is often referred to as the place "where the big rivers meet." Migration corridors following the three rivers constrict into one. Peak action in this area takes place during late October through November and into early December.

In small waters in this region, ducks and geese that tough it out can find refuge on larger waters that don't freeze over. They have to move south or starve when deep snow and thick ice shuts off feeding. Peak action in this region is late October through November and into early December.

Huge populations representing most of the species of North America from the north surge over this region. Canada geese from several populations have collected from across western-central Canada. Adding to the surge is a subspecies population roughly estimated at one million interiors and twenty thousand giants, which has nested on the southern shore of Hudson Bay and the western shore of James Bay. Migration corridors pass along east and west side of Lake Michigan, around the east side of Lake Superior, and on to toward southern Illinois. Wintering is in Wisconsin, Illinois, Missoula, along the Mississippi River valley to the northeast corner of Arkansas. Lesser snow geese numbering in the millions have nested in the western Arctic Region. Most of this population has lingered across Alberta and Saskatchewan. The Arctic Coast white-fronted goose populations, almost a million, pass through on route to the Gulf.

The migration of mixed interior and giant Canada geese population from along the southwest corner of Hudson Bay runs primarily along the eastern prairies of the Great Plains trending toward the Mississippi River. A small part of this population will winter along the Mississippi, mingling with other populations.

Some long migrating dabblers, notably pintails, mallards, widgeon, gadwall, green-winged, and blue-winged teal from Western Tundra, the

Boreal, and Southern Prairies also number in the millions. Mallards alone coming down this corridor are well over six million. A significant part of the total populations of canvasback, redhead, and scaup freshwater diver ducks is included in the surge. A minor part of the pintails passing along the Mississippi corridor branch off and go to the southern Atlantic Coast for the winter.

Canvasback migration routes follow this region, then diverge to the Gulf Coast along the Lower Mississippi or the east side of the Great Plains. Timing is into the northern Great Plains begins in September and surges into October. Some linger along the eastern edge of the Great Plains through October and November, then head down the Lower Mississippi before freeze-up during middle of December. Another corridor runs straight south arriving in lower Texas in November.

The mallard migration schedule for the Canadian population is to clear the northern providences through October. By mid-November they've gone south to join the US population. Mallard migration is usually pushed out of the north by weather through October. On to wintering grounds into November and December.

The wintering region with the largest population of mallards, about six million, is along the Mississippi flyway in the Upper and Lower Mississippi Regions along the Mississippi Delta through Iowa, Illinois, Kansas, Missouri, Arkansas, and Mississippi south into southern Louisiana and the Gulf coastal marshes. Some hold out in the Great Plains of the Midwest.
A relatively low number of northern pintail, 400,000, go down the Mississippi.

The gadwall's heaviest concentration of migration goes south toward the Texas, Louisiana, and Mexico Gulf Coast, arriving during November. A large segment of the population moving along this corridor winters along the way in Texas. Another corridor goes south along the Lower Mississippi then along the coast to the central and eastern Gulf States, arriving throughout November. Three-quarters of the population goes to Louisiana.

The densest corridor of blue-winged teal migration is between the Central Prairies and the East Texas/Louisiana coast. This migration trends across this region on the way. Departures from nesting areas are late September through early November. Movement across all regions toward the south and west surges during October. Long range migration to Central America and beyond continues through November.

Nesting corridors of smaller migrations of greater scaup, around 100,000, run the length of the Mississippi to the Gulf Coast and spread along the Texas Coast.

Most of the lesser scaup population, about three million, migrate through or from southeast Saskatchewan, southeast through October, then along the lower Mississippi to the Gulf coasts of Louisiana and eastern Texas. Most have surged into wintering areas by November.

About one million widgeon migrate along this region on the way to the marshes of the Lower Mississippi and Louisiana. Some will go on to Central America.

Around 2.5 million green-winged teal migrate through this region during September on the way to the western coasts of Louisiana and Texas, and interior and coast of Mexico. Most of the migration has reached the Texas Gulf Coast by November or early December.

Lower Mississippi River Region (Missouri, Tennessee, Arkansas; Mississippi; Louisiana)

The Lower Mississippi River Region is the default area that comes to mind for anybody with the slightest insight into waterfowl hunting. Dabbler ducks have always been drawn by green timber hardwood trees naturally flooded seasonally dropping acorns into shallow water. Now controlled flooding of hardwood stands has added hunting areas of eastern Arkansas around Stuttgart. Extensive rice growing throughout the area along with the green timber feed has added to the attraction of dabbler ducks. Wintering population densities of all species of geese and ducks are high all the way to the mouth of the Mississippi and spread along the coast. The large concentration of mallards is a big draw to hunters. Peak action is late November through January.

A lot of the action of the northern part of this region extends away from the Mississippi River and across Arkansas. In its completely natural state, about a third of the area of Arkansas was wetland or lowland subject to flooding. That area is defined by a line between the northeastern corner with Missouri to the southwest corner with Texas on one side, and the Mississippi River on the east. The Arkansas River and White River, with its Black River tributary, cut across the north to south lowland.

The area that lies between the Mississippi Rivers and Yahzoo Rivers is called the Mississippi Delta. This area, routinely flooded by the river every year, is referred to as the pin-oak flats, and is covered with downed acorns in the fall. Waters retreat annually so that the trees survive the flooding. Waterfowl hunters wade far out into the area, place a few decoys, and they're ready to call ducks straight down through the trees. When conditions are all in place, including the mallards, hunting flooded green timber provides the ultimate hunting experience.

Even if the green timber gets crowded, or the water is too deep, or it's a dry year and there's no water at all, or the acorn crop fails so that it's not such a great experience, the hunter still has a lot of other options. The farms on both sides of the river created by clearing and draining the original flooded land are also flooded, harvested, and flooded again. In the process, wasted grain missed by the combines becomes top-grade subsistence for the ducks, and it's more reliable than the hit-or-miss acorn crop. And the action from the hunter's perspective is more reliable.

The Mississippi side of the river is lined with management areas. As it flows through Louisiana and nears the Gulf, it transitions into the coastal marshes which are wintering areas for large populations of both ducks and geese.

Flooded rice field in the Mississippi Delta. These ducks working a flooded rice field in farmland immediately adjacent to managed areas famous for green timber mallard hunting. Flooded delta areas are heavily used when the water level and acorn crop are right. Otherwise, usually often, ducks move to better and more reliable feed.

Maggy works the big swamps of the Mississippi Delta.

A population of lesser snow geese from James Bay makes a mass departure around the first of November and surges non-stop toward southern Louisiana. The coasts of Texas and Louisiana often have a peak surge early December with snow geese arriving from South Dakota. The very large, eastern arctic lesser snow geese population, 4.2 million, has a migration surge headed south from Baffin Island in mid to late September. Large numbers are over southeast Hudson Bay and James Bay by mid-September. A major route south for this gathered population passes straight south non-stop to the Louisiana coastline, generally along or just east of the Lower Mississippi Region beginning in October and surging in November. This is the final stop of the Canada population from southwestern Hudson Bay. Numbers that make the complete trip are low. Wintering is mingled with other populations.

Most of the wood duck population nests over the entire eastern half of North America from the Great Lakes south. Wood ducks in the east leave the northern part of their summer range October through November and concentrate across East Texas, Lower Mississippi, and the Gulf States.

The ring-necked duck population migrating toward the lower Mississippi is estimated to be around 300,000 or more. It reaches the upper Mississippi in September and surges during mid-October. Migration of greatest numbers is straight south toward the lower Mississippi and Texas/Louisiana Coasts, arriving through November and into December.

Canvasback populations of 200,000 take routes to the Lower Mississippi before freeze-up during middle of December.

This is the destination of a lot of mallards and a lot of crazed mallard hunters. The mallards famously take a route that parallels the Missouri River to the delta of the Lower Mississippi from October into November. They migrate toward the nearest, highest quality and most abundant feed. That has evolved toward agricultural areas where they linger along migration corridors along the Central and Mississippi Flyways as long as the feed holds out and the temperature isn't low enough for freeze up. Flooded rice fields of the deltas along the Lower Mississippi are the final destination for many. Texas and southern Louisiana serve as terminal destinations unless the winter is unusually warm, and many linger to the north as long as food is available and the waters are open. Deep snow cover and only freeze up will move them on down the line. Greatest surge of migration is from the greatest density of nesting that would be southern Saskatchewan, Alberta, and Manitoba. Major corridors to the southeast out of this area are down the upper Mississippi and along the Missouri. Mallard migration is usually pushed out of the north by weather through October, and on to wintering grounds into November and December.

A significant number of pintails, about 400,000, passes along the Mississippi corridor on the way to the Gulf.

Heaviest concentration of gadwall migration goes south toward the Texas, Louisiana, and Mexico Gulf Coast, arriving during November. Three-quarters of the population, about three million, goes to Louisiana.

The population of blue-winged teal migrating to the lower Mississippi is around 200,000. The densest corridor of migration is between the Central Prairies and the East Texas/Louisiana coast. Migration surges during October.

Greater scaup migrations, around 100,000, run the length of the Mississippi to the Gulf Coast and spread along the Texas Coast.

Most of the population of lesser scaup migrates through or from southeast Saskatchewan, southeast through October, then along the lower Mississippi to the Gulf coasts of Louisiana and eastern Texas.

The American widgeon population, about one million birds, migrates toward the marshes of the Lower Mississippi and Louisiana coast. Some will go on to Central America.

Green-winged teal migration to the lower Mississippi is estimated to be around 200,000. Migration is protracted compared to other species, from first movement out of the far north in September until the end of the year until arrival of the flights that go all the way to southern Mexico and Central America. By November into December most of the migration has reached the Gulf coast.

Texas Region

North Central Texas is the southern extension of the well-drained plains south from the glacially-formed lakes and potholes extending down from the northern tier of states. Beautiful natural waterfowl habitat occurs scattered along the Central Flyway although some of the original rivers like the Platte are often drained by municipal water and irrigation systems. But the waters are still there, just in the form of reservoirs and irrigation storage. And the old prairies now produce feed in the form of crops, wasted grain and aquatic plants for ducks and emerging sprouts for geese.

East Texas has extensive infrastructure supporting crops and cattle operations and a string of numerous very large reservoirs that tie with those of eastern Oklahoma and continue along the border with Louisiana in the south to the coastal plains.

The Panhandle is typical of the high plains that front the east side of the Rockies from Canada through Mexico. It has natural seasonal wetlands of Playa Lakes in wet years, and human enterprise infrastructure of ranch stock ponds, power plant reservoirs reliably support waterfowl in this dry country. Small stock ponds may freeze over when cold fronts roll in from Canada, but larger waters will be open. Vast numbers of wintering ducks and geese drawn are by grain farming. Best action is November through December.

Gadwalls in weed bed on edge of stock pond. Typical of natural feed in ranching country. Feed is natural and the small body of water is man-made.

Texas has a lot of space and a lot of good waterfowl hunting spots. When Texas became a state, a stipulation of that deal was that Texas would keep its public lands. Therefore, the state of Texas, rather than the Federal Government, retained all of the land that had not been previously claimed.

So, when it comes to Most of it became private property. Hunting, Texas is the land of the lease. The hunter pays the owner and has sole rights to hunt wildlife, usually deer, quail, and waterfowl. Fishing is a different story. The big lakes, as we refer to them, are actually impoundments or reservoirs, and were made and are controlled by the Federal Government. These types of bodies are referred to as Army Corps of Engineer Lakes and are not unique to Texas. The big lakes have areas reserved as waterfowl sanctuaries, and other areas where hunting is allowed. There is a large number of small water impoundments created over fifty years ago by the Department of Agriculture for purposes of soil conservation on private land. These impoundments are leased for waterfowl hunting as part of a general hunting lease.

Most Texas hunters use a private hunting lease. Leases are most used for whitetail deer and bobwhite quail, but many include waters attractive to waterfowl and cultivated fields with wasted grain from summer harvest and emerging sprouts late in the season.

Sustained action occurs from early teal season in September through end of season with the conservation snow goose hunts in the spring.

An estimated lesser snow geese population of over two million winters in the Panhandle. Something less than one million crosses widely over East Texas toward the Gulf. Numbers vary in that very large flocks will be found in fairly concentrated areas. All subject to change.

Gadwall in channels of depleted reservoir. Larger bodies of water are distributed across the eastern side of the Great Plains. Most have been constructed by the Army Corps of Engineers and have been around for more than fifty years. Managed for recreation as well as water storage and flood control, they're often the best public areas for fishing and waterfowl hunting. The plains experience cycles of drought and flood leading to wide variation in water levels. Shallow upper ends form winter habitat for a wide variety of waterfowl.

Snow geese covering a reservoir. Over the high plains of the Texas Panhandle, the most reliable bodies of water during the migration and wintering are reservoirs and cooling ponds for power plants.

White fronted geese, population a little less than one million, make a fast traverse across the state north to south on their way to the coast of Texas and areas in interior Mexico. They will surge across Texas late in October.

A relatively small population of around 100,000 interior Canada subspecies often combine with other populations. Nesting is in the area of lakes of northern Manitoba and Saskatchewan. Migration is along the western prairies south into the Missouri River Valley of the Dakotas and down the Missouri, then on south to North Central Texas. Wintering is along migration route, heavy in southeast South Dakota, then very lightly south to Texas.

Mallards enter the Panhandle during October and November along a route through western Nebraska and eastern Colorado. A separate migration stream across eastern Kansas passes through eastern Texas on their way to the Louisiana Gulf Coast. Weather seems to influence the urgency of progress to the south.

The general migration pattern is a drift into Northeast and Central Texas from states to the north along the Central Flyway. Again, weather and feed seem to be the driver. Mild winters may hold mallards to the north of Texas. Population is estimated to be around two million across the entire region.

A canvasback migration of 150,000 runs straight south from the Prairie Pothole Region to Texas, arriving in lower Texas in November.

A relatively small migration of 200,000 northern pintail winters or traverses the Texas Region. Destinations are the Gulf Coast of Texas, the Texas Panhandle, and the east coast of Mexico. A significant number go on to the interior of Mexico and down the coasts of Central America.

The heaviest concentration of gadwalls migrates south toward the Texas, Louisiana, and Mexico Gulf Coast, arriving during November. A large segment of the population moving along this corridor winters along the way in Texas, about 700,000.

Blue-wing teal migrate in a long, very dispersed, continental-wide pattern. The densest corridor of migration is between the Central Prairies and the East Texas/Louisiana coast, estimated at around five million.

Light migrations of greater scaup, around 100,000, disperse along the Gulf coast and spread toward the Texas coast.

The lesser scaup population, about three million, migrate through or from southeast Saskatchewan through October, then along the lower Mississippi to the Gulf Coasts of Louisiana and eastern Texas. Some will go on over the Gulf to Central America. Most have surged into wintering areas through November. The American widgeon's arrivals into wintering areas surge during November into the Texas panhandle and Gulf Coast, one million.

Green-winged teal population in Texas is estimated to be around 400,000. Arrivals into the Texas Panhandle start in late September. By November into December most of the migration has reached the Texas Gulf coast; by the end of December to the east coast of Mexico and Central America.

Most of the wood duck population nests over the entire eastern half of North America from the Great Lakes south. Wood ducks in the east leave the northern part of their summer range October through November and concentrate across East Texas, Lower Mississippi, and the Gulf States.

Snow geese on power plant impoundment on a cold, foggy winter morning. The flat and generally dry Texas Panhandle is limited in bodies of water but covered by wheat fields. Wintering snow geese feed on wasted grain or sprouts across the state. Snow geese often gather by the thousands in water sanctuaries within range of feed. Pass shooting is good under these conditions with geese flying low through fog across flat terrain in foreground.

Redheads come by the hundreds to work vegetation along the edges of the bays of the Gulf. Redhead ducks from the Great Salt Lake marshes arrive in large numbers during November into December along the eastern Gulf Coast of south Texas and Mexico.

Destination of the greater part of the ring-necked ducks' migration is the lower Mississippi and Texas/Louisiana Coasts arriving through November and into December. Largest wintering concentrations are in the southeast Texas and Louisiana Coasts.

Working a redhead on the Gulf. Redheads come by the hundreds to work vegetation along the edges of the bays of the Gulf. Brush is thick enough to slide a boat under cover. Kimber has lots of business when things get popping. We've come to notice that most landscape shots taken by duck hunters have either a retriever working or a bunch of dead ducks. Credit: Kevin Preston.

Mexico Region

Nesting range of the Mexican duck is interior Mexico from the US border south, to the narrowing of Mexico east of the Yucatan Peninsula. During winter the population consolidates into the southern part of the range.

White-fronted geese arrive in interior central Mexico in November through January.

Redhead ducks from the Great Salt Lake marshes arrive along the Baha Gulf and Pacific coast during November into December and along the eastern Gulf coast of south Texas and Mexico in the same timeframe.

Mallards, about 300,000, move into northern Mexico from the Central Valley of California late.

Northern pintail's California population numbers around 1.8 million. The rest migrate from the Prairie Pothole Region to the Lower Mississippi, the Gulf Cost of Texas, the Texas Panhandle, and the east coast of Mexico. A significant number go on to the interior of Mexico and down the coasts of Central America. The rest of the Prairie Pothole Region population and the thinly spread population of eastern Canada go to the southern Atlantic coast, and some will move on to the Caribbean Islands.

Gadwall in Mexico are estimated at 100,000.

Blue-winged teal movement is across all regions toward the south and west surges during October. Long range migration to Central America and beyond continues through November. Mexico estimated at 200,000.

About half a million lesser scaup ducks migrate south and winter along the Pacific coasts of the US, Mexico, and Central America.

Green-winged teal winter along the Pacific coasts of the US and Mexico and by the end of December habituate the east coast of Mexico and Central America. A rough estimate population is 500,000.

Intermountain West Region (Montana, Idaho, Alberta, Utah, Wyoming, New Mexico, Nevada, Interior California)

This area is centered on the Great Salt Lake, a focus of migration routes that cross the mostly dry intermountain western US, not normally considered a major waterfowling area. The freshwater marshes around the Great Salt Lake are an attraction for waterfowl in a land otherwise dry.

Heavily populated migration routes pass through the area, and large populations stay in the area before moving on while a significant number winter in the surrounding area. Best hunting time is early October through November. Irrigation systems and the crops and pastures produced support. This region overlaps with the Pacific Coast Region on the west. Some migrations come down the Pacific Coast, then cross over into the interior. Irrigation systems and the crops and pastures produced support many transients and a significant population that winters in the area.

Salt Lake Marsh. A refuge in the desert for waterfowl.

Ducks on the Big Hole River, Montana.

Ducks working the hatch.

Close water and feed. Canadas on short walk from irrigation pond to hayfield. Water and hayfields make for a perfect habitat.

Nature of the total experience is diversity in widely scattered hot spots. For the region, September through early October is generally high action.

Migration of the entire population of cackling geese, about 400,000, is across the Gulf of Alaska to the Columbia River and on to wintering grounds in the Central Valley of California.

The Taverner's population, 300,000, crosses the Pacific to Skagit Bay of northwest Washington and on to the Columbia Basin to winter.

The dusky and Vancouver Pacific coast population of Canada goose population, 400,000 migrates across the Gulf of Alaska, a few to Queen Charlotte and Vancouver islands, to southwest Washington, then up the Columbia and south to winter in the Willamette Valley.

One of the lesser Snow Goose arctic coast populations passes through Freezeout Lake area of Montana peaking in the first week of November on their way to Utah and on into California by mid-November.

The Intermountain West population of western Canada goose population of 300,000 is scattered. Migration takes place in small flocks generally to the south, and usually not far, from the Columbia Basin to the Central Valley of California, from the Snake River to Nevada.

Mallards push through Alberta and the Intermountain Region during November. Their route to California goes across southern Idaho and on into northern California and the Central Valley during December. Some go on into Mexico. Almost one million migrate westward across the Intermountain Region and winter in the Columbia Basin of Eastern Washington. Along the Snake River of southern Idaho about 600,000 migrate; in the Central and Imperial Valleys of California, about 700,000 migrate.

On migration, a population of about 1.8 million pintails pass through the northern Intermountain West across Alberta and the Great Salt Lake marshes where some will winter. Northern Pintail wintering areas total are Central Valley of California and Sacramento Valley. Most of the western Arctic population migrates from the Prairie Pothole Region across the Intermountain Region to the valleys of California; some will winter there, while some will continue south to the western coast of Mexico.

An estimated half million lesser scaup ducks migrate south and winter along the Pacific Coasts of the US, Mexico, and Central America.

Around 1.3 million American widgeon migrate from the western area of the Great Plains through northern Intermountain Region to the Columbia and Snake basins, California valleys, and Mexico.

Green-winged teal in large numbers migrate to the Pacific Coast either directly or through the marshes of the Great Salt Lake. A small population moves down the Pacific Coast from western Alaska beginning in September through October before freeze-up, usually in early November. They'll winter along the Pacific Coasts of the US and Mexico.

Nesting area of cinnamon teal is highly concentrated in the marshes around the Great Salt Lake. Other significant nesting areas are between the mountain ranges of Oregon, Nevada, and California. Nesting is otherwise widely dispersed across the Intermountain West Region.

Cinnamon teal surge away from their nesting areas during September. Migration is concentrated in a relatively small range between nesting areas and wintering areas along the lower west coast of Mexico and across the interior of southern Mexico.

Pacific Coast Region (Alaska; British Columbia; Washington; Oregon; California; Mexico)

Lesser snow geese from the western Arctic by way of Utah arrive in California by mid-November. Some of the white-fronted goose population on the way to the Pacific Coast of Mexico will pass through the Imperial Valley during October.

Mallards journey into the Central Valley during December. Beginning in early September, the western Alaskan population of white-fronted geese takes a shortcut across the Pacific to Washington state and then on to the west coast of Mexico. The main surge is throughout September in the north and October in the south.

Redheads in relatively small numbers move along the Pacific coast to Baha during October, November, and December. Black, white-winged, and surf scoters spread along the Pacific from October on to the end of the year.

The northwest coast Canada goose population is composed of Dusky and Vancouver Canada goose subspecies. Range of this estimated as 400,000 population ranges along the Pacific Coast from southeast Alaska south to Oregon. Most of the dusky population migrates across the Gulf of Alaska; a few go to Queen Charlotte and Vancouver Islands, while most head to southwest Washington, then up the Columbia and south to winter in the Willamette Valley.

The Alaskan population of lesser snow geese gathers and will head first to the South coast of Alaska, then taking either a shortcut across the Pacific to the Columbia Basin, then down the Pacific flyway to Oregon or California, or along the Alaskan coast to Puget Sound Washington during October. The Pacific population, about 1.35 million, breeds along the western Arctic Coast, West Coast, and interior Alaska. They will migrate along the Pacific Coast to the central valleys of California to winter beginning in late October through November. Lesser snow geese from the Western Arctic by way of Utah arrive in California by mid-November.

Clacking goose migrate along the northwest Pacific Coast and interior and northeast Oregon into the Central Valley of California. Migration of the entire Alaskan population of cackling geese is across the Gulf of Alaska to the Columbia River and on to wintering grounds in the Central Valley of California. Population is around 400,000.

Taverner's geese, population 300,000, cross the Pacific to Skagit Bay of northwest Washington and on to the Columbia Basin to winter.

Many of the western Canada goose subspecies, a population of around 300,000, will winter in the Central Valley of California.

Beginning in early September, the western Alaskan population of white-fronted geese takes the short-cut across the Pacific to Washington state and then on to the west coast of Mexico. The main surge is throughout September in the north, October in the south. Some on the way to the Pacific coast of Mexico will pass through the Imperial Valley during October.

The black brant western population, roughly estimated at 300,000, winter along the southern US coast and the Baja Peninsula of Mexico. The easterly population migrates west around Alaska. Migration is southeast across the

Pacific to the Baja. They gather on Izembek Lagoon during September and surge on down the coast December through January.

Ducks of the Arctic Coast and adjacent tundra begin their move to the south in late August or early September.

Most of the long-tailed ducks in the western range scattered across Alaska and eastern Siberia, population estimated at 700,000, move along the Pacific Coast throughout October. Peak of migration is in mid-November.

Common eiders of the western main surge of migration is in September and October estimated at 100,000 round the Alaskan coast and winter on the southern coast of Alaska.

King eiders western population of about one million winter at sea along the coast of the Northern Pacific Coast to Puget Sound. Migration is unique, with long strings low across the water surface going around points rather than lifting over. They reach wintering areas in October.

The Western Alaska population of northern pintails migrates along two corridors: the first over the Pacific to Puget Sound, and the second from the Alaskan Peninsula along the Pacific to northern California. Most of the western Canada Arctic population migrates through the Prairie Pothole Region and across the Intermountain Region, to the valleys of California. Some will winter there, while some will continue south to the western coast of Mexico.

Some mallards are moving into the Central Valley during December. Joining the populations of western Canada and Alaska, some of the population on the western side of the prairies drop over into the Pacific Flyway toward central valleys of the West.

The black scoter population migration heads south along the Pacific coast to southern California. Arrival is September through December.

The white-winged scoter population is roughly 600,000. Wintering area for the western population is along the Pacific, which overlaps with the breeding area in western Canada and extends from the south coast of Alaskan all the way to Mexico.

Most of the surf scoter population, around 300,000, migrates to the Pacific and spreads from southern Alaska to the Baja during September through December.

Great Lakes Region (Minnesota; Wisconsin; Michigan; Illinois; Indiana; Ohio; New York; Ontario; Quebec)

This region sees large populations pass over on their way south. Overflying species predominate. Sea ducks are the primary group to winter on the Great Lakes after smaller waters have frozen.

Many migrating populations from throughout Canada pass over the Great Lakes Region. It's also the wintering area for large populations of divers, including several species of sea ducks. These large bodies of water don't freeze over and interrupt the feeding of diving fish eaters, whereas the smaller waters in the area freeze and drive the dabblers south. Marshes in shallow areas of the lakes themselves, which comprise much of the area outside the immediate vicinity of the lakes, support considerable numbers of dabbler populations.

This region also offers a wide variety of waterfowl hunting, including dabblers and sea ducks on big and little waters. Hunting seasons across this region officially begin and end according to regulated closings, but freeze-up, particularly for dabbler ducks, often precedes official closing.

Most of the long-tailed duck population starts moving out from their nesting areas along the Arctic Coast and tundra east of Hudson Bay in early September. At the same time, smaller populations to the east, along the west of Greenland, start to head south. Most of the large eastern population, estimated at over one million, moves to the southeast overland and around the shores of Hudson Bay through October. Surf scoters and long-tailed ducks fly over the eastern Great Lakes during flights from James Bay to the Atlantic. Many will winter on the Great Lakes, many more move on overland to the upper and middle Atlantic Coast. The peak of migration is in mid-November.

Most of the wood duck population nests over the entire eastern half of North America from the Great Lakes south. Wood ducks in the east leave the northern part of their summer range October through November and concentrate across East Texas, Lower Mississippi, and the Gulf States.

The large, eastern Arctic lesser snow geese population of about 4.2 million has a migration surge from Baffin Island in mid- to late September. Large numbers are over southeast Hudson Bay and James Bay by mid-September.

A major route south for this gathered population from James Bay passes through corridors across Michigan and Wisconsin general south over Illinois early October, and straight south non-stop to the Louisiana coast generally along or just east of the Lower Mississippi Region beginning in October and surging in November.

A Canada goose population composed of roughly estimated 350,000 interior and fifty thousand giant Canada subspecies nests around James Bay and winters as far south as Tennessee. Migration corridors run across Michigan, Lake St. Clair, and Lake Erie and its marshes. Wintering is along the corridors in Ontario, Michigan, Ohio, and in decreasing numbers to Tennessee and Alabama.

Range of the black duck is the eastern half of North America. Nesting and wintering areas have considerable overlap. Migrations are short and leisurely through October. Wintering area extends from the Great Lakes and Northeastern US regions along the Atlantic coast to the Gulf coast.

In October, redheads in significant numbers follow corridors to Lake Erie and Lake St. Clair, then take a turn south for Florida and the mid-Atlantic.

Canvasback populations of 350,000 migrate across this region. Migration to the east is along corridors that diverge, then unite, one across the southern Great Lakes, and another that crosses the Upper Mississippi. Both end at Chesapeake Bay. Migration surges across the Mississippi and Great Lakes during October and into the Chesapeake through November and December.

The mallard's Canadian population clears the Northern provinces by October. By mid-November they've gone south to join the US population. Mallard migration is usually pushed out of the north by weather through October, and on to wintering grounds into November and December. A relatively small population, half a million, migrates along the Atlantic Flyway to winter in the Chesapeake Bay and down the coast to South Carolina.

Northern pintail Prairie Pothole Region and eastern Canada populations on the way to the southern Atlantic coast cross this region. Northern Pintail population along the Atlantic Flyway is around 100,000.

About 200,000 gadwall pass through this region on the way to wintering areas of the Atlantic Flyway, primarily South Carolina.

Greater scaup migration corridors are long across the continent of North America to the Atlantic coast. Some pass over parts of this region. The long east-west migrations are dense, estimated at over 300,000, along the northern Atlantic and the Northeastern US.

A lesser scaup population of 1.5 million will cross parts of this region going southeast to the Atlantic Coast, then a large part will move south toward Florida. Most have surged into wintering areas through November.

Canadian East and Atlantic Maritime Region (Labrador, Newfoundland, New Brunswick, Prince Edward Island; Nova Scotia)

This region has a tremendous amount of shoreline. All with very high tides and shorelines with practically countless estuaries. The nearby ocean serves to suppress freeze-ups in this northerly region. It is a draw for both sea ducks and dabblers that stay rather than head south. Small waters are far removed from the coast, the region is covered with swamps and marshes, will eventually freeze up and move dabblers to the edge of the big waters or south.

The hunting experience is very diverse and convenient to large population centers of the Northeast. Of particular interest are black ducks and eider sea ducks, of the Canadian East and the Atlantic Maritime Provinces.

The greater snow goose, population estimated at 250,000, nests in a small area of northernmost Artic Islands and northern Greenland. Departure from nesting grounds is at the end of August and early September. There is a stop-over to gather on the St. Lawrence River at the end of September and early October. Many stop for a while on Delaware Bay before moving on to wintering grounds toward the coast of North Carolina and Back Bay Virginia.

The population of the Atlantic Canada north shore of the St. Lawrence and Newfoundland population is about seventy thousand. It is distributed along the northern Atlantic coast and migrates down the coast of Labrador through the Canadian Maritimes, along the coast of New England over Long Island, south along the Jersey shore and coastal Maryland, and into North Carolina. Wintering is spread along the southern part of the migration beginning thinly in Newfoundland and distributed in more significant numbers in the Maritimes and on to the south.

The Atlantic brant population, about 500,000, migrates across eastern Canada, uses James Bay as a staging area, and then winters along the New England and upper Atlantic coast. The population going to the eastern coast of the US departs the James Bay staging area in October surges into Chesapeake Bay in November.

The common eider main surge of migration is in September and October. The eastern population, estimated at two million at one time, travels east along the coast of Labrador and the northern Atlantic States. Surge is into December. The west coast of Greenland population simply moves offshore for the winter.

The eastern population of King eiders, about 200,000, migrates along Eastern Canada and Maritime and New England coast, the Gulf of St. Lawrence, and off the coast of Labrador from early September through October.

Most of the long-tailed duck population starts moving out from their nesting areas along the Arctic coast and tundra east of Hudson Bay in early September. At the same time, smaller populations to the east along the west coast of Greenland start south. Most of the large eastern population, estimated at over one million, moves to the southeast overland and around the shores of Hudson Bay through October. Many will winter on the Great Lakes, and many more move on overland to the upper and middle Atlantic cost. The peak of migration is in mid-November.

The black scoter eastern population nests in the tundra and open forest south and east of Hudson Bay. Migration for the black scoter consists of a short hop over to the Atlantic Coast in late fall. Migration begins slowly in September and builds along the coasts through December.

The white-winged scoter population, roughly 600,000, migrates overland to the east and winters along the full length of the Atlantic coastline.

The surf scoter total population is around 300,000. Some of the central population of about 100,000 migrates to the east and gathers from October on James Bay, then on to the Atlantic coast to join the small breeding population from east of Hudson Bay to cover the entire coastline by December.

The common merganser population estimates are around 650,000. Migration out of Canada is delayed until just before freeze-up. Its arrival along the Atlantic Coast, Great Lakes, across the Great Plains, Intermountain West, and the Pacific coastline occurs in late November.

The hooded merganser, with a population around seventy thousand, winters along the Pacific, Atlantic, and Gulf Coasts and adjacent areas inland. It arrives across northern states through November and on wintering grounds through December.

The red-breasted merganser population, around 240,000, winters on the Great Lakes and coasts of Northeastern United States, as well as south along the Atlantic and Gulf Coasts. Migration is from November through December along the Atlantic and Gulf coasts.

A small part of the northern pintail Prairie Pothole Region populations and the thinly spread population of eastern Canada cross this region on the way to the southern Atlantic coast, and some will move on to the Caribbean Islands. Northern Pintail wintering areas along the Atlantic Flyway is around 100,000.

The black ducks' migration, which takes place in October, is short and leisurely. Wintering area is most dense is the coast of Northeastern US coast, somewhat less around the eastern Great Lakes.

The canvasback population of about 350,000 migrate across this region and winter along the Atlantic Coast. About 200,000 of those pass to the west of the region and go on across the Gulf and interior Mexico. Migration ends Chesapeake Bay through November and December.

A relatively small mallard population, half a million, migrates along the Atlantic Flyway to winter in the Chesapeake Bay and down the coast to South Carolina.

Gadwall passing through this region are on their way to wintering areas of the Atlantic Flyway and number around 200,000.

Northeast United States Region (New York; Maine; Massachusetts; Rhode Island, Connecticut; New Hampshire; New Jersey; Pennsylvania)

This region has a very long saltwater shoreline, considering the tortuous path it follows. The freshwater Great Lakes and St. Lawrence River and seaway that border on the north effectively make it into a peninsula.

Details of a hunter's experience in both this region and its northern neighbor are practically identical. Migrations of the same species have the same timing, with only an offset of arrivals. Freeze-up occurs earlier and longer for interior Canada than it does for the US side of the Great Lakes and St. Lawrence, due not only because it's to the latter's southern location, but also the fact that it is surrounded by more big waters.

Dabblers and divers are to be found in the countless small waters of the area. Sea ducks are present along the coasts and offshore.

The big draw for dabblers is usually black ducks, considered by many to be the dabbler most difficult to take, more so than even the mallard. Northern pintails are also high on the docket. Freeze up of the small waters moves them to larger waters not iced over or on to the south. Game is on for the sea ducks.

Sea ducks winter along coasts of both southeast Canada and northeast US. There are two primary locations for hunting sea ducks: the shoreline, shooting off rock ledge, and shooting over decoys from boats, either slowly towing decoys well offshore, or anchored with decoys around boat. Hunters may put out on the ledge, decoys set, and then back boats off. After shooting, a boat should pick up the take. Nonresidents hunting with guides should hunt using the same techniques. Guide supplies boats, other equipment except guns, and skills. And the best also provide a lot of experience dealing with the Atlantic in early winter. Nonresidents hunting with outfitters would be wise to stay in a place at the recommendation of the local outfitters.

The nature of the total hunting experience tends toward success and sustained action on all types of waters. For many of the large populations of hunters in this region, it also proves to be a nice experience close to home.

Hunting seasons across this area are regulated to officially begin and end according to regulated closings, but inland marshes undergo freeze-up, particularly for dabbler ducks, which often precedes official closing. Offshore hunting for sea ducks goes on until season closing.

The rocky New England shore. Sea duck hunter's delight. Credit: Kurt Crowley.

Departure of the greater snow goose from nesting grounds occurs at the end of August and early September. There is a stopover to gather on the St. Lawrence River at the end of September and early October. Some head south over the next month. All leave the St. Lawrence at freeze-up at the end of November.

The Atlantic Canada goose population is distributed along the northern Atlantic Coast. The population migrates and winters down the coast of Labrador through the Canadian Maritimes and along the coast of New England and on into North Carolina.

The black duck populations in the United States nest and winter in locales that overlap. Large concentrations are in marshes around Chesapeake Bay area, with more distribution to the west. Movement into the Northeast from Canada runs through October.

The Atlantic brant migration traverses across eastern Canada. The population that migrates to the south in the US is estimated at 500,000. This group uses James Bay as a staging area in October, then winters along the New England and upper Atlantic, and surges into Chesapeake Bay in November.

The common eider eastern population, which varies widely but has been estimated at two million, travels east along the coast of Labrador and the northern Atlantic. Surge of migration for most of the eastern Canadian population takes place into December. The west coast of Greenland population simply moves offshore for the winter.

King eiders migration destinations are Eastern Canada and Maritime and New England coast, the Gulf of St. Lawrence and off the coast of Labrador. Eastern wintering population is estimated at 200,000.

Most of the long-tailed duck large eastern population, estimated at over one million, moves to the southeast overland and around the shores of Hudson Bay through October. Many will winter on the Great Lakes, while many more move on overland to the upper and middle Atlantic coast. The peak of migration is in mid-November.

The black scoter eastern migration consists of a short hop over to the Atlantic Coast in late fall and on to the south, September through December. Total population is around 500,000.

Best estimates of the total white-winged scoter population are roughly 600,000. The eastern population migrates overland to the east and winters along the full length of the Atlantic coastline.

The surf scoter eastern population is around 100,000. Migration to the east gathers from October on James Bay, then on to the Atlantic Coast to join the small breeding population from east of Hudson Bay to cover the entire coastline by December.

The common merganser population is around 650,000. Their migration out of Canada is delayed until just before freeze-up. Arrival along the Atlantic Coast, Great Lakes, across the Great Plains, Intermountain West, and the Pacific coastline occurs in late November.

The hooded merganser population, estimated around 70,000, winter thinly dispersed along Atlantic, and Gulf coasts and adjacent areas inland.

Migration is across northern states through November, wintering grounds through December.

The red-breasted merganser population is estimated to be around 240,000. In the east, the species winters on the Great Lakes, the coasts of Northeast, and south along the Atlantic and Gulf. Migration arrives along Atlantic coast through November, to the south and around the Gulf into December.

Pintails move south across the eastern Boreal, journeying along the Great Lakes and New England coastline. The northern pintail wintering area is along the Atlantic Flyway. This population of around 100,000 migrates from September through November.

The canvasback population, around 350,000, winters along the Atlantic. A drop in population over the last several decades has caused restrictions in bag limits, usually capped at one per day per individual. The eastern route to the Atlantic surges across the Mississippi and Great Lakes during October and into the Chesapeake through November and December.

The mallard migration in this area heads south from wherever they have previously nested. Mallards will linger in the north as long as food is available and waters are open. Deep snow cover and freeze-up, however, will cause them to head south.

The Canadian population of mallards migrates from the northern provinces through October, usually because of inclement weather. The fowls then journey to wintering grounds in November and December.

A relatively small population, about a half million, migrates along the Atlantic Flyway to winter in the Chesapeake Bay and South Carolina.

Gadwall total population in this locale is four million. Many move easterly from the Great Plains, across the Mississippi and on toward the Atlantic, arriving in Chesapeake Bay during October. Around 200,000 winter on the Atlantic Flyway, primarily in South Carolina.

The nesting greater scaups' total population is estimated at 500,000, with migration corridors spanning across the continent to the Atlantic coast. Denizens of these long east-west migrations are dense, estimated at over 300,000.

Lesser scaup ducks population of 1.5 million heads southeast to the Atlantic Coast, with a large part then heading south toward Florida. Most have surged into wintering areas by November.

The American widgeon population of about 200,000 migrates out of the northern Central Plains, and heads east to winter along the Atlantic coast and Florida.

Very few green-winged teal migrate east to the Atlantic.

The Southern Atlantic Coast and Piedmont Region (Delaware; Virginia; North Carolina; South Carolina; Georgia; Florida)

This area is rich in the old traditions of waterfowl hunting, with the heart of the region being the Chesapeake Bay. Here, lodges with walls and furniture are permeated with the smell of old tobacco, old whisky, old shotguns, and old money.

This southern region has significantly milder climate than its northern counterparts. Many hunting spots on many types of waters are available. The numbers of cold-water sea ducks available offshore is smaller here, while dabblers fill the sheltered coastal inlets and marshes. Black, white-winged, and surf scoters spread down the coasts. Redheads work the shorelines along the warm Florida shore. Freshwater ponds inland don't freeze. Canada geese from the north join the year-round residents along the full length of the shore.

Nature of the total hunting experience here is sustained action and tradition. Dabblers in brackish coastal waters intermix with sea ducks offshore. The tradition that surrounds the Chesapeake has both draws and downfalls. Famous blinds that surround the shore usually belong to the folks in a very high tax bracket, who may not be welcoming toward newcomers. Therefore, when hunting this area, it's best to hunt with a guide or outfitter who knows the area. Regardless, before you go, it's best to research public hunting areas and wildlife management areas out on the Bay.

With a short drive down the coast, you can get more bang for your hunting buck. The rivers of the Carolinas flow into the ocean through natural marshes and controlled wetlands. An internet search with the standard ducks and/or geese prefix and the name of a location will help you to find a good place to start. Public lands and waters that you can probably handle with your bass boat decked out with a camo cover. The experience will probably be better first time out with a local guide. Action improves toward the end of the season with late arrivals. The climate of this region is normally mild to the extent that small inland waters don't freeze over. Sea ducks are hunted offshore in the northern part but are less available in the south. Hunting mallards in brackish marshes of the Carolinas is an exciting experience.

The large population of 1.2 million Canadas winters along the New England and mid-Atlantic Coasts. This population is composed primarily of interior Canada subspecies with some Atlantics along the eastern reaches. It nests in the tundra of the Ungava Peninsula and adjacent Boreal Forest to the south. Corridors of migration run along the eastern shore of Hudson Bay, south through central New York and eastern Pennsylvania, to the eastern shores of Maryland, Virginia, and northeastern North Carolina.

A large population of non-migratory Canadas is distributed along this region from north to south. Numbers are hard to determine, but may come close to one million.

Range of the black duck is the eastern half of North America. Some very rough estimates based on rate of decline in the past few decades is around 500,000. Nesting continues toward the south to include concentrations in marshes around Chesapeake Bay, with a wider distribution to the west. Recently, mallard populations have encroached on black duck breeding sites. Mixed breeding where the two co-mingle has diminished the black duck population from the west. True, full-blooded black duck populations have been pushed to the east.

Wintering area extends from the Great Lakes and Northeastern US along the Atlantic to the Gulf Coasts. The densest area for wintering is the Northeastern US coast. Migrations are short and leisurely. Movement into the Northeast from Canada runs through October.

The total population of the canvasback is currently around 750,000. About half of the population winters along the Atlantic. Decreases in populations over the last several decades have required restrictions in bag limits, usually one per day per person. The largest migration is from the Prairie Pothole Region to the south and east. It begins along corridors that diverge, then unite, one across the southern Great Lakes and another across the Upper Mississippi. Both end at Chesapeake Bay. The eastern route to the Atlantic surges across the Mississippi and Great Lakes during October and into the Chesapeake through November and December.

A relatively small mallard population, about a half million, migrates along the Atlantic Flyway to winter in the Chesapeake Bay and down the coast to South Carolina. And finally, there are wintering mallards to be found scattered across North America in between all of the places cited.

Pintails of the thinly distributed nesting areas to the east moves south across the eastern Boreal, along the Great Lakes and New England shoreline. Northern Pintail wintering along the Atlantic Flyway number around 100,000, and pass north to south from September through November.

Many gadwall move east from the Great Plains across the Mississippi and on toward the Atlantic coast arriving in Chesapeake Bay during October. Wintering areas hold about 200,000 on Atlantic flyway, primarily in South Carolina.

A lesser scaup population of 1.5 million goes southeast to the Atlantic, then a large part will move south toward Florida. Most have surged into wintering areas by November.

The American widgeon migration of about 200,000 flies out of the northern Central Plains east to winter along the Atlantic Coast and Florida.

Ring-necked duck pass through the Central US during October and November. A large number, around 150,000, turns toward the southeast to Florida, arriving November. Fewer leave toward final destinations along the Atlantic coasts, with arrivals peaking during November.

Redheads reach Florida in November in relatively low numbers.

Best estimates of the eastern population of black scoter is around 500,000. Migration consists of a short hop over to the Atlantic Coast in late fall and on to the south. Migration begins slowly in September and builds along the coasts through December.

Best estimates of white-winged scoter population are roughly 600,000. The eastern population migrates overland to the east and winters along the full length of the Atlantic coastline.

The eastern surf scoter total population is around 100,000. It migrates to the east and gathers from October on James Bay, then on to the Atlantic coast to join the small breeding population from east of Hudson Bay to cover the entire coastline by December.

The common merganser is rare throughout this region. It arrives along the Atlantic coastline during late November.

The hooded merganser is rare across this region. Migration destinations are Atlantic and Gulf Coasts, as well as adjacent areas inland. It arrives across northern states through November and on wintering grounds through December.

The red-breasted merganser population, total around 240,000, a small part in this region, migrates along the coasts of Northeastern United States and south along the Atlantic and Gulf Coasts. It arrives along the Atlantic coast through November and around the Gulf coast into December.

The Gulf Coast and Coastal Plains Region (Florida; Alabama; Mississippi; Louisiana; Texas; Mexico)

Large populations of waterfowl gather across this Region, which intersects with the Lower Mississippi Region along the Louisiana coastal marshes. Sheltered brackish waters run the entire length of the coast. Many waterfowl populations arrive late in the year or into the next after a long leisurely trip. Prime action is late November through January.

Nature of the total experience for this region is sustained action improving toward end of the year with late arrivals. Southwest Louisiana's coastal marshes have prime action from late November through January. This action spills out and along the coast in either direction. This region boasts some of the smartest birds around, so you can add "the thrill of the challenge" to the long list of reasons to be out there. Here, white geese dominate along coastal plains, feeding on emerging crops of rice and wheat. Dabblers and divers both winter here in great numbers. Huge gatherings of redheads congregate along bays and shorelines.

As this area is far from large centers of population, it's best to get fitted out with some serious navigation equipment before you head out. This investment in knowhow and equipment will create some fun fishing after the ducks have gone. You'll need to be looking for a place to store all of those snow goose decoys.

A Google search for ducks or geese followed by name of a town in the area will help you find guides, outfitters, and lodges. A quick Internet search will also supply the perfect decoy set for the time and place.

The large eastern Arctic lesser snow geese population of 4.2 million has a migration surge from Baffin Island in mid- to late September. Large numbers are southeast by Hudson and James Bays by mid-September. A major route south for this gathered population passes through corridors across Michigan and Wisconsin over Illinois in early October, and straight south non-stop to the Louisiana Coast, generally along or just east of the Lower Mississippi Region beginning in October and surging in November.

A large population of predominantly lesser Canada subspecies to the west is composed of a very roughly estimated number one million, and ranges along the eastern Great Plains. Exact numbers are hard to pin down due to the many man-made waters used by migrating and wintering geese. The longest migration of Canada geese is across the Arctic Coast west from Hudson Bay including eastern Arctic islands. Most of the migration travels south across Manitoba through Devil's Lake, then stops and goes south toward Oklahoma, where significant numbers start to drop off and winter. Most keep on south over North Central Texas toward the vicinity of Houston. Some drop out along the way around the lower Gulf Coast until a few reach northeast Mexico.

The mottled ducks' year-round range is the western Gulf Coast from the Mississippi Delta near Texas and the east coast of Mexico.

Redheads arrive on the south Texas Gulf coast and lagoons.

The fulvous whistling duck can be found scattered around North America. They exist in significant numbers in a rather restricted area around the western Gulf, along the coasts of Texas and Louisiana in summer, and along the eastern coast of Mexico in the winter.

The black-bellied whistling duck is a permanent resident along both coasts of Mexico and Central America. A small part of the Gulf population migrates to lower Texas for nesting.

Most of the wood duck population nests over the entire eastern half of North America from the Great Lakes south. A much smaller population nests along the Pacific coast from Puget Sound to the interior valleys of California. Wood ducks in the east leave the northern part of their summer range October through November and concentrate across East Texas, Lower Mississippi, and the Gulf States.

The mallard has evolved toward agricultural areas where they linger near migration corridors along the Central and Mississippi Flyways while feed holds out and the temperature is habitable. Flooded rice fields of the deltas along the Lower Mississippi are the final destination for many. Texas and southern Louisiana are terminal destinations unless the winter is unusually warm.

The wintering region with the largest population of mallards, about six million, is along the Mississippi Flyway. This Flyway is comprised of the Upper and Lower Mississippi Regions along the Mississippi Delta through Iowa, Illinois, Kansas, Missouri, Arkansas, and Mississippi south into southern Louisiana and Gulf marshes. Some hold out in the Great Plains. Another large population of about three million or more move south along the Central Flyway through Colorado, Kansas, Nebraska, East Texas, the Gulf Coast, and the Texas Panhandle.

Northern pintail migrate to the Lower Mississippi, the Gulf Coast of Texas, the Texas Panhandle, and the east coast of Mexico. A significant number go on to the interior of Mexico and down the coasts of Central America. Populations along the Central Flyway, primarily the Texas Coast and Panhandle, is around 700,000; in Mississippi, a population of about 400,000 arrives late into November and December.

Gadwall fly out of the Dakotas and Minnesota by the end of October and move through Michigan, Wisconsin, Iowa, and Illinois. Heaviest concentration of migration goes south toward the Texas, Louisiana, and Mexico Gulf coast, arriving during November. A large segment of the population moves along this corridor, wintering along the way in Texas. Another corridor goes south along the Lower Mississippi, then along the coast to the central and eastern Gulf States, arriving throughout November. Some migrate southeast to South Carolina and Florida, while others travel the Gulf Coast of the US to coasts of Central America. Three million of the population goes to Louisiana, and the other 700,000 travel to Texas.

Blue-winged teal total population is around seven million. Blue-wings migrate in a long, very dispersed, continental-wide pattern. The densest corridor of migration is between the Central Prairies and the East Texas/Louisiana Coast. Not far behind is the next major corridor to the east, which crosses Florida on the way to South America.

Departures from nesting areas are late September through early November. Movement across all regions toward the south and west surges during October. Long range migration to Central America and beyond continues through November.

Corridors of smaller migrations of greater scaup, around 100,000, run the length of the Mississippi to the Gulf coast and spread along the Texas coast. A few turn off of the main east-west corridors and go straight to the west coast of Florida.

A lesser scaup population of three million migrates through or from southeast Saskatchewan through October, moving along the lower Mississippi to the Gulf Coasts of Louisiana and eastern Texas. Some will go on over the Gulf to Central America. Most have surged into wintering areas through November. An estimated half million migrate south and winter along the Pacific coasts of the US, Mexico, and Central America.

The American widgeon migration surges onto the Northern Plains in early September through October. Most move to the south and southeast across the Great Plains through October. Arrivals into wintering areas surge during November. About one million arrive in the Texas Panhandle and Gulf Coast, and another one million in the marshes of Lower Mississippi and Louisiana. Some will go on to Central America. About 200,000 will migrate out of northern Central Plains to winter along the Atlantic coast and Florida.

The total population of green-winged teal is around five million. More than half migrate through or from northwest Canada and the prairies to the south-southeast to the western Gulf coasts of Louisiana, Texas, and interior and coast of Mexico. Migration is protracted when compared to other species, from first movement out of the far north in September through the end of the year until arrival of the flights that go all the way to southern Mexico and Central America. Last of the population moves through the northern part of the Great Plains ahead of freeze-up, which occurs there between mid-November and mid-December. Arrivals into the Texas Panhandle start in late September. By November, most of the migration has reached the Texas Gulf coast; by the end of December, to the east coast of Mexico and Central America.

Chapter 11

Intangibles: Very Compelling Things and Nonthings

Before we get into the chapter pertaining to selection criteria, we need to consider aspects of duck and goose hunting beyond the physical reality of identification, shooting, habitats, arrangements, and locations. We'll get into misty memories associated with smells of pipe smoke and sleepy dogs drying on the floor in front of a fireplace with talk of flights swooping in over cold blinds. In other words, here we'll touch on the things that are kind of difficult to put your finger on. Like Eddie and Bart, just out there.

The Anticipation

Getting up early and heading out to sea in the dark is enough to make you wonder why you're out there. Then dawn explodes in the east like no other place. And that says why, even before about a thousand redheads come diving into the decoy spread.

Morning on the Gulf. Our friend Kevin Preston and his pals have the morning and the Gulf all to themselves. Companionship (lots of gun smoke), dogs, outdoor experience, from shot to sauce. . . . Credit: Kevin Preston.

Boat ride out on the Gulf. Credit: Kevin Preston.

Boat ride out on the Atlantic. Credit: Kurt Crowley.

Here they come. Credit: Kevin Preston.

Here they are. Just the instant a couple breaks to a few decoys. Texas stock pond.

Here they are. A couple thousand snows come over a big decoy spread. Illinois harvested cornfield. Credit: Kurt Crowley.

The Action: Making Shots and Memories
Eddie and Bart Share a Christmas Present

It was twenty minutes 'til early dark, sometime before Christmas morning. All of the regulars of their duck huntin' party were just getting done with late-night Christmas Eve gatherings or were shortly going to be leaving to have an early-morning Christmas. So it was just Eddie and Bart, and perfect conditions to hunt the favorite spot. The honey hole favorite spot changes from one place to another, one year to the next. But Eddie and Bart both knew when they woke up where they need to be today: a three-acre pond close by, good for four guns. But this morning, it would be just one.

The two of them made the five-minute drive out to the big pond and parked under a large pecan tree. Five decoys and one excited yellow lab came out of the truck with Eddie. They made the 150-yard, straight-line walk through the still-pitch-dark morning. Bart covered about 1,500 yards in his excited anticipation of the actual excitement to come. Retrievers just roll that way. With casts perfected by practice, Eddie scattered the five decoys out over the twenty feet of shoreline moss. No waders that morning. Eddie settled in beside a tree on the bank to relish his favorite time of the day with his long-time hunting buddy. Both man and dog enjoyed the moment together: an instant of pleasant anticipation of the action about to explode. Or not.

A hunter normally expects that the action, if any, will be stretched over an hour or so. But not that morning. As it turned shooting light, Bart attempted to suppress the audible sounds and shakes of the excitement of anticipation as he heard the ducks on the way in. Both hearts pounded with excitement. As the ducks whistled in, Eddie's internal dialogue started. *Not yet, not yet. Kill zone. Take 'em. One down. Miss. Two down. Reload. More comin' in. Take 'em. One down. Two down. Miss. Reload. More comin' in. Take 'em. One down. Miss. Miss. Reload. More comin' in. Take 'em. Miss. One down. Miss. Reload. They're still comin in! Waitaminute! That's six! Nine shots and six ducks. Limited out! Way less than five minutes. Better get Bart to work 'em baaaack!* Bart was into the water and retrieving ducks.

Eddie perceptibly sagged. This glorious morning, this wonderful Christmas present is devoured with a gusto that matches the speed of its delivery. With all the ducks in, Bart turned his attention to fetching in the decoys. He knew that this hunt was wrapped up. Luck and Christmas presents come in different flavors. Eddie smiled. Ducks were still comin' in. Just sit and enjoy the show.

Eddie's Tale of His First Duck—a Greenhead

I went along with my big brother Danny and his friend Bobby. The hunting tactics and techniques were age-old but effective for boys with lots of stamina and time but few shotgun shells and shotguns of limited firepower.

I had yet to take my first duck with the new shotgun I'd received on the occasion of my twelfth birthday. But even before I'd bagged a few ducks to obtain the credentials to consider myself as sort of a legitimate duck hunter, I had my heart set on that elusive trophy: a big greenhead. Mr. Big Daddy Mallard. Sir Francis Drake. The prize. Dinner for several.

This felt like the morning. Colder than a well digger's shovel. Colder than a witch's broom handle. You get the idea. The group operated to a master tactical plan. We'd check all the ponds in North-Central Texas. One of 'em was bound to have a bunch of ducks on the water restin' or feedin'. We'd sneak up on 'em from the dam side, "embankment" to city folks, and slip over the top and pop a big mallard drake before he could make a flap to get away.

We walked for miles. Boy, it was cold. Cold through my two pairs of blue jeans and through my three shirts. Cold through my big coat over the top of everything. Cold through my two pairs of socks on my feet. By now you Northerners (that's everybody north of the Red) are chuckling up your heavy woolen sleeves. We never really had warm winter clothes in Texas when we were kids. At least those of us of what we now refer to as "modest means," way out in the country about where the gravel roads play out. We just wore more of our not-so-warm clothes. All the garb would eventually get so heavy that the exertion from any movement would heat us up. All but our hands, that is. Those didn't get much exercise from carryin' all the weight. The solution for cold hands was another couple of socks. They became shootin' socks with the modification of a small hole on the right-handed socks (for the right-handed kids), just big enough to stick a trigger finger through. Of course the shootin' socks went into the wash with all the rest of the socks . . . they just didn't smell like feet. Nobody ever found out about the shootin' socks with the secret modification. But Mom always wondered how we managed to wear holes in our socks like that with our big toes.

We weren't very careful in the preservation of our clothing department, but the safety department was another story. Rules for use of the new long-barreled, full-choke Ithaca M-66 Super Single shotgun by a just-turned twelve-year-old was that a shell could be carried in the chamber, but the gun was to be carried broken open so that, with game in sight, it had to be snapped shut and the hammer pulled back before a shot could be taken.

The morning's march eventually took us to a favorite spot for fishin' and swimmin' and duck huntin' according to the season. A levee had been constructed to keep floodwaters off that part of the farm. Soil was bulldozed from alongside the embankment to form the levee so that a beneficial side effect was that a nice shallow slough of collected water alongside the levee. Trees were starting to grow up along the levee so that the place was a perfect setup for duck hunting. No ducks were on the water as we sneaked over the levee, so we sat down to wait and see if any action came our way.

It wasn't long in coming. A flight of ducks dropped in after their morning feeding. I completed the required sequence of manipulations to get the single shot into battery just as the ducks dropped in toward the water and I caught a big mallard drake in mid-deceleration. It fell like a rock into the water. I still remember Bobby's quote, "You got 'im, you go retrieve 'im." The water was only knee deep, so that was how far up my jeans froze like a rock on that cold morning. Flights of ducks kept coming in, maybe five or six in all. I might have been the coldest; I was certainly the happiest kid along the North-Central Texas segment of the Central Flyway going in that mornin'.

First Goose Rodeo in the Peanut Fields

A good friend, Joe Aston, hunts anything covered with feathers. Joe would be a wingshot, but his favorite hunt is turkey hunting. So, he thought he would try goose hunting with some of his friends, who, as enthusiasts, knew where to go for the best. In the case, the best was on the west side of North Texas in the sandy dirt where peanuts grow well. Peanut farming is restricted to certain areas with dirt loose enough to plow the peanut plants out of the ground without crushing the peanuts. Then combines pick up the peanuts and separate the peanuts from the roots of the plants. Like all combine harvests, a fair amount of the harvest goes through the combine with the trash and is left on the ground. But what's important to our interests is that geese are crazy about peanuts. And so it came to be that Joe was out in the dark surrounded by 2-D flat Canada goose decoys on his first goose hunt.

First task of his first goose hunt was to scoop out a depression in the soft loose dirt. The depression was meant to be shallow on one end to assist the goose hunter to pop up as the geese came within range. The hunter used field trash as camouflage. Shortly after he got fixed (with some difficulty since he didn't have any experience digging fox holes), down they came.

"Shoot!" It's difficult to pop up in good form if your rear end isn't downhill from your shoulders, as Joe found out the hard way. He had to roll over on one side and prop up instead of a pop up. It took him a little extra time to get in battery compared with the other shooters, who were up by this time blazin' away. As he tried to get in focus, a dead goose came rocketing down from the sky like a big bowling ball with feathers, just missing his head. That sort of thing tends to startle a person. As he tried to get over it, down came another, then another. *It was rainin' geese!* The storm was over in a matter of seconds.

Now that's what you call a waterfowl huntin' experience.

Hot Goose Action on a Cold Day on the North End of the Texas Panhandle

We knew that a Nor'easter was moving in and it would be cold the next morning as we checked out our prospective hunting area late in the afternoon. We were right. The blizzard had come through during the night, one of those West Texas Blue Norther-Whistlers. This one had horizontal snow and almost horizontal sleet mixed with a full-fledged West Texas sandstorm. But a little inclement weather didn't faze our tough bunch of goose hunters—Eddie, Kelvin, Chad, Joe, Frank, Mike, and Jim—as we checked over the prospects before daylight the next morning. We were still fired up over the scouting we'd been able to put together the previous afternoon. The geese would overnight close to a big feedlot where they could use the unfrozen lagoons. By that time, they'd been flying out to the northwest every morning. We had access to a large area where they were headed. That morning, we were waiting by the road as the snow blew and the sleet beat on the trucks through mist and fog thick enough to completely obscure anything over forty or fifty yards out. We rolled out of the truck cabs and started to waddle out across the field. It appeared to be a full section set up for irrigation with a well and pump in the center feeding a wheel-mounted irrigation pipe with sprinklers. It was a struggle in the heavy outfits, walking into the windborne sleet, snow, and red dirt. The closer spots started to look like good places to set up. Joe and a couple more of the guys made it as far as the well and pump and decided that was the place to stop. They'd just as soon freeze to death right there than kill themselves going farther.

Eddie, meanwhile, plodded on, full across the diagonal of the mile to each side of the square-section-sized field. But he eventually found what he was after—a place to settle in on a tall grass–covered terrace, close to the corner where one side formed a linear feature extended behind him, which would be breaking up the open space of the absolutely flat field as the geese popped over the side that extended off to his right. That's all it takes to gather the scattered geese into a string coming over: a little windbreak to disrupt the wind just enough to make it the avenue of least resistance. A single Canada appeared out of the fog, barely lifting over the fencerow to Eddie's front. He dropped it. Then a double. Another single.

Some of the stoppers finally got a few.

Wildfowl on the Table—a Tangible Intangible

The preservation of the kill and preparation for the table is a combination of ritual and culinary art. In this process, any duck or goose that is killed is meant to be consumed. If that's not your plan, then don't pull the trigger. Leave it for another hunter, or that coyote, for that matter.

New hunters need to be aware of the waterfowl taste test. This test provides insight into why seasoned waterfowlers eagerly pursue some species and pass on others. It further explains the more creative culinary processes required to make the lower rankings more palatable to less adventurous consumers. Some delight in the creative effort required to make the lower ranking species taste good, and not everybody has the same preference, which is just as it should be.

So, as a good pal of mine would say, here's the deal on what's generally agreed as the order of preference: any of the dabbler ducks rank above everything else. The majority of people prefer mallards, probably because they're usually larger than the other dabblers. The diver ducks follow, with the plant feeders being the best. The sea ducks take more creativity to cook, but, with fancy fixins, can be pretty tasty. Coots are one notch past sea ducks, but they're so far into the fancy zone that you can't tell if it's a coot or a carp.

The Collectibles of Waterfowling

The fascination with the artifacts of waterfowling that is collectively enjoyed by those "in the know," is extreme. The undeniable favorite of collectors is fine old shotguns, usually doubles, with a lesser fascination with new shotguns, which sport highly embellished autoloaders and sometimes slide actions. Another favorite are old guns, not so fine but representative of the guns used in the good old days of wildfowl hunting. These shotguns are more often than not representative of the American-preferred shotgun, the slide actions and autoloaders.

But the most devoted collectors of waterfowl artifacts are decoy collectors. Ahhh, the old decoys. Meticulously carved and colored by garnered hands, made before machines stamped them out en masse. You can feel its life if you hold one of these old decoys in your hand. But to actually own it takes money. Lots of money. To the tune of a million dollars or so. But if you've got it, use it.

Chapter 12

Hunting Arrangements

Designing Your Personal Hunt

This chapter is about designing your own little corner of the great big world of waterfowl hunting. It tells you how to methodically sample the entire array of arrangements and locations available. It's easier said than done, as the measure of success is personal for each of us.

OVERVIEW OF HUNTING ARRANGEMENTS

We'll make an overall review of approaches to arrangements, providing enough insight to get you started and think through the approach(es) that best match your preferences, resources, and temperament. Then we'll see how arrangements do or don't fit our locations introduced at the start of Part III. You can consider your hunting arrangements in terms of yourself as an individual, a member of an existing hunting party, or the founder of your own party.

Do It Yourself on Public Land and Water

You should try to hunt on nearby public land often with the necessary equipment required. This area is often waterborne, due to access being blocked by residences that front lakeside. Boats can often provide free access. Small boats are the best bet to avoid competition.

Guides, Outfitters, and Lodges

Engaging professional assistance is sometimes necessary whether fowling on public or private land. It is usually particularly helpful for the beginning waterfowler hunter. An experienced guide can teach you the ropes quite quickly. The "ropes" here pertains to waterfowling techniques as well as equipment. Some beginners may hunt with a guide for years, while many others will quickly learn to use their own outfit of gear and equipment.

Some hunters prefer hunting in distant places, while others enjoy going back to the same place time after time. When that place is close to home, it's an even better deal.

Private Property Arrangements

The "old money" connections approach to life and hunting works well and comes with the territory for those born to it. Hunting close to home takes place with all sizes of parties. The optimum arrangement for a hardened waterfowler would be to make a living farming or ranching and fit in a morning hunt whenever you can. Some farmers and ranchers are absolutely hell-bent duck or goose hunters, and sometimes become guides during the offseason. To engage one of these farmer/hunters, show up with breakfast, donate a designated amount, go to a spot selected by the guide, set out the decoys, and tuck in.

The Lease

A hunting lease amounts to a legal contract that gives you the right to hunt on private land. For leases of individuals or small groups, the transaction is binding for a set time—a hunting season, usually a full year. Large businesses headed by individuals inclined toward the outdoors often take leases on large tracts and use it for entertainment of clients.

Leases are most widely used in states with less public land available for hunting. Topping the list is Texas. Proceeds from transfer through sale or trade of state lands to private individuals and private sector businesses goes into the Texas Treasury or is used to pay for specific projects. A notable example here is the construction of the state capital building, which was built with the funds from a trade of extensive rangeland.

Create or Join a Club

In the case of a low-investment hunting club, a few individuals may get together and buy or get a short-term lease on a lake or marsh, or possibly put up a shack, trailer, or camper for temporary shelter. The group may later step up to bigger waters, ones with real clubhouses and work to improve the habitat. If the group stays together, members may come and go with a progression of improvements. At the higher end of the price range, there are elite duck hunting clubs that have been around for well over a century. These time-honored clubs call to mind exclusive entry and tradition.

In addition to improving habitat, individuals or groups will create their own private hunting preserve, their own "happy hunting grounds," so to speak. The first step is to locate and acquire a property with drainage suitable for conversion to some habitat pockets that can become, with a few modifications, optimum waterfowl huntin' spots, usually for ducks. This is because ducks are attracted to small waters.

After a search for just the right combination set of landform characteristics that make up the ideal hunting spot, it's amazing how quickly the required modifications can be accomplished. Bulldozers can create remarkable "improvements" in a few hours/days. It's usually less expensive than expected. And if you play your cards right, so to speak, the whole operation can sometimes be partially written off as business investment.

Arrangements for Hunting Other Regions

As established by this late point in the book, part of the pleasure of waterfowl hunting in these good new days is the convenience of communication and travel. If hunting any of the regions might appeal to you, the best way to do more research is the internet. Simply search "duck hunting guides" or "goose hunting guides", followed by the location. Doing your homework this way upfront will save you both time and money in the long run.

Arrangements for Hunting Other Continents

Hunting abroad is more complicated than choosing a locale spot. If you choose to use a booking outfitter in planning a trip abroad, the work required by a professional is a lot less than it would be for somebody way down at the start of the learning curve. But a big advantage for international hunting is that you can combine the waterfowl hunt with a big game hunt for about the same cost.

Not being international hunters ourselves, a lot of what we know comes from professionals in our extended network of friends and families. It seems that connections for international hunts tend to advertise in more conventional formats, in addition to the internet. These include: booking agents; outdoor sports shows; ads in outdoor publications; and talking to other hunters.

Refer back to Chapter 1 for a summary of waterfowl around the globe. We'll keep the continental organization and list countries where those waterfowl can be hunted.

Eurasian Waterfowl Hunting Destinations

Waterfowl hunting in Iceland occurs early, before ducks and geese migrate south across the North Atlantic to Europe. There are few hunters and lots of game in a wild setting. Costs are reasonable.

Waterfowl hunting in Russia is extended as waterfowl migrate the considerable distance across the north to south width of Central Russia.

Waterfowl hunting in Uzbekistan and Azerbaijan takes place in wintering areas for Asian waterfowl. These countries are making a concerted effort to bring more visitors into the country.

Waterfowl hunting in Sweden and Finland taps into a long tradition of hunting. A hunting trip for waterfowl might include big game as well.

Waterfowl hunting in the Netherlands is typical of that of most European countries. Hunting has traditionally been restricted to aristocrats. The new hunter has to undergo a long period of training to be allowed to hunt. Hunts then come at considerable expense, but with the experience of tradition and ceremony. An agent would be able to sort it out for you.

South American Waterfowl Hunting Destinations

Waterfowl hunting in Argentina and Uruguay have very high bag limits, nice accommodations, and reasonable cost. Many very different species are hunted along with some of the North American species.

New Zealand, Austrian, Pacific Waterfowl Hunting Destinations

Waterfowl hunting in New Zealand includes many species introduced from Europe and North America along with native exotic species.

African Waterfowl Hunting Destinations

Waterfowl hunting in South Africa offers exotic species, high bag limits, and a tradition of old world hunting. Prices are reasonable and big game hunting is available.

Chapter 13

Into the Future

The high population of waterfowl exists today thanks to people who cared. Those conservationists who intervened in efficient mass slaughter as an enterprise serving a market. The dynamics of waterfowl populations have evolved under authority of game management for about a century.

Ducks and geese have survived for a very long time as the prey species of an extended fearsome series of both long-extinct predators. Ducks are subject to a wide range of risks. Shotgun-wielding human hunters are an obvious risk but are controlled by fish and game management authorities. A greater risk is loss from disease, often directly associated with insufficient nutrition, a factor which correlates directly to loss of habitat. That's quantity as well as quality of habitat which can be and is being addressed by both private and government organizations. Cyclic drought that completely dries up the shallow pothole ponds and lakes of the prairies of central and southern Canada, as well as the northern states of the US is beyond control. Natural predators tend to decimate the population. Arctic foxes, raccoons, and coyotes all have enough speed and strength to down a duck or small goose. Their most detrimental effect is preying on nests and the young. Large fish also pose a threat, as they methodically pick off hatchlings following their mother single file.

Consider the complexity of the interacting elements of the overall system that controls the wellbeing of waterfowl in general, and the populations of particular species. A system composed of natural elements and human impact interact with one another to affect the wellbeing of waterfowl. Two examples of these factors are overkill and drought. There are many others, obviously, some of which we as hunters have control over, and some of which are out of our hands completely. Other factors, such as environmental decay, are even more troubling, as they are beyond our everyday notice.

Combines have been designed to increase the speed of harvest. Modern combines have wide cutters that are detachable in a few moments. This added speed is worth its weight in gold as it is able to cover big acreages during the, sometimes narrow, windows of favorable weather. Modern fertilizers can also now produce yields several times greater than a few decades ago. This increased production inevitably produces waste; waste that attracts waterfowl.

Harvested grain fields were slim pickings several decades ago when shocks of grain were carefully hauled to the stationary thrashing machines. The grain was emptied into individual bags, causing little to no waste. Tom learned this concept firsthand during his childhood from a grandfather and great-grand-father while, with his dad, he "helped" with the harvest.

Combines working cornfield. Credit: JoAnne Airhart.

Migratory wildfowl have turned to the high-quality grain there on the ground for the taking, which has become essential in light of the continuing erosion of natural feed. This new habit of feeding also explains the preference of many ducks and geese to work the grain fields adjacent Waterfowl Management Areas. And even further, this change in farming has become the reason many savvy hunters spring for the outfitters deal of hunting leased fields rather than the sometimes-restrictive public land.

This is merely an example of a system-level interaction that is obvious to humans. There are many more we as humans don't know about and questions that we don't have the answers to. For example: "Why is the population of sea ducks disappearing?" The exact answer is now unknown.

Conclusion

That about covers it. Here's a quick recap:

Starter level requires just a shotgun and knowing how to use it. That includes knowing what to shoot and what not to shoot. Further, a dozen decoys and waders can take you up a notch in the places in terms of where you can operate. From there, you can start to decide if you're going to enjoy duck hunting. Or not.

To further enhance your experience, pick up a little, beat-up secondhand boat to get started. From there, you can get to the other side of the cattails and brush along the bank with a clear shot to that little pocket where those ducks are gonna splash in.

A couple months in, and you've now felt that chill when the wings come whistling in out of the dark. And seen some sunrises that break slow enough for you to enjoy the show as a slough yawns wakin' up. You're starting to measure the beauty of a piece of water by the stuff growing in it and the cover along the bank.

Along the way, you'll know when it's time to get a pup. He or she will soon become the best pal you'll ever have. Period. Months, years, and then decades will pass with the seeming blink of an eye. And remembering that pal will make your eyes tear when the great-grandpup pulls a silly stunt that reminds you of a morning a long time ago. You will by this time have reached the point of enlightenment that you've realized; it's not about shootin' ducks or geese at all.

About the Authors

TOM AIRHART

Tom was born into a world of farming and family, with hunting and fishing as time permitted. He was the curious kid thrust into all of it, initiated by four active generations of teachers. Over time, small game and seasonal waterfowl hunting on the farms evolved to Texas whitetails and elk throughout the West. He's also spent time fishing on the creeks, ponds, large reservoirs, and other bodies of water across North America. Along the way, he's garnered a lot of new friendships with amateur and professional water outdoorsmen, who fished in spring and summer, hunted waterfowl during fall and early winter. Tom was now finds himself among those who try to pass it along to grandkids and the great-grandkids and beginners everywhere. Unable to find a good elk hunting book for beginners, Tom wrote *The Elk Hunting Guide* in 2013. Facing a similar situation in regards to waterfowl hunting, he endeavored to write this book with Eddie and Kent. Fate and Eddie's dad, Bill, brought the three of us together, and here we roll.

EDDIE KENT

Eddie's first memories involve tagging along behind two older brothers, hoping to get in on the huntin' and fishin' action. And he did. The timeline is a little fuzzy, but according to his dad, friend and contemporary of Tom, by the time that he could keep up, he was already good at shooting the greenheads and had trained his first retriever. His greatest joy next to duck and goose hunting is introducing a young person to the sport. The young person constantly with him hunting, shooting, painting decoys, or whatever action is going, is daughter Ivy. She's already an instinctive wingshot in her own right. Eddie is often engaged in conversation, but seldom about his skills, so his coauthors will have to do it. We consider him to be world-class, in all things about waterfowl hunting.

KENT RAYMER

Kent Raymer has been duck hunting for over twenty-five years. Contrary to Tom and Eddie, Kent grew up in the 'burbs, then moved to the country. He's seen the best of both worlds through the eyes of a dedicated waterfowl hunter. Kent was first invited along on a guided trip just out of high school and, somewhere between "Shoot 'em!" and "Reload!" has been hooked ever since. He's hunted in a myriad of environments from stock tanks to open water lakes, flooded timber to salt water bays, from limits in ten minutes to getting skunked more times than he cares to count. His favorite hunting spot is anywhere his youngest daughter, Claire, and son, Peyton, happen to be hunting. His extended network of waterfowl hunting pals keeps our group up to date on what's going on across North America.

Index